Unbroken

ANGELA STERRITT
Honour the Dead, Fight for the Living,
Honour the Living, Fight for the Dead

Angela Sterritt

Unbroken

My Fight for Survival, Hope, and Justice for Indigenous Women and Girls

GREYSTONE BOOKS
Vancouver/Berkeley/London

Greystone Books Ltd.
greystonebooks.com

Cataloguing data available from Library and Archives Canada
ISBN 978-1-77164-816-5 (cloth)
ISBN 978-1-77164-817-2 (epub)

Editing by Jennifer Croll
Stylistic editing by Paula Ayer
Copyediting by Dawn Loewen
Proofreading by Jennifer Stewart
Fact-checking by Sarah Berman and Angela Sterritt

Jacket art by Angela Sterritt: *Honour the Dead, Fight for the Living,*
Honour the Living, Fight for the Dead, acrylic on canvas
Jacket and text design by Jessica Sullivan
Printed and bound in Canada on FSC® certified paper
at Friesens. The FSC® label means that materials used for
the product have been responsibly sourced.

Permission for all reporting originally conducted for the
CBC granted by the Canadian Broadcasting Corporation.

Permission for reporting originally conducted for
The Dominion and Open Canada granted by each publication.

Every effort has been made to ensure accuracy and
credit sources. Information that will allow the publisher
to correct information or update references is welcome.

Greystone Books thanks the Canada Council for the Arts, the British Columbia
Arts Council, the Province of British Columbia through the Book Publishing Tax
Credit, and the Government of Canada for supporting our publishing activities.

Canadä

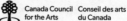

Greystone Books gratefully acknowledges the xʷməθkʷəy̓əm (Musqueam),
Sḵwx̱wú7mesh (Squamish), and səlilwətaɬ (Tsleil-Waututh) peoples on
whose land our Vancouver head office is located.

A NOTE TO READERS

THIS BOOK TOOK AN OCEAN OF COURAGE. As I cut through parts of the past I'd rather put behind me, I was often sinking in my own trauma or learning how to hold it in kindness and love. But the strength it took the family members of missing and murdered Indigenous women and girls to trust me, to share their stories, and to travel intimately with their pain of losing a loved one, in many cases horrifically, was unmatched. It unearthed unimaginable suffering.

While in some ways this is a dark and harrowing read, in others it is beautiful and loving, filled with all the care and compassion Indigenous people live in and give. This book, amassed from years of difficult conversations, recognizes and explores the full, complex picture of violence against Indigenous women and girls.

In reading this work, you will visit the depths of long-lasting and intergenerational trauma that is the direct result of colonial violence and genocide.

In my search for justice and healing, this book touches on difficult themes like suicide, assault, violence, and childhood abuse. Mostly, though, I am searching to honour the hope and love that permeate the spirits of all our people.

In my news stories I provide trigger warnings on articles that could cause victims or readers trauma. For this book, in addition to this warning, I'm hoping to send an offering of love, kindness, and care to blanket and comfort you as you take this journey with me.

Nee diit t'aakwdiit dimt
kw'asindiithl oots'inim
Our spirit is not broken

Contents

In Memoriam

FOLLOWING ARE THE NAMES of Indigenous women and girls who were murdered or went missing in British Columbia along the Highway of Tears (the stretch of Highway 16 between Prince George and Prince Rupert) or along adjoining Highway 97 or 5. The names, ages, and other details come from a wide range of sources: family members, police records, media reports, books, websites, *Forsaken: The Report of the Missing Women Commission of Inquiry*, Volume I (2012), and testimony from the National Inquiry into Missing and Murdered Indigenous Women and Girls. There are most likely more names I was unable to find or confirm. The women's and girls' Indigenous communities are listed as they identify themselves, as their communities identify them, or as they may be identified by media sources. I was not able to confirm some.

HT means Highway of Tears (Highway 16) murders or disappearances. For solved cases, the race of the killer is listed as WT (white), IN (Indigenous), or UN (unknown). SK means killed by a known serial killer.

1967   **Rose Roper**, 17, Secwepemc and Tŝilhqot'in. Murdered, solved (WT)

1969   **Gloria Levina Moody**, 26, Nuxalk. Murdered, unsolved (WT)

1971   **Jean Sampare**, 18, Gitxsan. Missing (HT)

1972   **Velma Duncan**, 18, Stswecem'c Xgat'tem. Missing

1976   **Coreen Thomas**, 21, Saik'uz. Murdered, solved (HT, WT)

1978   **Mary Jane Hill**, 31, Nisga'a. Murdered, unsolved (HT)

1978   **Monica Jack**, 12, Nlaka'pamux. Murdered, solved (WT)

1970–79   **Tracey Clifton**, age unknown, Tsimshian. Missing (HT)

1981   **Jean Kovacs**, 36, Nation unknown. Murdered, solved (HT, IN, SK)

1982   **Nina Joseph**, 15, Tl'azt'en. Murdered, solved (HT, IN, SK)

1989   **Doreen Jack and family**, 26, 26, 9, and 4, Cheslatta Carrier. Missing (HT)

1989   **Cecilia Nikal**, 15, Wet'suwet'en. Missing (HT)

1989   **Helena Tomat**, 17, Syilx. Missing

1989   **Alberta Williams**, 24, Gitxsan. Murdered, unsolved (HT)

1990   **Donna Charlie**, 22, Kwadacha. Murdered, solved (HT, IN)

1990   **Delphine Nikal**, 15, Wet'suwet'en. Missing (HT)

1993   **Theresa Umphrey**, 38, Pukatawagan. Murdered, solved (HT, WT, SK)

1994   **Alishia Germaine**, 15, Nation unknown. Murdered, unsolved (HT)

1994   **Roxanne Thiara**, 15, Anishinaabe. Murdered, unsolved (HT)

1994   **Ramona Wilson**, 16, Gitxsan. Murdered, unsolved (HT)

1995   **Lana Derrick**, 19, Gitxsan. Missing (HT)

1996   **Diane Stewart**, 42, SnPink'tn. Murdered, unsolved

1999   **Monica McKay**, 18, Nation unknown. Murdered, unsolved (HT)

1999   **Amanda Jean Simpson**, 4, Métis. Murdered, unsolved (HT)

2001   **Ada Elaine Brown**, 41, Tahltan. Murdered, officially undetermined, unsolved (HT)

2004   **Jacqueline Bob**, 41, Tsq'escenemc and Esk'etemc. Missing

2004   **Kayla Rose McKay**, 13, Gitxaala. Family dispute police claim of no foul play (HT)

2004   **Thelma Pete**, 53, Simpcw. Murdered, solved (UN)

2005   **Tamara Chipman**, 22, Wet'suwet'en. Missing (HT)

2006   **Aielah Saric-Auger**, 14, Lheidli T'enneh. Murdered, unsolved (HT)

2007   **Bonnie Joseph**, 32, Yekooche. Missing (HT)

2010   **Cynthia Frances Maas**, 35, Blueberry River. Murdered, solved (HT, WT, SK)

2010   **Emmalee McLean**, 14, Nisga'a. Family dispute police claim of no foul play (HT)

2010   **Natasha Montgomery**, 23, Nation unknown. Murdered, solved (HT, WT, SK)

2011   **Summer Star Elizabeth Krista-Lee (CJ) Fowler**, 16, Gitxsan. Murdered, solved (UN)

2013   **Immaculate (Mackie) Basil**, 26, Tl'azt'en. Missing (HT)

2013   **Samantha Paul**, 26, Tk'emlúps te Secwépemc. Murdered, unsolved

2013   **Destiny Rae Tom**, 21, Wet'suwet'en. Murdered, solved (HT, IN)

2016   **Caitlin Potts**, 27, Samson Cree. Missing

2016   **Deanna Wertz**, 46, Nation unknown. Missing

2017   **Frances Brown**, 53, Wet'suwet'en. Missing

2018   **Cynthia (Cindy) Martin**, 50, Gitxsan. Remains found, unsolved (HT)

2018   **Jessica Patrick-Balczer**, 18, Lake Babine. Murdered, unsolved (HT)

2021   **Carmelita Abraham**, 33, Takla. Murdered, solved (UN)

2021   **Christin West**, 36, Saik'uz and Lake Babine. Murdered, solved (HT, UN)

The following non-Indigenous women and girls were murdered or went missing along the Highway of Tears or adjoining highways:

1970   **Helen Frost**, 17. Missing (HT)

1970   **Micheline Pare**, 18. Murdered, unsolved

1971   **Mary Thomas**, age unknown. Missing

1973   **Pamela Darlington**, 19. Murdered, solved (WT, SK strongly suspected)

1973   **Gale Weys**, 19. Murdered, solved (WT, SK strongly suspected)

1974   **Monica Ignas**, 14. Missing (HT)

1974   **Colleen MacMillen**, 16. Murdered, solved (WT, SK)

1978   **Santokh Johal**, age unknown. Missing

1979   **Janice Hackh**, 16. Missing

1981   **Roswitha Fuchsbichler**, 13. Murdered, solved (HT, IN, SK)

1981   **Maureen Mosie**, 33. Murdered, unsolved

1987   **Mary Jimmie**, age unknown. Murdered, unsolved

1989   **Marnie Blanchard**, 18. Murdered, solved (HT, WT, SK)

1989   **Elsie Friesen**, 34. Murdered, unsolved

1992   **Maureen Sullivan**, 31. Murdered, solved (HT, UN)

1999   **Deena Braem**, 17. Murdered, unsolved

2002   **Nicole Hoar**, 25. Missing (HT)

2004   **Barbara Lanes**, 57. Missing

2005　**Amanda Gore**, 20. Murdered, unsolved
2006　**Julie Oakley Parker**, 33. Missing
2009　**Jill Stuchenko**, 35. Murdered, solved (HT, WT, SK)
2010　**Loren Leslie**, 15. Murdered, solved (HT, WT, SK)
2011　**Madison Scott**, 20. Missing (HT)
2014　**Kendall Moore**, 17. Murdered, solved (HT, WT)
2014　**Anita Thorne**, 49. Missing (HT)
2017　**Nicole Bell**, 31. Missing
2017　**Traci Genereaux**, 18. Murdered, unsolved
2017　**Roberta Marie Sims**, 55. Missing (HT)
2020　**Crystal Chambers**, 34. Murdered, solved (HT, UN)
2021　**Shannon White**, 32. Missing

The following list of Indigenous and non-Indigenous women who were murdered in or went missing from Vancouver is an edited version of the one in Wally Oppal's *Forsaken: The Report of the Missing Women Commission of Inquiry*, Volume 1 (2012). Oppal says: "Having considered various options for defining the extent of this list, I have decided that my fact-finding mandate includes all the women missing from the DTES [Downtown Eastside] whose disappearances were or could have been reported within the Terms of Reference who were not subsequently found alive or whose death has not been attributed to natural causes, including the [serial killer Robert] Pickton victims not initially on the missing women posters" (pp. 33–34).

1978　**Lillian O'Dare**, 34. Murdered, unsolved
1983　**Marlene Abigosis**, 25, Pine Creek First Nation. Missing
1983　**Rebecca Guno**, 23, Nisga'a. Missing
1983　**Sherry Lynn Rail**, 27. Missing
1985　**Sheryl Donahue**, 25. Missing
1986　**Elaine Allenbach**, 21. Missing

1988 **Taressa Williams**, 15, Semiahmoo First Nation. Remains found in Vancouver

1989 **Elaine Dumba**, 34. Missing

1989 **Ingrid Soet**, 30. Missing

1991 **Nancy Clark**, 25. Murdered, DNA found on Pickton farm

1992 **Elsie Sebastian**, 40, Pacheedaht. Missing

1992 **Kathleen Wattley**, 32. Missing

1993 **Sherry Baker**, 25. Missing

1993 **Gloria Fedyshyn**, 29. Missing

1993 **Leigh Miner**, 35. Missing

1993 **Teresa Triff**, 23. Missing

1990–94 **"Jane Doe,"** age unknown. Murdered, DNA found on Pickton farm

1994 **Angela Arseneault**, 17. Missing

1995 **Catherine Gonzalez**, 26. Missing

1995 **Catherine Knight**, 28. Missing

1995 **Diana Melnick**, 20. Murdered, Pickton charged

1995 **Dorothy Spence**, 32, Sandy Bay Ojibway. Missing

1996 **Tanya Holyk**, 20, Skatin. Murdered, Pickton charged

1996 **Sherry Irving**, 24, Líľwat. Missing, Pickton charged

1996 **Olivia William**, 21, Lake Babine. Missing

1996 **Frances Young**, 36. Missing

1997 **Cindy Beck**, 33. Missing

1997 **Andrea Borhaven**, 25. Murdered, Pickton charged

1997 **Cara Ellis**, 25. Murdered, Pickton charged

1997 **Cynthia Feliks**, 43. Murdered, Pickton charged

1997 **Marnie Frey**, 24. Murdered, Pickton convicted

1997 **Helen Hallmark**, 31. Murdered, Pickton charged

1997 **Janet Henry**, 36, 'Namgis. Missing

1997 **Maria Laliberte**, 47, Nation unknown. Missing

1997 **Stephanie Lane**, 20, Métis. Murdered, DNA found on Pickton farm

1997   **Kellie Little**, 28, Nuchatlaht. Missing

1997   **Jacqueline Murdock**, 26, Takla Lake (Carrier
        Sekani). Murdered, DNA found on Pickton farm

1997   **Sharon Ward**, 29. Missing

1998   **Marcella Creison**, 20. Missing

1998   **Sarah de Vries**, 28. Murdered, Pickton charged

1998   **Sheila Egan**, 19. Missing

1998   **Michelle Gurney**, 29, Nisga'a. Missing

1998   **Inga Monique Hall**, 46. Murdered, Pickton charged

1998   **Ruby Hardy**, 33, Biinjitiwaabik Zaaging
        Anishinaabek. Missing

1998   **Angela Jardine**, 27. Murdered, Pickton charged

1998   **Kerry Koski**, 38. Murdered, Pickton charged

1998   **Tania Petersen**, 28. Missing

1998   **Julie Louise Young**, 31. Missing

1999   **Wendy Crawford**, 43. Murdered, Pickton charged

1999   **Jennifer Furminger**, 28, Nation unknown. Murdered,
        Pickton charged

1999   **Jacqueline McDonell**, 22. Murdered, Pickton
        charged

1999   **Georgina Papin**, 34, Enoch Cree. Murdered, Pickton
        convicted

1999   **Brenda Wolfe**, 30, Kahkewistahaw. Murdered,
        Pickton convicted

2000   **Dawn Crey**, 42, Stó:lō. Murdered, DNA found on
        Pickton farm

2000   **Tiffany Drew**, 24. Murdered, Pickton charged

2000   **Debra Jones**, 43. Murdered, Pickton charged

2001   **Sereena Abotsway**, 29, Nation unknown. Murdered,
        Pickton convicted

2001   **Yvonne Boen**, 33. Murdered, DNA found on
        Pickton farm

2001   **Heather Bottomley**, 24. Murdered, Pickton charged

2001 **Heather Chinnock**, 30. Murdered, Pickton charged

2001 **Andrea Joesbury**, 23. Murdered, Pickton convicted

2001 **Patricia Johnson**, 25. Murdered, Pickton charged

2001 **Dianne Rock**, 34. Murdered, Pickton charged

2001 **Angela Williams**, 31, Tlowitsis. Murdered, unsolved

2001 **Mona Wilson**, 26, O'Chiese. Murdered, Pickton convicted

2004 **Sharon Abraham**, 39, Sagkeeng. Murdered, DNA found on Pickton farm

Preface

Waiy woh,
it is time

A MOVEMENT RISES

WHEN I LEFT THE STREETS, I had dozens of sketchbooks filled with my drawings, poetry, and reflections. My words traced my dreams and fears, and my imaginative illustrations told stories about love, friendship, and my struggles with both. They were a way of leaving the dimension of reality, in which I was a member of one of the most vulnerable groups of people in North America.

For several years as a teen and young adult, I lived homeless, Indigenous, and female in the downtown neighbourhoods of Vancouver and hitchhiked from city to city all over Canada and the United States. In these spaces, I watched as girls and young women like me turned up on missing posters with frightening regularity. I saw how little we seemed to matter; how authorities dismissed concerns about violence against us and ignored us when we disappeared. I wanted answers, but I was vulnerable, painfully shy, and socially awkward by nature. So I kept my head down and scribbled words and sketches, looking up just to nod or shake my head if anyone spoke to me. My pen became my counsellor, helping me flesh and flush out the transgressions of those who had abused and abandoned me and, later on, those whose fists and blows would normalize violence in my world.

My writing cast a shadow on those who victim-blamed and shamed us street kids for how we lived—for begging and for sleeping in parks, in abandoned buildings, and under bridges, often beat up and worn down. We'd describe ourselves as anything but victims, but we were not survivors or warriors either. We were reinventing ourselves by escaping dysfunctional homes and violence. We were fighting to change the course of our lives and the narratives placed on us, butting up against stereotypes and building community. And the small handful of us who were Indigenous, who carried an intergenerational historical pain, were guided by the same power our ancestors wielded within themselves during and following the hardest times of their lives during colonization. I then used my pen to transcend my suffering, and that pen became a tool of strength and resilience. I was not subhuman like the colonials believed. I was superhuman like my relatives who survived one of the worst atrocities in human history—a genocide fraught with targeted starvation, abuse, apartheid, assimilation, and attempted annihilation. As I chronicled my struggles, my strength and survival were proof: the colonials had failed.

When I started writing this book in 2015, I thought back to my journals that would be paramount in writing an accurate portrayal of my story. But every time I tried to write, an emotion too intense to bear ran through my veins. My tears would flow and flow, and rarely could I stop. My counsellor, that pen, was failing me.

But then I remembered what helped remedy my pain for years before that—illuminating a path for others to share their stories. I had blazed my own trail as a radio and print journalist when I was a teen leaving the street, drawn to share Indigenous stories that were hidden, left untold, or tucked away—stories many unbelieved unworthy of telling. Writing then for community and Indigenous newspapers and magazines, and hosting radio shows at local and student stations, I shared stories of Indigenous girls in prison, Elders vying for land rights and title, or the lack of resources to find missing Indigenous women and girls.

But in 2004, when I landed my first job with Canada's national public broadcaster as an on-air researcher, those stories became harder to tell. Many Indigenous people, like me, felt at the time that CBC and other mainstream media outlets failed to cover many Indigenous stories with the same respect, accuracy, rigour, and ethics as every other story. When I pitched Indigenous stories to CBC and other mainstream news outlets, executives and producers cast them away with the same excuses other Indigenous journalists had heard—that the public didn't care about Indigenous stories because they were too depressing, or they didn't understand them. But our lack of coverage made us complicit in the public's apathy, and I knew I couldn't remain silent. My pen emerged as an agent of change that could give Indigenous people a voice and the equality they deserved in media coverage.

Reflecting on this, I began to realize that perhaps it was possible to share my own story in this book if I could weave it through other Indigenous people's stories, much like those I have been privileged to tell as a journalist over the last two decades. As I thought about the places I'd lived and all the women and girls like me who didn't survive, I realized I could use my voice to raise theirs.

Sharing my own story is relatively new. I've hidden it for years to fit in and to survive. When I was living on the streets while attending high school, I would find trendy clothes in alleyways or thrift stores so I could look like the other kids who had homes and money. When I finally graduated grade twelve from the Vancouver School District's Adult Education program, I gave the valedictorian speech at a ceremony at the prestigious Lord Byng Secondary School. My grades were so high during my political science undergrad at the University of British Columbia (UBC) that the department chair offered me the opportunity to do an honours degree. In most of my jobs, I just seemed like a hard worker who was focused and kept my head down. But the trauma clung deep, until I started to realize I was not alone.

In 2008, a year before I graduated with a Bachelor of Arts degree from UBC, I decided to give back to a neighbourhood where I had spent time. I was hired as a support worker and then a mental health worker at a centre in Vancouver's Downtown Eastside for self-identified women and their children looking for shelter from conditions of poverty and violence. Most were Indigenous. Almost always their trauma substantially outweighed mine, and I often didn't feel equipped enough to provide the emotional and mental support or guidance they needed. There was so much going on for all of them—heavy grief, hell in their past and current lives—and for most, it had roots in their childhood experiences with colonialism. Many had severe mental health conditions and illnesses and were self-medicating. Most were desperate to have their basic needs met with housing, showers, clothing, and food—all of which we provided.

I hid there at first too. I hid my own trauma—but it was among these women that I realized how it loomed in almost everything I did. The Downtown Eastside was one of the only places I couldn't overachieve to conceal my past. And it was in this neighbourhood that I met some of the most powerful Indigenous women who were also survivors of violence. They taught me how to speak my truth and to stop hiding. Gitxsan and Wet'suwet'en matriarch Gladys Radek and Haida power-house Bernie Williams were speaking up about mysterious disappearances of Indigenous women and murder investigations that had lagged, were tenuous, or were nonexistent. They planted seeds for me to dig deeper and ask more questions about the disenfranchisement and dismissals of Indigenous women.

These female forces organized marches for missing and murdered Indigenous women and girls (MMIWG) every year, attended vigils, and spoke to any leader or journalist who was willing to listen. They taught me about their matrilineal cultures that mirrored mine and showed me how to intertwine our identity with aspirations to lift up Indigenous women's voices.

Bernie and Gladys fought hard but often saw little change. Still, they were unwilling to give up. There was pain, but there was power and love. And there was a movement building that few could ignore.

Like tiny pebbles that trip off a craggy cliff, breaking calm water that ripples, pooling into coiling waves, swelling into billows—it was a series of events that cascaded, culminating in a tidal wave that pushed the hearts of Canadians to care about the overwhelming violence committed against Indigenous women and girls in these lands. Since the 1970s, along a 725-kilometre stretch of Highway 16 from the northwest coast across the northwest and central interior of British Columbia, dozens of women and girls have gone missing or been murdered, with many of their disappearances still unsolved and the killers still unknown. Year after year family members have called for answers from police and for action from governments. After decades of marching, holding symposiums, walking to Ottawa, sharing stories in the media, and postering along that highway, now called the Highway of Tears, people started to open their eyes to the reality.

When 22-year-old Wet'suwet'en mother Tamara Chipman went missing on the Highway of Tears in Prince Rupert in 2005, her aunty Gladys Radek and others in her family relentlessly implored the media and authorities to pay attention to the alarming number of Indigenous women and girls who had gone missing, or were murdered, along that highway and others in the area. It was one of the first cases where an Indigenous woman's disappearance resulted in press conferences on the highway, media coverage, and a substantial investigation. Just over a year later, on the west coast, after more than a decade of loved ones demanding an investigation into more than seventy missing women from the Downtown Eastside, many of whom were Indigenous, the trial of serial killer Robert Pickton began. With more media attention on the Highway of Tears and all eyes on the Pickton court case, a chill ran through British Columbians as it became eerily clear that Indigenous women were less safe than other women in the province.

When I worked in the Downtown Eastside, Shawn Atleo, then National Chief of the Assembly of First Nations, was one of the first national leaders to visit women and family members of the missing in the neighbourhood. It was the first time I heard a high-profile politician call on the federal government to hold a national inquiry into MMIWG. It felt like a sacred moment. People were starting to listen.

But it wasn't until years later that the entire nation of Canada fully grasped the magnitude of just how many Indigenous women and girls were missing and murdered in Canada. In 2014, Tina Fontaine, a diminutive 15-year-old Anishinaabe girl, was found wrapped in a bag in the Red River in Winnipeg. The uproar around her murder pushed more Canadians to probe why and how Indigenous women and girls were being murdered at alarming levels. The heartbreaking tragedy fell on the heels of a report by the Royal Canadian Mounted

Police (RCMP), *Missing and Murdered Aboriginal Women: A National Operational Overview*, which demonstrated that Indigenous women are overrepresented in statistics of missing and murdered women. It revealed that rather than the initial recorded number of 500, there were nearly 1,200 known missing or murdered Indigenous women and girls in Canada.

While disparate, these moments were braided together by common threads—relatives, survivors, friends, and advocates spooling painful stories together with hope to press on. Their stories were habitually swept under a rug by an indifferent public, yet loved ones trudged forward in often seemingly sinking mud. Wave after wave, they pushed against the undercurrent to be heard, shaking the vines, shedding light on the cracks, and illuminating a dark tale that has haunted this land for decades.

The questions family members, reporters, and advocates asked at the National Inquiry into Missing and Murdered Indigenous Women and Girls in 2016 to 2019 shared a common theme: How did this egregious disparity in Canada stay hidden from minds and news coverage for decades? For one, the idea that Indigenous women do not matter is deeply embedded in this country's foundation. European settlers cast Indigenous women and their families as subhuman—heathens and savages who didn't have the genetic makeup to make progress in white society. And because of the way colonialism enforced men's superiority, in particular through sex-based discrimination legislated in the Indian Act, Indigenous women were displaced from their leadership roles and relegated to being at the behest of men.

The colonial hangover of systemic anti-Indigenous female violence means that many still live in fear that each day we—or our daughters, sisters, aunties, mothers, or grandmothers—leave the house, we might not make it home. And the darker our skin, the deeper the racism and the more vulnerable we are to violence and injustice.

Indigenous women are more likely to die prematurely or experience violence than any other race of women in Canada. While making up only 4 percent of the female population, Indigenous women and girls in Canada made up almost 25 percent of all female homicide victims in this country between 2001 and 2015.

IN SOME WAYS, despite the setbacks, Canadians—including journalists—are changing their perception of Indigenous women and girls from stereotypes or objects of doom and gloom to people of resilience and strength. As a mixed-race person, I've also experienced that shift in thinking. I've had to admit that I too have unconscious bias about Indigenous people and have let the stereotypes sink in deep. But I've found hope by listening to the younger generation, who challenge and transform the status quo in our own communities.

Less than a decade ago, the stories of MMIWG were not believed and not considered worthy of conversation, coverage, or even due diligence. Executives and producers, mostly white, have consciously or unconsciously inserted their biased perspectives on Indigenous people into our stories. Reporters in CBC's newsrooms across Canada were barred from using the word *survivor* to describe residential school survivors, as laid out in CBC's official language guide at the time. Instead, we were directed to call them only *students*. As Indigenous reporters, the message that we felt was being relayed to us, again and again, was that we could not tell the truth unless it was more aligned with a colonial way of thinking that erased, diluted, or softened Indigenous experiences. It took years of Indigenous reporters working hard behind the scenes to convince gatekeepers that these stories mattered and deserved ample coverage, and to start to imagine shattering bias against us.

In 2008, in the lead-up to Prime Minister Stephen Harper's apology to residential school survivors, then CBC reporter Wab Kinew led a successful charge to allow CBC journalists to use the term *survivor* and change the wording in CBC's language guide. And in 2012, a constellation of events lined up to drive more transformation. In the winter of 2012, during the Idle No More movement events across the country, for the first time in my career I would look at the TV, turn on the radio, or open an online story and see multiple diverse Indigenous people sharing their stories, rather than one Chief or one white person speaking on our behalf. I saw what I had yearned to see for years: the real, undiluted truth. Once people seemed more willing to listen, the truth came rushing out.

Following the RCMP's *Missing and Murdered Aboriginal Women* report acknowledging what many family members had been screaming for years—that there were nearly 1,200 known Indigenous women and girls missing and murdered in Canada—the final report of the Truth and Reconciliation Commission of Canada dropped like a bomb in 2015. It laid bare the direct links between residential school, the foster care system, and the high number of MMIWG. In the same year CBC News, under the leadership of Connie Walker, created a database compiling 287 cases of MMIWG. The *Globe and Mail* and the *Toronto Star* followed suit with projects dedicated to MMIWG, including daily news coverage with investigative components.

Incremental changes in media coverage have helped raise the profile of some cases and propelled officials to respond to the crisis. However, there are still Indigenous women and girls going missing and being murdered at disproportionate levels today. And there are still glaring problems with the way the media handles Indigenous stories. When the final report of the National Inquiry into Missing and Murdered Indigenous Women and Girls came out in 2019, media were the first to rail against commissioners' use of the word *genocide* to describe colonial violence. I knew then that a subject—the media—that I had initially given a small role in my book was something I needed to address more acutely. And the more I interviewed family members of MMIWG for this book, the more responsibility I felt I bore as a journalist to help my industry colleagues, the gatekeepers of information, do better. Likewise, the more responsibility I personally felt to investigate the cases of those family members' loved ones—to honour their lives more respectfully, to find answers with more rigour, and to lay out all the context and the many layers and years of colonization that have brought us here.

In writing this book, I tried my best to find justice for Indigenous family members. But it has been hard. Often their loved one's likely killer or killers had died before I could find answers. A source I was relying on to verify facts also died while I was writing this book. In many cases, police would not provide me with information, so I was forced to file several Access to Information and Privacy requests—even for straightforward and mundane questions such as "How many staff members of this task force are currently investigating missing and murdered women and girls?"

But my worst fear was that speaking to family members would be retraumatizing to them—that writing this book would unearth emotions and dredge up hard memories and cause harm. Ethics is a pillar of journalism that many forget, but we have an obligation to be mindful of and mitigate the harm our stories may cause to those they include. When it comes to disenfranchised or vulnerable communities, our ethical duty is even higher.

I was also concerned that including my own story could be perceived as disrespectful to the family members. Would my story overshadow theirs? Would including details of my own life take up space that otherwise could be used to amplify theirs? That apprehension is something that I am still struggling with. I survived. Their loved ones did not.

But I knew that by sharing my own experiences—close up, personal, sometimes awful and violent—others could see how vulnerability and cycles of violence work. I am sharing my experiences because I want everyone to understand what it's like to be thrust into a world of unpredictability and vulnerability, but also to be a part of a world of hope and love. And most of all, if you are a survivor, I want you to know: I see you, I hear you, I believe you, and you are not alone.

MY OWN STORY begins on Vancouver Island and moves to Vancouver, to the streets of the downtown neighbourhoods and cities in the United States, then weaves through Prince George near the Highway of Tears, to Yellowknife, Toronto, Winnipeg, and back to Vancouver. Along the way, I both experienced violence and lived alongside women whose experiences and knowledge pushed me to pursue journalism and report on women and girls who are marginalized, missing, or murdered. My own experiences living in Prince George gave me context for my later investigations into women and girls like Ramona Wilson, Gloria Levina Moody, and Tamara Chipman; similarly, my writing on the Pickton investigation is underlain with what I know of the Downtown Eastside from some of my time spent there. For years, navigating the trauma in my life, from the abuse I experienced at home, to street life entrenched in unpredictability, to violence in relationships, I've found that I was not the only one who bore scars from the shrapnel of colonization—far from it. Searching for answers about my identity and vulnerability took me on a journey where I learned about Indigenous women whose lives often mirrored or shared themes in mine.

There is ugliness in this story, but there is also beauty. The light in the darkness comes from the family members, friends, and advocates who've transformed the narrative about their loves ones: from marginalized, uncared for, and abhorred, to loved, honoured, and memorialized. Ultimately, they fight for the lives of women and girls in future generations.

And to understand their stories—of those who have survived, and for those who cannot share—you have to begin at a time that has been erased or warped by the colonials, a time when Indigenous women were revered as the backbone of our communities.

1

Adaawk, *oral history*

BEFORE IT WAS
THE HIGHWAY OF TEARS

GITXSAN IS THE NAME of my people on my father's side. Translated to English it means "people of the river mist." As you travel the dewy highways and roads that ribbon the northwest of British Columbia, it's clear why. Glacier-crowned mountains, misty zephyrs, and lush forests cradle the rushing waters from the Xsan (Skeena River) that runs along part of Highway 16— now infamously known as the Highway of Tears. The artery connects today's Prince Rupert to Prince George and a number of Indigenous communities in between. It's an area I've cherished since I was a young adult. I'd often pull my car over on the highway, just to listen to ravens smack their wings overhead, watch steelhead pop their gills out of the rapids, and feel the crisp air blow from the snowy mountaintops.

Nestled within the most northern reaches of the highway are six of my Nation's villages—Gitanmaax, Gitsegukla, Gitanyow, Kispiox, Gitwangak, and Sik-E-Dakh (Glen Vowell). These communities speckle our traditional territory—an area about five times the size of Prince Edward Island. Each distinct village is home to 400 to 700 people, or 800 to 2,500 if you include off-reserve members. Some are graced with towering and intricately carved totem poles, others are known for their summer rodeos, and still others boast peaceful mountainous landscapes. I am registered with Gitanmaax, a community born out of a tiny summer village first called Ansi'suuxs, or "place of the driftwood." In English, Gitanmaax (first called Git An Maa Hixs) means "people who fish with burning torches" and is rooted in our creation story about a woman who gave birth to part-human and part-canine children who eventually sustained the community with their unique fishing skills. While it is the band I belong to today, my lineage stems from Kisgegas, a now abandoned village farther north. Both communities are about a fourteen-hour drive northwest from what is now Vancouver, or about five hours northwest from Prince George.

While those from far away may see these lands, near what is now known as the Highway of Tears, as merely characterized by danger and despair, we see them as so much more. Oral histories and archaeological evidence show that my people lived in the northwest of what is now called British Columbia, building huwilp (house groups), families, and villages, at times struggling and at others thriving, for ten thousand years at least.

My childhood was filled with my dad's stories of living at home in Gitxsan territory, of our culture, and of his travels. His tales helped me journey in my imagination to our rugged gentle lands of fireweed, red cedars, and rivers, absorbing our rich cultural history—much different from where I was born and grew up by the ocean in a small, largely white town on Vancouver Island. His stories instilled a curiosity in me about the expansiveness of the world, but also about how I belonged in it. Many of his narratives were of our Gitxsan relatives fighting to keep our land, our distinctiveness, and our relations, which in turn shaped my identity, knowing I would have to be brave and outspoken if I wanted a place in this world.

By age 9, I was captivated by the pieces of our culture he'd sprinkle throughout our conversations. He'd tell me stories about how the Gitxsan, Tsimshian, and Nisga'a once lived together in the northwest region as one people in an ancestral village known as Temlaham, long before they dispersed throughout the northwest. These stories were chronicles of a landslide and great deluge and how our Nations built our communities back up after the natural disaster. After long phone calls with his cousin, my uncle Neil Sterritt, my dad would tell me about our adaawk (oral history), which traces the history of our land told in pictures in formline designs carved on house fronts and in totem poles, and delineated through modern-day relationships. When I was living in Prince George as a young adult, over emails, Neil would describe to me how our matrilineal lineage is connected to the lax gibu (Wolf clan) and how, up until he died in 2019, his father, Neil Sterritt Sr., was Wiik'aax ("big wings"), the head of the House of Wiik'aax. It is a name and role my grandfather Walter Sterritt—Neil Sr.'s brother— was groomed for since he was a young man. Neil Jr. said foot messengers used to bring my grandfather small gifts as he was being raised to fill the leadership role. But Grandpa decided to focus on his family and work rather than become the miin wilp (head) of the House of Wiik'aax, and eventually Neil Sr. (after once declining) agreed instead. These stories learned from my dad and uncles are ones I hold close to my heart, since my grandfather died before I was able to process memories, when I was a baby.

Uncle and Dad shared that our Gitxsan trickster, or transformational figure, Wiigyet, created our natural world of rivers, oolichan runs, and light and darkness—in folly, spite, and pure selfishness. In my younger years, I was not taken by these stories, which often seemed long-winded rambles. I didn't relate to their clever and philosophical messages until much later in life. But they gave me a sense of the creative wisdom of our people and inspired the curiosity and imagination that would later draw me to visual art, literature, and storytelling.

Wiigyet is said to be craft without wisdom, and power without any regard for consequences. To me, Wiigyet holds up a mirror to us, making fun of the weaknesses that make us human. As I got older, I became more enamoured of these stories, and my thirst to learn grew. When I lived on the street, they became a metaphor for survival; they reminded me that even in chaos, with ingenuity and acceptance of the ever-changing world around us, anything is attainable. If not a teacher, Wiigyet pushes us to ask questions about our intentions and to laugh at ourselves when it all stops making sense. The tales also taught me about myself, and about my Gitxsan culture—one that puts our women at the centre of everything. My uncles didn't share much with me about the roles of our women, other than that we are a matrilineal society. But I later learned much more from Gitxsan women and Elders while living in Prince George and in Vancouver.

Before she passed on, Gitxsan Elder, artist, and author Judith Morgan shared much of her knowledge of our culture with me for CBC stories and then in long informal phone calls. Judith was excited to share as I keenly soaked up her knowledge. Before the colonials dug in, she said, Gitxsan women held revered political and social roles. Most women in northwest Indigenous societies had, and in some ways still have, authority and decision-making power over the land—fishing holes, berry grounds, and sacred sites. Judith said that Gitxsan women continue to hold sigidim haanak' (female Chiefs) names, and once controlled our territories. By our cultural law, in order to hold a Gitxsan name or hold a seat in our feasts, I need to be adopted by a high-ranking member of my family or another family's house, since my Gitxsan lineage stems from my paternal line and we are a matrilineal society. While I've made attempts to go home, connect with my family, and participate in Gitxsan events when I can, I often struggle with this, thinking: Do I, as a mixed-blood city kid who lives so far away, belong, and is it my place to try? It is something I still grapple with, knowing how critical identity and especially my role as a woman are in our Nation. Still, it is my responsibility to learn about where I come from, on both my Gitxsan and white sides, how we got here, and how to heal from the wounds of colonization.

Before settlers helped themselves to our territories and built roadways for resource extraction, my relatives carried deer hides, furs, and oolichans along a major trading route known as the grease trail. My people would pack heavy boxes of valuables, namely oolichan grease, often using cedar rope tumplines. The route started at Gitlax'aws—a Nisga'a fish camp where inland Indigenous groups stayed—and extended all the way to the Gitxsan village of Gitanyow. The trade of grease for furs, seaweed, and seafood sustained our traditional economies for generations. But that trade and the trail that supported it were disrupted by the colonists trying to make their mark in the northwest.

Europeans entering Indigenous territories for the first time were shocked seeing the high-ranking and leadership positions Indigenous women held in their communities. "It was not long before [Europeans] realized that to dominate the land and the people that were occupying it, they needed to disempower the women," writes Kim Anderson in *A Recognition of Being: Reconstructing Native Womanhood*. Removing us from the land was a critical part of the colonial empire-building project.

Scores of ships visited my Nation's territories and the northwest region from the 1700s to the 1800s, loaded with settlers in search of resources to fund European and American economic and political expansion around the world. With the newcomers came major changes for my people—many of them painful and devastating.

In 1862, a steamer ship known as the *Brother Jonathan* carried mining prospectors from California to Vancouver Island. The vessel was also transporting smallpox—a deadly virus endemic to the European population. The virus spread north from Victoria when officials forced visiting northwest Indigenous traders back home. As a result, smallpox eventually killed off many northwest Indigenous people, including 30 percent of the Gitxsan population. At least thirty thousand Indigenous people died over the next year, leaving mass graves, empty villages, traumatized survivors, and societal collapse. It is part of what has been called the "red holocaust" or the genocide of Indigenous people. Genocidal intent, some scholars have said, is clear knowing the government of the day limited vaccinations for Indigenous people—those with no natural immunity—and refused to mandate a general quarantine, two strategies that would have at least contained the epidemic. Unlike the vaccination efforts happening in the east of Canada at the time, any efforts colonists made to manage smallpox in British Columbia appear to have been disorganized, to say the least. To protect themselves from the disease, the colonials evicted Indigenous people at gunpoint, burned villages to the ground, and towed away canoes full of the dead.

Many Indigenous people and scholars today believe that governments benefited from this inadequate response to the crisis: not only did the lethal outbreaks devastate communities, but there were fewer people alive and healthy to stand up to the crime of land theft, and therefore governments could avoid providing compensation to Indigenous people for the massive land grab that followed. While there is little proof that the Hudson's Bay Company deliberately killed Indigenous people by gifting blankets infected with smallpox, as is sometimes rumoured, there is evidence that the disease was used as part of germ warfare. As early as 1763, for example, the British had used blankets exposed to smallpox in their attempt to subdue the Indigenous uprising led by Chief Pontiac of the Odawa. Even with this well-documented history, some journalists and politicians still refuse to admit a genocide took place in Canada and neglect to acknowledge how it connects to land dispossession. Just a year before the smallpox epidemic, in 1861, the governor of the Colony of Vancouver Island, James Douglas, was fundraising to extinguish Aboriginal title and move Indigenous people from huge swaths of their traditional territory to tiny, remote tracts of land the colonials called reserves, in order to make room for further white settlement.

Like the fur traders who came into the region earlier, miners passing through Hazelton en route to the Omineca goldfields in the early 1870s used the grease trails for travel and to transport minerals. Crews widened these trails so settlers could pack goods by donkey and horse train.

Those like my great-grandfathers, and later their children, contributed to and enjoyed some of the benefits of the booming logging, fishing, and mining industries, but too often the newcomers, in particular the miners who arrived in droves, showed little to no regard for Gitxsan life, culture, or concerns. Still my people stood their ground, fighting to protect the land that had sustained them for centuries.

In 1872, four years before the Indian Act was created, careless prospectors failed to extinguish a campfire near a Gitxsan village. The blaze spread to twelve Gitsegukla longhouses and twelve totem poles, burning the entire village to the ground. When the miners refused to compensate the Gitxsan Chiefs— as required by our law—the Gitxsans blockaded Skeena River traffic, preventing supply ships from getting in. The colonials sent in two gunboats to the mouth of the river, where Gitsegukla Chiefs met Lieutenant-Governor Joseph Trutch. There, he granted the Chiefs $600 in compensation, which in today's dollars would be about $13,000—not a lot for an entire village including totem poles that today are worth $25,000 to $60,000 each.

Over the years following the fire, the Gitxsan resisted further encroachment, erecting several other blockades to prevent the theft of our lands and the denial of Aboriginal rights and title.

In June of 1909, without consultation with or compensation for the Gitxsan, settlers started to build wagon roads from Hazelton to Kispiox. In my uncle Neil J. Sterritt's book *Mapping My Way Home*, the late Wiilaxhaa, who was part of my family's house group and a Gitxsan land rights advocate, explains how, on the advice of his Sim'oogit (Hereditary Chief), he wrote a letter to the road foreman that said, "Please do not come through our town. If you are willing to build a road through our town, the land is reservation and we want to get paid for the land." The foreman ignored the request. That fall, when crews started road building, Kispiox community members took and hid the road crew's equipment. When Sim'oogit Gamgisti'ltxw attempted to address the situation, the foreman hit him, leading to a small brawl with the crew members. Wiilaxhaa outlined that further fights took place, saying the "whites" incited and carried out the violence but the Gitxsans were jailed, some for several months, because white officers took the settlers' stories as truth. "Every day, right up to this day, the white men are always after the Indian... And we overlook it all and lay the blame on the government," Wiilaxhaa said.

It was not just governments and police, as Wiilaxhaa states, but the entire settler population that was rapidly moving into my family's territories, using the idea of Indigenous sub-humanity to maintain white dominance. It wasn't just an idea. Dehumanization of Indigenous people was actually part of a framework of international law—the Doctrine of Discovery—used by explorers like Christopher Columbus. It stated that in God's eyes, we were subhuman, and lands not occupied by

Christians could be discovered and claimed. And that was used as legal and moral justification for colonial dispossession of sovereign Indigenous Nations. It gave the settlers an assumed legal right to move in and push us out.

When I hear stories of my great-grandmother Luu Uuxs ("inside the copper" in English) spending days in the bush carrying behemoth bentwood boxes filled with huckle-berries, or of grandfathers when they were as young as 12 hunting mountain goats to feed their community, or even stories of simply surviving those colonial days, I think of my people as superhuman. Our stories map a supernatural trajectory—one that fuses our spirituality, our creation stories, and our land, all of which the colonists attempted to chop up or erase. Learning how our ancestors took the remaining fragments and put them back together, reclaiming their names, land, languages, and feast hall system, is what gives me hope. In my darkest days, I recall these histories—a constant reminder that I too can heal my broken path.

DESPITE MY ANCESTORS' BEST EFFORTS to preserve their land, our grease trails were covered with and intersected by railways, logging roads, bridges, mills, bars, and roadways, and the ancient trade route was eventually destroyed. My ancestors watched the lush forests slowly become well-trafficked roads.

I've travelled the highways from Vancouver to Prince George and then through my home territory many times since I was a baby, but more often as an adult. In 2016, while conducting research for this book and going to visit my cousin, then the mayor of Hazelton, I drove westward from Prince George and then north along Highway 16. Haunting plywood billboards plastered with pictures of the faces of young missing women jumped out from the side of the highway, every 10 to 20 kilometres. Posters stuck to gas station receptacles and on store windows made it hard to forget the reality that dozens of women and girls have gone missing from or been murdered here since the 1970s. And all that made me think not only of my family's history of being removed from this land, but also about my own vulnerability—memories of travelling alone, hitchhiking along dark highways, and being among those who could easily be ripped away.

While those haunting images terrified me, I took comfort in the undeniable beauty and power of the land and water that the highway cuts through. After I left Hazelton and continued west, then south, the salt-licked air swelled from the Pacific as I neared the once booming fishing town of Prince Rupert. Handsome yellow cedars edged the highway and sun-soaked mountain ranges gazed from the horizon. The smell of rich soils and dripping conifers were reminders of the rainforest that once stood where the highway now rests. Travelling up and down Highway 16, every so often you see a wall of fog rising from tributaries like smoke and unfolding like clouded wings pushing apart the rocky cliffs and imperious mountains. From the crusty crags in Rupert, I saw tiny archipelagos sprawl across the ocean, sopped up by mighty waves. Fishers pulled black cod, red snapper, crab, and salmon from nets and traps.

And the landscape reminded me of our Gitxsan territory, just as rich and beautiful as this. Grandpa Walter and his brother, my great-uncle Neil Sr., kept up their health in their younger days by running up and down the mountains on traplines in Xsan watersheds. When Neil Sr. was around 92 years old and I was in my early 20s, I visited him at his house that overlooks the rushing Xsan, and he shared stories with me about what life was like before these lands were chopped up, spit out, and disfigured by men who dreamed of cashing in on the rivers, trees, earth, and people.

My great-grandmother Luu Uuxs, who also went by her English name, Kate Morrison, was born in 1882 into a world that was being transformed by settler colonialism and the resource extraction that Europeans wreaked. In my uncle Neil Jr.'s book *Mapping My Way Home*, he describes Luu Uuxs's strength. Carrying my great-uncle Neil Sr., a baby at the time, on her back along with supplies, she transported my grandpa (her eldest child) in a toboggan pulled by five dogs. She would mind family camps, as well as a garden and the children, while the men hunted for moose, rabbit, and grouse. But she could also fell and peel an 8-metre cedar tree between lunch and supper, and later managed their family's rental cabins. But as colonization dug its patriarchal claws into Indigenous communities, Indigenous women and children were the first to be stripped of their power.

That loss of self-determination and land is a common thread that links many of the women and girls who have gone missing or been murdered. Many were ripped from their land, families, and communities during colonization—through residential school, the Sixties Scoop, the child-welfare system, or gender discrimination legislated in the Indian Act. And those who live along the Highway of Tears face added vulnerability due to the remoteness of their communities, which comes with a lack of services, limited access to education, and unreliable or unaffordable transportation.

These vulnerabilities have made it easier for at least three serial killers to prey on women in these lands over the last few decades. It's hard to reckon with, emotionally and intellectually, and it's even more difficult to untangle.

Trying to find answers—about what happened to the women, who killed them, and why so little has been done about it—comes from a place of discomfort for me because in many ways, it's personal.

I WAS FIRST HELD in the northwest when I was just a baby—when my Newfoundlander mom and Gitxsan and Irish dad drove up from my birthplace of Campbell River to spend time with family. Dad was a longtime logger with charisma and a love for nature, but he also suffered from trauma that he coped with by using alcohol and drugs. Mom was a legal secretary who was hardworking and tenacious and could find any file for a lawyer. She was gregarious, loyal, and loving, but she didn't always make the best choice in men. She met my dad at a bar in Prince George after moving there with her sister, my aunt Mary, one of her eleven siblings from Bell Island, Newfoundland. She grew up poor and would share stories about how many potatoes she peeled to feed the huge family. She was an incredible mother who was kind and patient.

Because my mom passed away from cancer when I was barely 20 and still figuring out my own life, I don't know much about her young adult life. "She was vulnerable and that was her strength and weakness," Aunt Mary tells me over Facebook Messenger, a platform we've used to communicate since 2009. Her time with my dad was rough, Mary says, and my mom was constantly moving in and out of crisis. After they met, Mom moved with my dad from Prince George to Black Creek, a town about 35 kilometres south of Campbell River, for logging work, and I was born not long after. Dad also had a 9-year-old daughter from a previous marriage, whose mother had died not long before, so my mom took her on as her own. From faded and flap-cornered square photographs, I've gleaned memories of our little family's trips back to my dad's homeland to visit relatives.

My understanding of my father's early life is also convoluted, blurred by the beer- and cider-influenced stories he shared with me over the years. His five siblings—two brothers and three sisters—dispersed from Gitxsan territories in scattered timelines: born in faraway hospitals, or heading into the wilds of settler-Indigenous logging or mill industries at young ages, or getting married and moving to other towns. My dad's stories, framed in living-room pictures, illustrated his love of blue robin eggs and white spirit bears of the coastal forests, and his regrets for cutting those forests down.

When I was around 11 years old, after half a 2-litre of peach cider, he brewed up memories from Glen Vowell, where my grandfather was born, and from Manson Creek, where he died, and then Kispiox, where his Gitxsan family's ties were spooled. Dad also spoke of later days when disputes and rivalries broke out between kids in the largely white-populated Hazelton and Gitxsans in the Gitanmaax reserve, up the street from the house where he grew up. In the 1950s and '60s, he'd lament, kids would literally throw rocks at each other across the invisible divide.

But the stories he told that stick with me the most are the ones from more recent history: of my Gitxsan uncles—warriors, he'd call them—"who knew the white man's laws inside out," using legal texts as weapons to fight for Gitxsan rights and title to the land. In white-man courts, in a 1997 Supreme Court of Canada case that would famously become known as the *Delgamuukw* case (named after a Gitxsan hereditary Chief who brought it forward), my relatives used songs, dances, maps, testimony, and genealogy to demonstrate our cultural and traditional laws (ayook) that dictate our responsibility to our lands. But for those representing the colonial laws, like former Supreme Court of British Columbia chief justice Allan McEachern, who presided over the original 1991 Gitxsan-Wet'suwet'en land claim case in *Delgamuukw et al. v. The Queen*, Indigenous people had no rights to the land. In his decision, he asserted that the Gitxsan and Wet'suwet'en people lost their title to the land at the time of colonization because they were primitive peoples incapable of holding proprietary interests, with lives before contact that were (as he stated, quoting Thomas Hobbes) "nasty, brutish and short." My uncle Neil J. Sterritt countered that argument with anthropological evidence demonstrating that our system of government was equally sophisticated even though it diverged from colonial ideals. He explained that in our Aboriginal law, the land, the plants, the animals, and the people all have spirit—a foreign sentiment to the colonials, who thought of the natural world as merely something to extract and profit from.

"These are our Gitxsan heroes: our family," my dad would say, introducing a shy 11-year-old me to them on our East Vancouver back porch. I remember thinking that they didn't fit the mould of an "Indigenous warrior." They wore jeans and T-shirts, had short hair, big moustaches, and light skin, and joked and laughed a lot, telling stories about the trial and growing up "up north." They were a stark contrast to the camouflaged, stoic, and violent "Native warriors" in movies or the headdressed and loinclothed "Indians" I'd seen in textbooks. And they butted up against the perceptions that still surface today in my conversations with non-Indigenous people, who sometimes expect to see a romanticized version of us, always in regalia and practising "rituals." Often I hear people longingly say, "But I never see the Indigenous people; where are they?" as if expecting us to perform our Indigeneity for them. I always say, "You might not expect it, but we are lawyers, doctors, students, mechanics, activists, teachers, journalists, just like you." We do not exist just within the framework of many non-Indigenous people's notion of culture. But we are also frequently seen in a less romanticized way. As a kid, seeing my respected Elders and uncles depicted as greedy, primitive, or lazy in popular literature and in the media planted the seed for me to start telling our own stories with the bedrock of accuracy they deserve. From that time on, I began to slowly grasp the thick discrepancy between the reality for my people and how outsiders perceived us.

Dad also boasted of different, less heroic times. From innocuous ones, like feeding grapes to hungry raccoons in Stanley Park, to darker ones, like "shrooming" in his logging loader while cutting down spruce trees and red cedars. About a week after an accident, just before he started to lose his mind forever to dementia, he told me that the many bruises all over his face and body were a consequence of drinking hard while operating his loader.

Sterritt stories always contain dark and light elements of adventure and travel, migration and rootedness, which are common themes for many mixed-blood families, whose tributaries are as varied as our lineage. But with my dad's stories, there were also elements of duplicity and trickery, much like in the layered legends of our creator Wiigyet. These stories gave me further impetus on my path as a journalist—of constantly yearning for a truth, one that is often unclear and at times even warped.

Most of my dad's side rode rough waters throughout their child, teen, and adult lives, battling family demons like sexual abuse and domestic violence, and surviving sinister histories wreaked by dubious government policies. Indian agents following the Indian Act forced my community to stop using our language, Gitxsanimx, and put an end to practising our ceremonies and traditional laws—in the end all spoken about in secret, slowly drifting away from the next generations' vernacular and psyche. As recorded in countless documents, Indigenous people, from the late nineteenth century and into the twentieth, faced two options: voluntarily assimilate through the Gradual Civilization Act of 1857, or be forced to assimilate, often violently, through residential school, apartheid, and dislocation. The British push for assimilation was reinforced by the long-standing colonialist view that Indigenous people had an inferior culture that showed we were not as intelligent or as capable as European settlers.

My dad told me my grandfather Walter joined the Canadian government's voluntary enfranchisement program as a young man, gaining the "privilege" of assimilating into Canadian society and thus gaining full Canadian citizenship. Some of my relatives told me Grandpa Walter did it so he could vote; others said it was so he could drink at a bar like the whites. But in early 2020, one of my Sterritt cousins shared a chilling reality with me, one that hurts to think about: He did it so that his kids wouldn't have to suffer at residential school. Instead, his children would attend the white and mixed school in town that was not characterized by brutal physical, sexual, and mental abuse.

But, ironically, anyone who did not assimilate and was determined to be "Indian" through the federal government's Indian Act was afforded certain provisions, like health care and education, as compensation for the land that was taken. Still, one could lose that status involuntarily if they went to war or to university, or if they were an "Indian" woman who married a non-Indian man. Strangely, a white woman could gain status if she married an "Indian" man, something my own mother was offered (but rejected, she told me, because she was not the one who was oppressed and didn't feel she had a right to it).

My dad's extended and immediate family, many married to white partners, relocated away from their home territory for logging and mining work and blended into other towns and urban centres, like Prince George, Mission, and Campbell River. Not every Indigenous person had that choice. Those who were darker-skinned faced more racism and didn't have the financial mobility to move away and start over.

As my dad descended into the depths of dementia in 2018, the memories he shared with me were faded and muddled and near gone. The last time I visited, before he passed into the spirit world in 2020, I'm sure he had no idea who I was. But his earlier days, consumed by liquor, weed, cocaine, and acid, were not much different. It was often an unpredictable haze that I was forced to navigate. But it was not all bad. Now that he has passed on, the kinder memories often seep in. When I visited him on weekends as a child after my parents split up, for example, he would tell me bedtime stories about his time in the bush, the window open with the cold winter air breezing in as I curled up in layered quilted blankets. Or the time that he must have sensed I was being bullied physically and mentally by what felt like the entire female population of my high school, and he picked me up and took me to McDonald's at lunch so I didn't have to endure hiding in bathrooms another day. He taught me to be streetwise and take care of myself by looking at people's body language for prompts of their behaviour to come, something I now recognize as a trauma response. He taught me how to drive his Blue Bird bus when I was 11—the one I would sneak into later after he pushed me into the throes of the street when I was 14. There was good in him. But a lot of the negative overshadows that.

My aunties were curt about and dismissive of the past and I assume many, like me, have various levels of trauma and stress disorders, though I'm not sure they would ever admit it. Other, less talked about, invisible barriers prevent me from wanting to dig deeper and explore my ties to long ago. One of my biological paternal uncles, who is now deceased, was a pedophile who sexually assaulted and molested many of my cousins and other family members. It has resulted in triggers I still experience almost every day, decades later. Dredging up and reliving these memories is not on my bucket list, but they're also mysteries that pull me in, compelling me to find out more and search for the why and the how. It is much easier to comb through the parts of my roots that grow the strongest.

MY FIRST ENGLISH WORDS as a baby were *light* and *mama* because my mom used to flick the light on and off to help me to get to sleep (it must have made sense at the time). My first Gitxsanimx words came much later in life, in my early teens and 20s. They were *adaawk* (Gitxsan oral history), *gwe'a* (meaning "poor" or "pitiful," sometimes in culture and wealth), and *Amsiwaa* (the word we use for white man). All three words are significant, connected, and demonstrate my early Gitxsan political education. Our adaawk is encapsulated in our feasts, totem poles, relationships, and creation stories. My connection to the word gwe'a isn't just about being raised without my culture, but about helping me understand why and how economic and social policies of the past still play out today—like how the Indian Act still determines who is and who is not an "Indian" in Canada. And Amsiwaa: the ever-present conflict inside and outside of me, like a battle that encompasses everything stubbornly, persistently. A reminder that I too, as a woman who is part white and part Gitxsan, carry the burden of responsibility for what happened on these lands. Rather than move through the world like a chameleon using my white or Indigenous identity to my advantage, I've chosen to use both as a point of responsibility. While I recognize my pale skin as holding privilege, few don't know I am Indigenous, as I make a deliberate choice to voice who I am and where I come from.

As Wiigyet teaches us, humans are not perfect. Gitxsans did not live in a world that was absent of conflict, difficulties, or even war. Oral stories explain how our villages, like other human societies, fought battles over territory, marriages, laws, and jealousy and sometimes faced casualties. It meant, as my uncle Neil J. Sterritt points out in his book, that Gitxsan lands changed, expanded, shrank, and overlapped throughout our history. Conflicts within our territories were often brought to an end through negotiations that recognized and respected different cultural laws. But a new type of violence cascaded into Indigenous lives when the colonials started trickling in from Europe.

Residential school created a long-lasting legacy of intergenerational trauma in the way it destroyed families, forcibly removing children from their homes and subjecting them to priests and nuns who committed unimaginable physical, sexual, mental, emotional, and spiritual abuse. The mere admission of such atrocities wouldn't come until more than a century after many of the institutions first opened. But even as late as 2021, the experiences of some residential school survivors—at the St. Anne's residential school in Ontario, of being strapped to an electric chair and shocked while being laughed at by nuns, an experience repeated over and over for years—would not be considered enough for compensation by federal government lawyers. We know now from documents and testimony that the federal government's plan to violently assimilate Indigenous children was real—but it was an epic failure, and a tragedy that many will be trying to understand and reconcile for perhaps another century, or even longer.

Like other mixed-heritage Gitxsans I know, my direct family members never attended residential school, so I've always grappled to find answers to why many of my relatives were so dysfunctional. Dad often told me about how hard it was for his family to watch their territory be ripped away from them ("bulldozed right from under them" was the phrase he used), just the same as their culture, clan and kinship system, and language. When he helped me get my Indian status card when I was 11, he underscored what it meant and what it didn't. It was not a privilege; it was not free stuff—it was a crumb the federal government gave us for the vast amount of land it took from us. His explanation of land dispossession and assimilation—two key assaults of colonization—does not directly explain the abuse and violence in my family, but it sheds light on the trauma, the loss, the disconnection, and the way we were colonized and assimilated into a European culture that saw us as inferior and subhuman.

During my trip up Highway 16 in the fall of 2016, the late and fiercely respected, never to be forgotten Nisga'a warrior (a title I use rarely) Preston Guno asked me to speak at a conference about Indigenous girls and sexual abuse. I stood in a gymnasium in Burns Lake, a town about two hours away from Gitxsan territory, and spoke to a group of about forty Indigenous people. I talked about being from a family where many of us were sexually abused and about the violence I experienced on the street. I realized once again, even there, sharing these experiences, that my ability to hide, to mask my pain, was strong. After I spoke, so many women came up to me and thanked me for my words, all with versions of "I would have had no idea you went through all of that." Concealing my past with blazers and blush and decorative words and the emotionless flair of a journalist forced all that pain down to a point where I'd forget all that I had survived. But now I was allowing my veneer to crack and reveal my vulnerable inner self. Before then, every time I had shared, no matter how strong I felt at the start, I would wind up feeling guilty, shameful, and defenceless, like my shield had collapsed for all to see my wounds, and my ever-present scars. But here I felt strong. I knew I was among sisters, and I felt them catch me in a safety net of understanding.

One of those kindred spirits was Brenda Wilson, a force to be reckoned with—a humble, smart, beautiful, well-dressed, well-spoken, and esteemed Gitxsan woman. Brenda lost her baby sister, Ramona, to the Highway of Tears in 1994. Watching Brenda sing the Women's Warrior Song, tears streaming down her poised face, and speak of who her sister was and how she disappeared, I could not help but tear up myself thinking of all she had been through.

And I also thought about how her sister's fate could have easily been mine.

2

Nee dii sgithl ts'ixts'ik loo'y, *I don't have a vehicle*

SHE COULD HAVE BEEN ME

IN THE 1990S, and into the early 2000s, teenagers locked themselves in their bedrooms, listened to music their parents loathed, and rebelled against the rules—much like the teens of today, minus the viral TikToks, Instagram Stories, and snide subtweets. We didn't hear about the news seconds after it happened. The online world hadn't yet moulded the human psyche, nor had its patois started buzzing through high school walls and office dividers. The state-of-the-art CD was replacing the old-school tape, and brick phones were still a gag on *Saved by the Bell*. It was rare for a person as poor as I was to have a mobile phone, but I wasn't a typical teenager with a typical bedroom. I had no home, and because of that, no landline. I knew I had to find another way to communicate, so I used email on library and school computers and then cheap mobile phones I'd buy at pawnshops. But earlier, in 1994, the year Ramona Wilson went missing, most people had very limited or no access to cell phones, high-speed internet, or email. Social media didn't exist. There was no way to get instant messages out to millions in times of panic, worry, grief, or loss. And without the trust of journalists to share their stories at the time, Indigenous people relied solely on more sluggish methods of communication—word of mouth, homemade missing posters stuck to telephone poles, and door knocking.

It was also a time when predators relied more on physical highways than electronic byways. The Amber Alert system and the use of DNA evidence in court were both still in their infancy. And it was still an era when the general public, the media, and in many cases the police didn't consider missing and murdered Indigenous women and girls (MMIWG) to be an important issue. For Brenda Wilson and the scores of other people who have lost loved ones along the Highway of Tears, the institutional failures of the police and media and the pain they've caused still reverberate through their lives every day. Many still see no possibility of justice for their loved ones. And even though it's hard for me to talk with people about losses while they're still grieving, it's an important part of finding out why there have been so many women and girls—by my count, at least seventy-five—missing or murdered along the Highway of Tears and adjoining highways.

Among those, Ramona Wilson's story stands out to me. Like me, she was Gitxsan and belonged to the Gitanmaax band, she was living away from her traditional territory, and if she were alive today, she would be not too much older than me. My heart skips a beat whenever I read about Ramona. I reflect on my experiences as a vulnerable teenager hitchhiking my way across North America in the late 1990s, thinking of how similar my background was to Ramona's and imagining what could have been my own fate. Hearing that she was a poet reminds me of myself as a teen, filling pages and pages of sketchbooks with prose and poesy. She had faith in a higher power, which draws me back to my belief then in divine beings and supernatural forces that interlaced my life as alternating saving graces.

As the summer orange sun faded behind the slopes of the Ts'edeek'aay mountains in Smithers on Saturday, June 11, 1994, 16-year-old Ramona was getting ready for a dance. The graduation event was 75 kilometres away at the Gitanmaax community hall in the town of Hazelton. She had just finished eating her favourite food, ham and pineapple takeout pizza, in front of the TV with her mom, Matilda Wilson, and her older brother. By then, at 28 years old, Ramona's sister Brenda was living on her own with her two young children. That evening, she'd made her way to a barbecue at a house a few doors down from her mom's. Amped for a night of celebration, Ramona laced up her pink-and-white high-tops, pulled on her white sweatshirt and acid-washed jean jacket, and waved goodbye before making her way out into the night.

If she hitchhiked or got a ride from friends, her route would have taken her from the west side of Smithers and north along Highway 16—an artery that in this area traces the path of the Bulkley River (Xsi'yeen Andoo). If her ride picked her up near her Railway Avenue home, she would have looked out the window and seen the Smithers Golf and Country Club, gone around Kathlyn Lake, passed the Smithers Airport and then Moricetown—about halfway there—before she made it the full hour away to the dance in Hazelton, the town that her reserve and mine, Gitanmaax, is nestled within. Brenda says when she arrived at the barbecue, another attendee told her that Ramona had stopped by. She herself never saw her there. "I only heard that she stopped by, because she had to walk past that house to get to [Smithers]."

But she never made it to the dance.

That night, when her friends didn't see her, they assumed she had attended another community graduation dance or had a sleepover at a friend's home in Moricetown. Summer was well on its way and the season's spontaneity was taking hold. But Ramona was the responsible one in her friend group, and her friends and family expected to hear from her soon. When Matilda still hadn't heard from her daughter on Sunday, she started to make calls to friends and family, places Ramona hung out, and local hospitals.

On Monday, when Ramona didn't arrive at school, Matilda and Brenda started to panic even more. After school, one of Ramona's best friends, Kristal, called the Smitty's restaurant where Ramona worked as a dishwasher. But she didn't show up there either, and Kristal knew Ramona would never have missed work.

Matilda started to ramp up her efforts to find her daughter and called the Smithers RCMP to file a missing person report. However, Brenda says officers suggested Ramona had run away or just needed some time away from the family, something that didn't make sense to her given their close relationship. Brenda says what stands out from that time is how they were judged by the police and the community, for being a single-parent family and being Indigenous.

"I don't think it was taken seriously," Brenda tells me by telephone from her home in Prince George. She says her family was forced to do the legwork of trying to find her baby sister. "We had to do our own posters, and if I wasn't working at the Friendship Centre as a program director, we wouldn't have had any support at all," she says. She and her family also set up and operated a tip line that was run out of the centre. "I was able to reach out to co-workers at the Friendship Centre, and face to face, and say, 'This is serious, this is the second person [at the time] to go missing.'"

A few years before Ramona's disappearance, on June 13, 1990, Wet'suwet'en teen Delphine Nikal went missing. She had gone to visit friends in Smithers, about 16 kilometres from her home in Telkwa, and was last seen by two friends hitchhiking east from Smithers on Highway 16. Shortly after Ramona disappeared, three other Indigenous teen girls also went missing from nearby communities. Roxanne Thiara, 15, was last seen in Prince George in July 1994. One month later, she was found dead near Burns Lake along the Highway of Tears. Alishia Germaine, 15, was last seen at the Prince George Native Friendship Centre in December 1994. She was later found slain near an elementary school by Highway 16. And Lana Derrick, 19, was a college student visiting family in Terrace when she went missing in the early hours of October 6, 1995. RCMP said she was last seen at a gas station on Highway 16, but her family believes she was seen alive after that at her friend Clarice's house in Terrace.

Brenda says that after her sister went missing, even with rising fears of a serial killer in the area, authorities often left her in the dark. "We had to initiate all those searches and get media to cover the stories," she says. Though there were journalists who wanted to get the word out, in a town that seemed to care little about Indigenous women and girls going missing, they had to fight to tell their stories. "Sometimes media gets a bad rap, but I always stand up for them because they've always been so helpful to our family, and anywhere I can help them I do," she says.

As for the larger community in Smithers, Brenda says she was constantly let down. Rumours laden with stereotypes about Indigenous people being "incompetent parents," "drunks," and "always in trouble with the law" were commonplace, she says. In early 1995, she and her mother organized a benefit dance to fundraise for the search and a reward for finding Ramona. But it wasn't a success. Instead it was overshadowed by a fundraiser for a missing white woman. That spring, Smithers citizens and business owners rallied around a series of events for Melanie Carpenter, who went missing from Surrey, a city more than 1,100 kilometres away. At the time, an editorial in the *Interior News* (Smithers) expressed their disappointment. "Why did Matilda not benefit from the generosity of our corporate citizens in her campaign to find her daughter?" the paper asked. As Brenda says, "It was another slap in the face, you know, trying to get support from our community. We just probably broke even. Meanwhile, the Melanie Carpenter Benefit Dance was in the thousands." Furthermore, police quickly identified a suspect in the Carpenter disappearance, 37-year-old Fernand Auger, and a warrant was issued for his arrest.

Brenda says it's the stereotyping of Indigenous people and the racism against us that has historically meant Indigenous women who are missing or murdered are given less attention than white women. "The way Indigenous women are seen as 'the squaw' or 'the drinking Indian' brought about by colonialism" has led us to this discrepancy, she says. Academics, journalists, and advocates have written extensively about how tropes of Indigenous women either as the idealized Indian princess or as a squaw—a highly offensive and derogatory slur suggesting Indigenous women are impure, barbaric, and dirty—are frequent in popular literature and media and work to undermine our humanity and credibility. These pervasive stereotypes foster violence against Indigenous women, girls, and two-spirit people. And in the past, the scorn we've received from the general public has made our Indigenous stories easier for the public and journalists to ignore.

IN THE LATE 1990s and the early 2000s, stories about MMIWG were scarce in newspapers, online, or on radio and television. I've read stories about missing women and girls along the Highway of Tears from this time, mostly from community papers and later blog posts, some of which read like conspiracy theories. But most of the information came word of mouth. Behind the scenes were desperate parents, siblings, or relatives searching for clues as to what happened to their loved one, but often it felt like those who had the power to uphold their voices or help solve cases didn't care. When there was coverage in mainstream outlets, it often had an overarching narrative implying that vulnerable girls and women had somehow brought situations upon themselves, or they'd just run away. Family members and advocates have called this out as victim-blaming, and it continues to this day.

Historically, it's been common for law enforcement to lay blame on victims of violence and people who have gone missing, no matter their background. In North American news reports and documentaries from the 1960s to the early '90s, police would tell parents that perhaps their missing child "just ran away." In 1982, for instance, Noreen Gosch's 12-year-old son Johnny Gosch, a white boy from West Des Moines, Iowa, disappeared while delivering papers. Police deemed him a runaway and told the Gosch family that a child's disappearance would not be recorded until they'd been missing for seventy-two hours. Noreen Gosch has spoken publicly about how uninterested the local police and the Federal Bureau of Investigation were in searching for her son, even with witness evidence that he had been kidnapped. To help find her son, Gosch spoke to the media and distributed his picture in newspapers, in flyers, and on buttons. Eventually Johnny's image was one of the first to be put on the side of a milk carton, in 1984. That spawned a worldwide movement of pictures of missing kids on cartons that lasted until the Amber Alert system started in 1996 in the United States, and 2002 in Canada.

Though most of the children on milk cartons were white, as were nearly all the high-profile cases of missing girls and boys in the 1980s and '90s, Indigenous, Hispanic, and Black children went missing at a higher rate. This also holds true for missing adults, so much so that the term "missing white woman syndrome"—said to be coined by Gwen Ifill, a Black journalist and author—is used to explain the media's fascination with missing women who are white, pretty, and from middle- or upper-class backgrounds. And it was a missing white woman who brought attention to the high number of missing and murdered women and girls along the Highway of Tears, even though many

Indigenous women and girls had disappeared from or were found murdered in the region for several years prior.

When I interview retired RCMP officer Wayne Cleary for this book, he tells me that since the 1960s, upwards of fifty-nine women, many Indigenous and some as young as 12, have gone missing or been murdered along or near the Highway of Tears or highways connected with it. Yet it was not until 25-year-old Nicole Hoar—a white tree planter who was hitchhiking from Red Deer, Alberta, to Smithers, B.C., to visit her sister—went missing in 2002 that the public, the media, and the police started to pay attention. Her case received tremendous national coverage and sparked a full-scale multimillion-dollar investigation into the Highway of Tears murders not long after, even though more than twenty Indigenous women were murdered or had disappeared before her without a fraction of this attention. In documents I obtained about the case through Access to Information and Privacy requests, RCMP officers acknowledged this disparity, stating that the police force may "be met by criticism from Aboriginal communities and support groups who may view this search as an example of tremendous police resources and effort being allocated into an investigation into a non-Aboriginal victim." The RCMP followed significant leads (a suspect is now in jail for killing his brother but has never been charged with Nicole's murder). In 2022, Indigenous family members of women and girls who went missing or were murdered along the Highway of Tears still speak of not seeing the same spotlight on their loved ones missing or murdered today.

As a journalist working for mainstream media today, I can clearly see there's still a grave discrepancy in the ways Indigenous and non-Indigenous (particularly white) women's and girls' disappearances and murders are handled by police in Canada. For years Indigenous family members and advocates have pushed to shed light on the overrepresentation of Indigenous women and girls among the missing and murdered, but for years they were not believed. To show that the situation was at a crisis, advocates started to collect data.

From 2005 to 2010, Sisters in Spirit, a project developed by the Native Women's Association of Canada, compiled statistics on violence against Aboriginal women, recording 582 cases of missing or murdered Aboriginal women in Canada. It was the only organization at the time focused on listening to and recording family members' stories and collecting and disseminating the numbers of MMIWG in Canada. However, in March of 2010, the federal Conservative government under Stephen Harper cut funds from the research project and redirected the funds to other departments, with the largest portion directed toward policing and the criminal justice system, and toward creating a National Centre for Missing Persons and Unidentified Remains. Sisters in Spirit was forced to close at the end of March 2010.

It would take until 2014, two full decades after Ramona Wilson went missing, for Ottawa to initiate the Missing Children/Persons and Unidentified Remains (MC/PUR) database in order to address the disturbing number of unsolved cases of MMIWG. However, the data was not restricted to Indigenous women (or even broken down by race), even though funding for the database had been diverted from Sisters in Spirit. In 2015, CBC reported that the database was still not complete due to technical problems and had not yet contributed to solving any cases.

Out of the 32,759 missing persons (adults) listed in the federal government's database in 2019, we still don't know how many are Indigenous. According to the RCMP website, "the information is gathered primarily through an electronic connection with the Canadian Police Information Centre... an established infrastructure for sharing information between police agencies." "Additional information," it continues, "may be entered directly by CMPUR [Centres for Missing Persons and Unidentified Remains] members." The Canadian Police

Information Centre system collects criminal records and information on wanted persons, people who are on parole or probation, stolen vehicles, stolen property, and missing persons. Police agencies are responsible for inputting the data and ensuring the integrity of each file, though in 2020, the Canadian Association of Chiefs of Police admitted that improving the consistency of reporting and addressing gaps in data collection remained a goal. The RCMP's website warns that "there is some subjectivity in the original CPIC [Canadian Police Information Centre] data that populates the Missing Children/Persons and Unidentified Remains Database, and it may not be consistently completed nor maintained by agencies." This means that individual officers input the information into the database, and the way they record that information may be tainted or influenced by their feelings or opinions. For example, police with implicit bias against Indigenous people may decide not to add names into the system if they feel the person may be not actually missing but rather—as I have often heard—on a drug binge, in another province, or just unwilling to be found.

Indigenous youth and adults that are missing have historically been considered transient or partaking in high-risk behaviour to a higher degree than white people, to the point where their disappearances are sometimes not deemed suspicious. But that is not an accurate portrayal. A 2009 academic report called A Comparison of Aboriginal and Non-Aboriginal Missing Persons in British Columbia Where Foul Play Has Not Been Ruled Out found that in the cases the authors reviewed, "The most common probable cause of the missing person cases among Aboriginals and non-Aboriginals was a kidnapping; however, Aboriginals were much more likely to have this probable cause than non-Aboriginals." The report also found that among both groups, there was a high rate of unknown reasons for being missing (46.7 percent for non-Indigenous and 43 percent for

Indigenous). Both groups had a low rate of cases of being run-aways (both under 2.5 percent).

At a CBC Prince George town hall I spoke at in 2016 about the Highway of Tears, Mary Teegee, executive director of Carrier Sekani Family Services, commented that if some fifty women and girls had gone missing from an affluent neighbour-hood in B.C., such as West Vancouver, there would be much more alarm from the media and action from the police.

As a journalist monitoring media coverage, I can attest that Mary's assessment is accurate. Even with CBC, the *Toronto Star*, the *Globe and Mail*, and other media showing more recent ampli-fication of coverage of MMIWG stories, media still go into a frenzy over missing white women, while missing Indigenous women, in most cases, rarely get the same attention.

In the late fall of 2017, 56-year-old Annette Poitras, a white woman from the Vancouver suburb of Coquitlam, lost her way while on a dog-walking hike. She was on a gravel trail that curves around Eagle Mountain, about ten minutes away from home. During the three days she was missing, reporters from all major television news stations arrived with satellite trucks, doing live hits for their top story each night. Hundreds of sto-ries were published or broadcast by mainstream media outlets across B.C. in those three days and after she was rescued. In the months that followed, there was even a book written about her experience (that I was assigned to cover as a television reporter at the time). I have personally never witnessed or heard of this level of coverage when an Indigenous woman or girl has gone missing—or has even been murdered—so seeing it was surpris-ing, to me and other journalists.

One month before Poitras went missing, 53-year-old Fran-ces Brown, a Wet'suwet'en woman, had been mushroom pick-ing north of Smithers when she disappeared. Local Indigenous community members organized ground searches for weeks, and RCMP and search and rescue crews searched extensively for seven days. Yet there were no cameras, no satellite trucks, and just a handful of local online and radio stories. She is still missing. One explanation could be that Poitras went missing from an area near a large city that television reporters could easily get to, while Brown went missing from a remote area near a small northern town, where there are few mainstream news outlets. Still, the leaders making decisions in newsrooms can choose which stories we give more attention and suggest the ways that we cover them.

And the problem isn't just what stories producers and executives in media decide to dedicate resources to. Our reliance on institutions like the RCMP, rather than on family members' accounts, also reveals our bias, often against Indigenous women and their families.

In April 2016, the year before the dog walker went missing, Deanna Desjarlais, a 27-year-old Cree woman, disappeared. During a CBC interview with me at the time, Desjarlais's friends and family said they had not heard from her for nearly three months—when she travelled from Saskatoon, Saskatchewan, to Vernon, B.C. At the time, the Vancouver Police Department said publicly that Desjarlais had been seen in Vancouver and Surrey, and that officers were tracking her travels to determine where she could be. But family members told me they felt the police were not taking it seriously.

Tragically, her body was found in September 2016 in a wooded area in Surrey. When Desjarlais went missing, I was a casual temporary employee working almost full time at CBC and freelancing at other outlets. At that time, writing about MMIWG at CBC was challenging—stories I pitched were questioned and there was a push to rely on the police's account of a woman's disappearance or murder rather than the family's, even if there were questions about systemic racism within the force, or about its inaction or lack of investigation.

Cate Friesen, a white woman who was then the executive producer of CBC Aboriginal (now called CBC Indigenous), was one of the only producers keen to publish the Indigenous stories I pitched, regardless of their complexity and sensitivity. She agreed to publish my story about Deanna's family members' concerns about her disappearance and then another story after she was found dead. However, once my story on Deanna's death was published, another white CBC executive questioned the validity of the family's statements, claiming their allegations that police were not taking their concerns seriously were not backed up by the police themselves. While it is common journalistic practice to allow authorities to respond to allegations, even after I made the call and received a reply (a full denial from police), an executive assigned a new article to be written by a white journalist that was focused on the RCMP's efforts—rather than those of the family members—to find answers about her death. One year later, an inquest found fault in the police investigation of Deanna's murder. The report made recommendations to several arms of the provincial government, from the solicitor general to the minister of housing, to improve policing standards on missing person investigations, supply more low-barrier housing for Indigenous women, and increase culturally appropriate support services.

JUST AS DEANNA'S FAMILY AND FRIENDS waited for months to find answers, the search for Ramona Wilson would go from weeks to months, until the worst news came. Seven months after Ramona went missing, the RCMP received an anonymous tip about the case. The caller claimed that Ramona's body was behind the Smithers airport. Because of the limited technology of the day, the police were unable to trace the call and couldn't gather more information about how the tipster knew those details. They conducted a search of the area and found nothing. Then, ten months after Ramona went missing, with support from the Calgary-based Missing Children Society of Canada and family craft and bake sales and fundraisers, the Wilson family was able to offer a $10,000 reward for information on her disappearance. Two days later, on April 10, 1995, two young boys ATVing near the Smithers airport found Ramona's remains in a wooded area just off Yelich Road. Police reported that the clothes she wore the night she went missing were discovered where her remains were found, along with several items in a small organized pile a few feet away. Police also uncovered a small section of rope, interlocking nylon ties, and a small pink "brass knuckles" type of kids' water gun. Her high-top runners were never found, but Brenda tells me that according to forensics experts, that could be because animals are attracted to the scent of shoes and may have dragged them away.

To this day, no one has come forward to claim responsibility for Ramona's death. Through news articles, Matilda has suggested that her daughter may have been the victim of a hit and run by a local who put her body behind the airport, since the horse trails her daughter was found on are difficult to find, navigate, or even know about for outsiders. However, Brenda refutes that theory, saying there is no evidence that her sister was hitchhiking. All she and others know for sure is that Ramona was asking friends and family for a ride to get to the dance.

Hearing that Matilda had a strong feeling that her daughter was hit by a driver while she was hitchhiking (or perhaps just walking along the highway) piques my curiosity. Not because I necessarily agree with the theory, but because of how easy it can be to disappear into the dark without a trace along the Highway of Tears. Anyone who has driven it at night knows how dim it is. There are no lights aside from car headlights on many of the long rural stretches of the highway, where the terrain is dark forests speckled with small communities. On past trips of my own, driving with my young child in the back seat, I've been terrified when cars would fly by with their high beams on, fearing I would end up in a ditch. Sign after sign announced that there was a new upgrade being completed—a new passing lane, a new rest area—all necessary things, but I wondered why the safety of truckers was prioritized over that of locals, many of whom have been forced to hitchhike for years without an accessible and affordable transportation system. Still, there is no conclusive evidence that Ramona was a victim of a hit and run. The B.C. coroner's office provided me with a report that offered no new clues as to how she died, and the RCMP say they continue to investigate.

The RCMP has never released any information about the autopsy to the family or the public, saying it is an ongoing open investigation and that is its policy. Via email, RCMP spokesperson Janelle Shoihet tells me that "in an on-going criminal investigation, the cause of death may be important not to release until the investigation goes to trial or is otherwise concluded." Shoihet says officers look at each case individually. As of 2022, Matilda and Brenda have no idea how Ramona was killed—a heartbreaking reality to live through, never having closure.

Unlike Ramona, I was not killed on my way to mark a high school rite of passage, leaving my loved ones in darkness, to spend the next thirty years in heart-wrenching wondering. In many ways I was lucky to live, but in other ways, I was unlucky in life.

MY MOM DIVORCED MY DAD when I was 2 years old and married my stepdad, a warehouse manager originally from Manitoba, not long after. They were typical working-class parents raising a family—that sometimes included his two daughters from his previous marriage—in Campbell River.

My biological dad came in and out of my life, at some points every weekend, at others closer to once a month. The visitations were often dramatic and dark. Dad was often under the influence of alcohol or drugs on my visits, and while I do not have clear memories of him abusing me as a baby and toddler, I do not know if he didn't. I do know that he did not protect me from potential abuse from his friends or relatives, because he was so often inebriated. It is a hard, hard reality to reckon with, that I was unprotected by those whose job it was to keep me safe.

The visitations became less routine when my biological dad moved to Vancouver. A few years later my mom and stepdad moved to what would later become their retirement condo, and I moved to a new elementary school where I didn't adjust well. I was bullied first by girls, and then by boys, hitting me with two-by-four pieces of wood. It was an incredibly depressing and lonely time. Not sure what to do, my parents decided to send me to my dad's in Vancouver to start off fresh in a new school there.

Moving in with my biological father at 11 years old was a hairpin turn of a transition: from my stable, blue-collar, middle-class parents' home in a west coast fishing town to East Vancouver, where my dad lived with his wife in a home that was rough around the edges, physically and emotionally, to say the least.

Dad was a logger, but as I remember he was often at home, doing side gigs like bootlegging and renting out illegal suites in his basement. The companies he worked for, like MacMillan Bloedel and Weyerhaeuser, were shuttering and he had to make ends meet. His wife, a woman I struggled to connect with in any way, was a border patrol and corrections officer who had been with my dad as long as I could remember. To earn allowance, I would clean mould out of beer bottles in our East Van backyard, in a shed that became a makeshift home brewery, and hand out flyers for my dad's delivery service.

My dad was often drunk, hungover, or "buzzed," usually sipping from travel mugs or cups poured from a 2-litre bottle of peach cider. Driving his white '69 Chevy with a giant Donald Duck sticker on the side, he would shove his plastic mug in the improvised cup holder and sip or slam his cider wherever we drove. He once recklessly drove over a concrete meridian to do a U-turn when he realized he was going the wrong way. Another time police arrested him for drinking and driving and the rest of us had to cab home. And then there were moments that more clearly showed me he didn't have the tools to be a healthy parent.

One time, when I was still 11, my dad was on an overnight binge and returned home in the early afternoon. I had just made a sandwich to eat in front of the TV and had left lettuce remnants on a cutting board in the kitchen. When he asked me sternly to clean it up, I said, like most preteens will do, "In a minute." With a bad hangover, patience is hard to come by, I suppose. Before I knew what was happening, my dad grabbed my hair and arms and dragged me across the room and up the stairs. As I screamed for help, he held me up against a wall at the top of the staircase and held a pillow over my mouth. Soon after his hands gripped my throat. Later that day I could hear Dad telling family members on the phone that I just had a "temper tantrum."

Hearing of the bruises and cuts on my neck, face, and wrists, my mom flew to Vancouver from Campbell River and took me to the hospital so a doctor could check for internal injuries. While I had external wounds, seen by my mom and recorded in medical documents, my dad adamantly denied he did anything to me. Over the years, he would lie to my uncles, aunts, and sister, saying I was making up the (mostly mental and emotional) abuse, and he rather than I would be believed. Years later the hashtag IBelieveHer would resonate with me more than any other. Forgiveness came later.

In a traumatized state, just trying to get through the shrapnel of the catastrophe of living with my dad, I made the hard decision to move back in with my mom and stepdad. Back in Campbell River, I had a good start at my new school. I joined the cheerleading squad and was dating a popular basketball player. I had a best friend. But later that year, the bullying started again and I began to self-sabotage. I started to hang at the smoke pit and with the "wrong crowd." I stopped studying. I fought with my mom a lot. Like most teens, I was struggling with a new independent identity but I was also really traumatized, lonely, and suicidal. I tried to kill myself with a bottle of Tylenol. When I threw up, I could hear my parents whisper that they thought I ate too much candy that day. But the worst was yet to come for me. I was struggling, anxious, on edge, and talking back a lot, and I imagine it was tough to deal with me as a parent. But we didn't talk about the outcomes of trauma then. The narrative was more about tough love. My stepdad, while a good guy, was very hyper-cleanliness focused and a perfectionist, and after I decorated my entire room with collage-style postering, it was the last straw for him. I came home one day, and all my boxes were packed. We don't talk about it today. He is all I have now and I don't want to lose another family member. But the pain, the betrayal, and the confusion feel like bullets buried deep in my chest, still today. And while my mom has passed on now, I still wonder why she never fought for me or protected me more, and sometimes the hurt pulses through my body.

Just a year and a half after moving in with my mom, I reluctantly moved back in with my biological dad, where the spiralling down spun fast.

The bullying in Vancouver was worse than in Campbell River. Mouldy sandwiches in my locker. Chased by girls trying to beat me up after school. It became, after a while, just a way of life. Some people didn't seem to like me, no matter where I went. I never really fit in anywhere. Looking back, maybe the juxtaposition between my white, stable, healthy, loving mom and my unstable, alcoholic Gitxsan and Irish dad twisted my sense of self—who I was, or how to present or pretend to be for the world. I went through life at home and school on edge and high alert with little knowledge of what could come next. In these times, I thrust myself into my writing, where I could privately express my full self without judgment or fear.

At the start of grade nine, after years of bullying and an unstable home life, I wrote in my diary that I felt like killing myself, again. It was a free-writing type of entry, and a sort of emotional spilling—getting the dark wounds out as words on the page. But my dad's wife found the diary one day at the bottom of the stairs and read it. When she showed it to him, instead of asking what was wrong or making some calls to get a counsellor for me, he immediately told me I needed to check in to the mental hospital on my own or "get out of the house." I was barely 14. I took the bus to St. Paul's Hospital, terrified that I would not be believed once again. But after sharing with the house psychologist that it was my dad who had mental health and addictions issues, and that I was just surviving as a teen, he saw the situation for what it was and wrote my dad a note, saying I was a normal teenager, experiencing pain.

Not long after that, my dad pulled out a phone book, pointed to the numbers for the Ministry of Children and Family Development and told me to make arrangements for foster care. The alternative, he said, was to grab a sleeping bag and live on the street. Terrified, I phoned social services, but as a teen I was lower priority and they could not find a placement for me immediately. Still, my dad's decision was made.

My first night on the street was scary. I stayed up all night in a twenty-four-hour coffee shop, going to the bathroom every hour to try to sleep on the tiled floor for as long as I could. I eventually tried to sneak into my dad's rundown Blue Bird bus, which was parked in his backyard beside the mini home brewery. But hours later, while he was tripping on acid, he found me and told me to go into the house, where we called social services again. My life from then on was a succession of group homes, foster homes, and various levels of street life, often not making contact with my family for months.

RAMONA WAS PART OF A LOVING FAMILY when she disappeared. She had a lot going for her, Brenda says. She was a high school student; the youngest in her family, she babysat her older sisters' kids regularly. She and Brenda played on a women's baseball team together. She held a solid job at Smitty's and had been hired to work for the summer as a peer counsellor for the Smithers Community Services Association. One of her only vulnerabilities, some would say, was being Indigenous. According to statistics gathered by the National Inquiry into Missing and Murdered Indigenous Women and Girls, Indigenous women are twelve times as likely to be murdered or missing as any other women in Canada and sixteen times as likely to be murdered as white women. When it comes to intimate partner violence, Indigenous women experience it more frequently and more severely than non-Indigenous women. Simply being Indigenous and female is a risk. In the national inquiry's final report, the commissioners write: "Even when all other differentiating factors are accounted for, Indigenous women are still at a significantly higher risk of violence than non-Indigenous women." While awareness about MMIWG has grown, especially since Ramona's death, the number of Indigenous female victims of homicide has increased over the past several decades.

For Indigenous women and girls who live in remote areas, like Ramona, the risks of murder and violence are exacerbated by limited accessible transportation. The lack of safe ways to get around was one of the things Ramona and I had in common.

While she hitchhiked with her friends to places nearby, I hitchhiked across Canada and the United States. For me, it was often a way of escaping the hard reality of being abandoned and living on the street. For her, like many in remote areas of B.C., it was often the only way to get from place to place.

When I travelled the highway in 2016, I saw scores of billboards within villages and along the highway promulgating the idea that hitchhiking was dangerous, if not deadly. More recently, in 2022, while travelling to my home territory for a CBC podcast, I saw those signs again and couldn't help saying to my colleague, "Shouldn't those signs say 'Don't kill women' instead of 'Don't hitchhike'?" Eerily, I saw scores of Indigenous women and men hitchhiking despite those billboards. As Gitanyow leader Wanda Good (whose cousin Lana Derrick went missing from the Highway of Tears in 1995) puts it, "If you are a mom and need formula for your baby, or food, and don't have a car, what would you do?" Reserves, set up in the 1800s and 1900s by colonial authorities aiming to isolate and alienate Indigenous people, not only were created on unfertile land, but also did not and still do not get the same funding as municipalities or provinces. Therefore, they often lack essential services (like hospitals and schools), public transportation, and retail establishments.

And Indigenous people in rural and remote areas have more to contend with than just inaccessible transportation. As Brenda Wilson explains, colonialism caused poverty and racism that has led to legislated and systemic barriers. First Nations people, under the Indian Act, also still do not have the legal authority to possess land on their own reserves, as that land is owned in trust by the federal government. The structure as it stands makes it difficult if not impossible to run or own businesses on reserve land. Racism and ongoing colonial violence also limit access to the job market, adding more economic roadblocks.

While I faced hardships and lived in deep poverty at some points in my life, I also had privilege, even while living on the street. I grew up in the city and had, in comparison, unlimited access to transit and all the amenities that were just a SkyTrain away.

Still, my existence was stamped with unpredictability and rocked by consistent violence—realities of being homeless, being a ward of the state, and being a young woman without the security and safety net of family. My blanket of protection was often the man or men I surrounded myself with—but sometimes that man would be the least safe person for me, or for anyone.

While still only 14 years old, I found my own shared rooming house in Kerrisdale and enrolled at Kitsilano Secondary, far from the East Van schools where I was bullied. Another Kits student, Brianna (not her real name), and I became close, and after the realities of paying rent as a teen in a house with a bunch of adult (some very creepy) men, attending school, and working part time became too much for me, I began sleeping in her mom's laundry room. That lasted until her mom found out and kicked me out, and the streets became my rocky road.

Brianna would sometimes stay with me on the street—sleeping in abandoned cars, under bridges, or in bank ATM vestibules. We also began to cross into the United States to meet up with her younger cousin Gina. While my dad did not want me staying at his home or with his family members, we remained in contact. Since I was legally still a child, he'd write me permission notes to present to guards at the border crossing in White Rock, saying he was allowing me to go fishing with tribal members on the Lummi reservation (something that was not true). Today, post 9/11, I can't imagine any border guard granting a child permission to cross into another country with simply a handwritten parental note. But with an Indian status card, at that time, border guards respected (or maybe just didn't quite understand) the Jay Treaty, codified into U.S. immigration law, which guarantees Aboriginal Peoples the right to trade and travel between the United States and Canada. We made the trek by thumb, often.

One September day, Brianna's dad refused to write a note for her to cross the border, so I went on my own. Close to Bellingham, as I stood with my thumb out on the side of the road, a white man in his mid-40s with pressed clothes and a trimmed beard picked me up in his grey SUV. When he offered to buy me dinner on that chilly autumn night, I did not say no. As I quickly learned, street life offers little predictability when it comes to eating, and you do not always have the choice of when or how you will receive sustenance or shelter, so when opportunities arise, saying no is often not an option. Over the course of two hours, he fed me so much alcohol, and so little food to absorb it, that my head spun. During the car ride to the warm home he offered, the whole vehicle whirled around me and I struggled to control my wasted body. When we arrived at the house about forty-five minutes later, he opened the front door and I staggered in, noticing that it was strangely empty. I naively thought I had arrived at a safe place to pass out for the night and was too drunk to be afraid of what might come next. In a waterbed, I felt like I was drowning when he attempted to rape me. Thinking fast, in survival mode, I faked a seizure until he finally backed off and fell asleep. As dawn broke, I got away, walking to the nearby town of Snohomish. When the traumatic experience felt submerged enough, I stuck out my thumb and made my way back to Canada. I didn't tell anybody about what happened to me because I felt careless for hitchhiking in the first place.

Later, when I was still living on the street and travelling across North America and I saw stories about Ramona in newspapers, I thought, as I often do today, *That could have been me.* I could have been dead and gone, with little more than a trace. The thought haunts me almost daily.

When I drive past Smithers on my way home in Gitxsan territory, I think about Ramona and other young women whose lives were taken along the highway, far too early. We still do not know how she met her fate, but it takes me back to how many times I stuck out my thumb or was with an abusive boyfriend or in a dangerous situation.

For a vulnerable young girl, it was petrifying being tossed onto the streets alone, without family, money, or safety. Going at life solo, freshly bruised by abandonment by my parents, was not easy. I carried the resulting rage, and the mistrust of those who were supposed to support and love me, for much of my life. Often, on counsellors' advice, I will imagine that as a girl I was protected from the abuses I experienced. I visualize that it was me, saving myself, ensuring that no one could hurt me— and if they did they would be held accountable. My early sense of betrayal spurred a fight in me to shield others from harm, a feeling that lasts to this day. I am fiercely protective of my son, my girlfriends, and Indigenous people. Only now, it is not my imagination that I use to safeguard others, but my voice, my pen, and my stories.

I didn't roam the highways forever. Eventually, I found myself settled in a part of Vancouver where many travellers and people without homes wind up, a place that has a sense of community but that also holds great vulnerabilities.

3

K'emk'emeláy, *the place of many maple trees*

FEAR ON THE STREETS

THE LAND HERE opens up like a palm from a fist. Coniferous mountains push up from the shore as waves crinkle across the Pacific. Colossal red cedars and western hemlocks hug the slopes of the Ch'ich'iyúy Elxwíkn ("twin sisters") and other towering mountains. Cedar scents blow through legions of trails that circle the rainforests as lush moss drips from bigleaf maples—the namesake of what now sits smack at the centre of this striking sight. K'emk'emeláy means "place of the maple trees," or more specifically, of many maple woods or groves of maple woods. "This was one of the names for Vancouver, where we would harvest trees higher than some skyscrapers," says Marissa Nahanee, a Skwxwú7mesh cultural leader, who is also a close family friend. The maple wood was used for homes, paddles, and tools like bows and arrows, she tells me. Some Skwxwú7mesh people have shared that this is just one name for the coastal city, with most titles describing smaller villages or areas used for gathering wood or plants, fishing, or hunting animals for food and clothing. Leḵ'leḵ'í was one of the names to describe what is now called CRAB Park, near Gastown, the neighbourhood that shaped the beginnings of what is now known as the city of Vancouver.

Where now stands an iconic steam clock and upscale art galleries and furniture shops once grew swaths of devil's club, huckleberries, and salal bushes in an understorey of the rainforest. Frogs hopped in the swamps, while grouse waddled from the woods. Indigenous people thrived on the wealth of the waters too, including the oysters and mussels on the pebbly shores that wrap the land. Before it became one of the most expensive cities in the world, this area was a gathering place used by the Sḵwx̱wú7mesh (Squamish), səlilwətaɬ (Tsleil-Waututh), and x̱ʷməθkʷəẏəm (Musqueam) for thousands of years.

Much like the land around the Highway of Tears, the once generous, resource-rich rainforest was cut up and slashed through by the new colonials who came to the coast in the 1800s. Settlers turned the shoreline into a seaport that gave way to logging booms, the Canadian Pacific Railway, and the Hastings Mill sawmill, and later to roads leading to businesses like the Globe Saloon, owned then by John "Gassy Jack" Deighton. Until 2022, his statue stood prominently in Maple Tree Square at the junction of Carrall, Powell, and Water Streets, the former site of his saloon in the neighbourhood named after him, Gastown.

Deighton, called Gassy Jack for his talkativeness, had two Sḵwx̱wú7mesh wives during his life, one just a girl named Quahail-ya or Wha-halia, 12 years old. According to Sḵwx̱wú7mesh oral history, the girl eventually ran away from her much older husband when she was 15. T'uy't'tanat–Cease Wyss, a Sḵwx̱wú7mesh woman who wrote a poem about Quahail-ya, says her bravery makes her a role model for Indigenous women. Gassy Jack's statue was defaced by red paint on at least one occasion and was toppled by a crowd of protesters during the Women's Memorial March in February of 2022. Indigenous women have said his former wife Quahail-ya, now long deceased, should have a statue to replace his.

In the early 1900s Gastown stretched from today's Downtown nearly to Main and Hastings. The Downtown Eastside was once the most important retail, political, and cultural centre of the city, encompassing Chinatown, Gastown, and Strathcona. It boasted a street car, a city hall, a library, a theatre, upscale hotels, and a museum. In the 1950s, though, shops and theatres moved toward Robson and Granville Streets, and as tourist traffic deteriorated, the hotels became rundown. By 1965 the Downtown Eastside neighbourhood started to face a steep decline, shaped by hard drugs and an influx of mentally ill patients released from institutions without being given resources like supportive housing. Its deterioration was amplified by arguably the harshest factor, the federal government's deficit-cutting agenda that put a halt to social housing in the '90s. And that's when I stepped onto the scene.

The neighbourhood was then known as one of the poorest postal codes in Canada. As a bright, creative, and sassy teenager, I didn't plan to live on the outskirts of the Downtown Eastside. I was ambitious. As a girl, I had dreamed of becoming an artist, a model, or a business owner. Looking back at my school records and reliving the instability and trauma, I don't recall having space to imagine living out any dream I had. I rarely was anywhere for longer than two years. I was sometimes in survival mode as a child. But as a teenager, surviving the circumstances I'd been placed in gave me a better understanding of the world that was sharply divided by privilege and power on one side and disfranchisement and exclusion on the other. My experiences gave me aspirations of achieving something beyond my own success: I wanted to change that world. Nonetheless, there I was, a teenager living in downtown Vancouver and the Downtown Eastside in a single-room occupancy—a term I see now as just a euphemism for "shifty hotel." Single-room occupancies line poorer areas in North American cities like Toronto, New York, and Vancouver. They are typically rundown residential hotels characterized by small rooms with just enough space for a bed, a chair, and if you are lucky, a sink and a dresser. In the beginning these units in the Downtown Eastside housed itinerant labourers, but with the changes in the neighbourhood, like the Hastings Mill closing down, the buildings shifted to mostly housing low-income people who spent most of their welfare cheques on the rent.

The single-room occupancies I lived in were infested with bedbugs, dealers, and perverts. They were usually in various stages of disrepair, with sinks that often didn't work and poor ventilation. Nobody held the slumlords accountable for not fixing the faulty ventilation, lack of running water, and broken windows. These places were not set up to safely house vulnerable teens. Creeps would grab me and other young women in the hallways or try to lure us with free beer or weed, or worse, try to break into our rooms at night. Our complaints to the hotel manager were met with eye rolls or, even worse, more lecherous advances from the hotel staff themselves. For me, the unpredictable and unregulated structure of these accommodations was just another part of the street life I'd become accustomed to.

When I shifted from couch surfing and group homes to living more permanently as a street person, one of the ways I could get away—from the cold of the winter, from under bridges or in doorways, or from the desperation of taking up creeps' offerings of their homes—was to get a social worker to help find housing. Many of us street youth would enter a system that promised to give us more independence but was often just as precarious and dangerous as living on the street. Social workers often treated us with disrespect too. A group-home parent named Tom Littlewood, who supported me when I was a teen, recently told me that a social worker once called me "that dumb little Indian who would never learn," something that pained Tom so much he had to hold himself back from punching him out.

The system I became entrenched in worked like this: As someone who was considered "at risk" and a current or former child in the care of the Ministry of Children and Family Development, I would visit the Adolescent Services Unit office, which was run by the ministry. That unit would decide if I should get a youth agreement, which meant I could access income assistance to help cover housing costs. Single-room occupancies were among the only places I and those in similar circumstances could afford with the roughly $350 that the government would provide for housing at the time. Back then, I considered living in these units as placing me in the upper echelons of street culture's hierarchy. But using hotels to house kids in care or leaving care has been criticized in several reports in Canada going back nearly a decade.

Manitoba's Child and Family Services placed a 15-year-old Anishinaabe youth, Tina Fontaine, in a hotel shortly before she was murdered in 2014. B.C.'s Ministry of Children and Family Development put a Métis 18-year-old, Alex Gervais, in a Super 8 hotel in Abbotsford, where he jumped or fell to his death from a fourth-floor room in 2015. One year later, B.C.'s representative for children and youth, Mary Ellen Turpel-Lafond, issued a report that found the Ministry of Children and Family Development had housed twenty-four children, many Indigenous, in hotels in the first quarter of 2016, something she called "disturbing." Turpel-Lafond called for the ministry to "reduce and eliminate the use of hotels as placements, even in emergency situations," saying hotels are not appropriate places to house children or youth. In 2016, the ministry banned the non-emergency use of hotels as placements for youth in care and required that contracted caregivers for emergency hotel stays be vetted on par with foster parents.

I stayed in one of the "better" single-room occupancies, known as the Piccadilly, on Pender Street. It shuttered in 2007 for fire-code violations. It was closer to Granville Street and farther from Main and Hastings, where then, like today, all the street action was—a noisy and frantic scene that includes a kind of open-air drug market where people openly smoke crack with makeshift pipes and shoot opioids. It is a place that I see as one manifestation of deep trauma, where hurt people are in need of mental, emotional, and spiritual healing, accessible and safe health care, and proper housing that society is failing to provide them.

As a street kid, I was living with my own trauma and was coping the best way I could. A friend I grew up with recently described the time we spent on the street as teens in this way: "We were reality averse." When I told her I wasn't sure how much I wanted to divulge in my book about our lives then—in particular our coping mechanisms—she told me, "It's your book, you should do what you want, but if you're trying to tell your story, drugs were sometimes a part of it."

It wasn't so much that we were addicted, but we took whatever we could get our hands on, she explained. Another friend reminded me that we were dealing with a lot of trauma (from constant abuse, assault, and abandonment), but we were also teenagers experimenting with life.

But we were not immune from the threat of addiction. At the time, when I was 17, I had been living in an abandoned building between the Downtown Eastside and downtown Vancouver with my boyfriend, Mark. I was exhausted and hadn't slept all night when I found out he had died of a heroin overdose. It was a shock, as I had never done the drug before, and neither had he to my knowledge. No one was sure if it was accidental or a suicide. Like most of us, he had grown up abused. He was half Cree and half white and was born with six toes on each foot. After his white adoptive parents had the extra toes cut off, he spent most of his early years in the hospital recovering, and he still walked with a limp when I met him. He used to tell me that his adoptive parents were racist and treated their biological white child well but abused him. He was traumatized from severe physical and mental abuse and often took out his rage on me. I had become seriously isolated as a result, and his death meant grieving, for the most part, alone. In the days following his overdose I struggled with the enormity of my grief, trauma, and loneliness and started to mask it with substances.

In the darkest days of my grief, I attempted to take my life in the bathroom of a Burger King but failed.

There was a joke some of us youth shared on the streets: "We can't even kill ourselves right." Thinking back, so much of our dark humour came from very real, not-so-funny traumas that filled us with self-hatred. That humour, and the darkness from all we'd been through, is what bonded us as street kids. But my trauma was not done rippling through my life. I was barely 17, didn't have a grade twelve diploma, and couldn't imagine living to 25 at that point. I was sorting through a lot.

When my abusive father forced me to leave home at 14, I was left to negotiate a child-welfare system and street life that made the yo-yoing home life of children of divorced parents seem secure and stable. Swinging from group home, to foster home, to independent living, to shelter, to single-room occupancy, to abandoned building, to car, to bridge was my reality. I never took men's offers to trade a warm bed for sex, but when you live in squats, you often need to cuddle up to whoever is beside you to keep warm, and sometimes that could mean a man.

During the same years I lived in the Downtown Eastside and downtown Vancouver, I spent a period of time living homeless on the road, travelling. During that time I became close with a white man named Joel. I was attracted to him because he was frightening to many, and I thought that would help protect me.

On the streets, this is currency. But one Friday night, Joel and I were walking a puppy for a friend, and Joel started to laugh and kick the puppy. I didn't think it was funny and got between him and the dog. He stopped kicking the puppy and lashed out at me instead. Blow by blow, he beat me into oblivion, smashing my head and bare face into the pavement. As I came to, I watched three men chase him off, with the puppy trailing behind. As far as he knew, he had left me for dead. Afterwards, I couldn't see properly; the whites of my eyes were red and my swollen face shades of purple, black, and blue. I was unable to walk for weeks, in the care of a friend.

As hard as it is to admit, I took Joel back. I remember the youth worker and the terrified look on her face when she saw me walk away with him. In a Mohawk ceremony decades later, a female Elder gently told me, "We have to be careful and cautious of where we turn to for comfort in this life." It was a warning I wished I had heard years earlier.

BUT FOR THE MOST PART I STEERED hard and consistently from creepy men's company. It's anyone's guess how, even with the street smarts I felt I had, I survived violence, manipulation, and the challenges of the elements. And while it's a survival tactic—chosen or not chosen—for many women on the street, I never did become involved in sex work. While I was never judgmental of it, there also just always seemed to be something that pulled me away from that part of the street, and in many ways I feel grateful that I didn't have another layer of trauma to contend with. But street life was traumatic in other ways.

It was common for my friends and associates to die early in life of overdoses, accidents, and suicides. A lot of my friends saw their "street shelf life" as no longer than 25 years old. My attempts to kill myself at an early age were related to the constant bullying and instability and abuse at home, constant reminders, I felt, that I didn't deserve to live and couldn't deal with the pain anymore. On the streets, suicidal ideation and attempts were the results of piled-on trauma, of constantly escaping or surviving violence. But sometimes, death on the streets was a terrifying reality. At an organization called Street Youth Services, where many of us took refuge for free food or other resources, there were "bad date" sheets hung on a bulletin board, beside missing person posters, job listings, and apartment rental advertisements. Sometimes the sheets were pages long. They outlined cis- and transgender women's disclosures of men's violence against them during what were supposed to be exchanges of sex for money. They gave descriptions of men, or sometimes a licence plate, and what they'd done to the sex worker. They were often brutal accounts. I would flip each page gingerly with hesitation and scrunch my face up, shocked that anyone could treat another human this way. Maybe those sheets were what discouraged me and my friends from wanting to enter a trade where we could earn more than from panhandling. Or perhaps it was something even more sinister.

IN THE LATE 1990s and early 2000s, I'd read the headlines about missing women who had lived on the street and those who had gone missing from the Highway of Tears, many of whom were Indigenous. I'd turn the pages of the newspapers slowly, not sure I wanted to read what was on the next page. At the time I was focused on trying to get off the street and move on to a new life. I was finishing my grade twelve at a community centre, trying to find stable housing, and looking at a future that had become totally foreign to me. After years of living on the streets, things that seem normal and mundane to other people, like eating at a table or using a bathroom in a home or even having a shower or changing your clothes, become things you need to get reaccustomed to. You also need to adjust to a life where you don't constantly look over your shoulder in anticipation of violence, never sure who to trust. It is a slow process to leave what became your family, your norm, your life on the street. I was terrified not just of ending up back there, but of what could very easily have happened to me. I was also scared not just to hitchhike again, but to even drive those highways that connect the Lower Mainland to the interior and the northwest of B.C. By then, the corkboards and newspaper articles announced that upwards of fifty street women were missing from the Downtown Eastside of Vancouver—a terrifying reminder of my own vulnerability and what I had survived.

Hearing about these missing women was also alarming for the journalists who were investigating these shadowy stories, something I would discover over the next few years. In 1999 I made my first entrance as a radio broadcaster, right back in the neighbourhood I was so anxious to leave. A teacher from the Gathering Place, the learning centre where I was getting my grade twelve, gently pushed me to apply to a program at CFRO-FM, Vancouver Co-op Radio, to learn how to tell stories on the radio to a local audience. The advert pinned to a pillar at the centre strongly encouraged Indigenous people from Canada and Latin America to apply. I was hesitant and told her that I thought I didn't have the skills, but she kept insisting, saying she had a feeling I'd be good at it, knowing I was a good writer and was expressive with my words. I thought about it for a while, feeling reluctant and filled with self-doubt. But then I thought about the time I'd been introduced to radio when I was 14.

I was living in a group home, and during a moment of desperation, learning that I had nowhere else to go and trying to understand the abandonment and the abuse I'd experienced, I had locked myself in the bathroom and picked up a razor, trying to end it all. The home parent, Tom Littlewood, knocked at the door and when I told him to go away, he told me he'd found my suicide note. Through the door, he told me, "You're a great writer." Stopped in my tracks, I started to think less about the pain and more about the potential of my life. When I finally opened the door, he told me about the Vancouver Co-op Radio station where his friend hosted a poetry show. Not long after, he took me there. Meeting her inside the station, eager to teach me the ropes and train me how to broadcast across the airwaves, for once I felt like someone believed in me.

Now, years later, with my teacher nudging me to apply for a project that seemed beyond my capabilities, I thought back to that experience and realized that maybe this was a path I could walk. Later, I would learn that by walking this path, I would help blaze a new trail along the way, mending my wounds by helping to heal others.

And so I plucked up the courage, applied, and was astounded to get an interview. I'll never forget the white male interviewer asking me, "So you are Native, but how are you connected with your culture?" and looking disappointed when I told him I grew up in East Vancouver and was quite removed from my culture. It seemed that he wanted to hear about me drumming and sing-ing and holding a rattle in a sweat lodge, but that wasn't me. Still, I got the job.

Vancouver Co-op Radio was then based in a building at the edge of Pigeon Park at Hastings and Carrall, in the heart of the Downtown Eastside. We made long-form documentaries on Latin American and Canadian development issues, with the latter part of our coverage largely being in the Downtown East-side of Vancouver. Another Indigenous woman in the group and I eventually used the skills we learned to cohost a radio show where we interviewed Indigenous political leaders, art-ists, and youth, played music, and sometimes just chatted about being Native youth.

I was just learning about what it meant to be a journalist. I was inspired by Co-op Radio host and veteran radio broadcaster Gunargie O'Sullivan, whose weekly show When Spirit Whispers aired and still airs some of the most powerful conversations with Indigenous people I have ever heard. I was also in awe of the journalists who were driven to uncover the truth and who were telling stories with impact that forced the public to look squarely in the face of awful realities. And there were journalists then who were taking on one of the most horrifying stories of our time, one that was unfolding right there where I spent time as a street youth and was now working, in the Downtown Eastside.

VETERAN JOURNALIST LINDSAY KINES is widely considered by other journalists, family members of missing and murdered Indigenous women and girls (MMIWG), and cops as the first to break not only the story of MMIWG in the Downtown Eastside of Vancouver, but also similar stories along the Highway of Tears. He started covering the stories in the late 1990s when he was with the *Vancouver Sun*, and he is credited with being the first reporter to dig in and repeatedly question police officials about the missing women—pushing them to step up their investigation.

In 1997, Kines wrote a story about the disappearance of Janet Henry, a Kwakwaka'wakw woman, after her sister Sandra Gagnon contacted him hoping to further publicize her case and garner support to find her. "At that time, I had no idea she was one of a larger number of disappearances. I did a follow-up piece in 1998, this time interviewing Janet Henry's [13-year-old] daughter about her quest for answers in her mother's disappearance," he tells me during an interview for a 2015 article.

The way Kines wrote about Henry stands out for how humanizing it is. He describes her as going on picnics and sitting by the water with her sister Sandra, and about Henry's daughter giving her a necklace with the word *Mom* engraved on it. He writes about the communities in Alert Bay and in the Downtown Eastside that loved and respected the 36-year-old mother. He also mentions that she was on welfare and had a substance abuse problem, but it isn't the focus of the story, nor does it lead the narrative about who Janet was. This contrasts with the CBC's history of disrespectful coverage of MMIWG (which has seen great improvements over the years). When I look at old CBC television news stories about missing or murdered women from the Downtown Eastside, much of the language used is dehumanizing, constantly referring to the women, for example, simply as "prostitutes" without further context. Even after Indigenous reporters at CBC spent years building up our MMIWG database and strengthening our relationships with the family members, errors were made—for example, leaving out pertinent information or depicting Indigenous women and girls as statistics or stereotypes.

Kines's stories are road maps for how all media should be reporting on MMIWG, even though they were written at a time, starting in the 1990s, when there was much less of a public push for better coverage of Indigenous people than what we see today, in great part due to social media. At the end of the first story Kines wrote on Henry, he includes a quote from a family member about how much her family loves her and wants her to come home. Then he describes Henry and asks people to keep their eyes out for her. Kines reveals Henry as human—as a woman, a mother, a respected community member—rather than just detailing how her life may have ended.

In April 1998, Wayne Leng, a single, middle-aged white man who worked in the automotive industry, was searching for his friend Sarah de Vries, who had gone missing from the Downtown Eastside in the same year. Leng tells me she was mixed race—Black, Indigenous, Mexican Indian, and white—and was adopted as an infant. She was last seen on the corner of Princess and Hastings by a woman Sarah had become fast friends with and who Leng says would not want to be named. Leng told police that he was dedicated to finding her because he had faith that she could one day leave the street, lead a good life, and contribute to society, even though it was clear that she was unable to return his love. He set up a toll-free line to collect tips from the public that could lead to where she was.

Through this tip line, Leng learned about scores more women who were missing from the same neighbourhood. But many of the concerns he shared with family and other friends of the missing women were met with silence from police and much of the media. Leng tells me he was having trouble getting any journalist to write about de Vries when he heard that Kines had covered cases of murdered women. He had also read Kines's stories about Janet Henry. So he reached out to Kines, whom Leng described as "very caring"—a quality many journalists lacked—bringing him de Vries's photographs and journals in hopes that a story on her would put public pressure on police, who he felt were failing missing women.

Kines took what evidence he had compiled from Leng and other family members and questioned the police sources he knew in the Downtown Eastside. "I was able to confirm that police were investigating a spike in disappearances from the neighbourhood. My story ran in July 1998 under the headline 'Police Target Big Increase in Missing Women Cases,'" Kines says. His article shed light on Vancouver city police concerns about the number of women involved in the drug and sex trades who had gone missing. By then, the police had a list of sixteen women who had been reported missing over the past ten years, including five in the year he wrote the story. At the time, police told Kines that "there is no indication that a serial killer is preying on the women." Detectives told him they were investigating the possibility that some women had died by suicide, by accidental drug overdose, or by homicide in disputes over drugs.

But Downtown Eastside youth agencies were terrified for the women for very different reasons that didn't place them at the centre of their own demise. In Kines's article, John Turvey of the Downtown Eastside Youth Activities Society said, "It is phenomenally dangerous out there. If you don't go missing and you don't end up dead, the likelihood of getting assaulted, raped, kidnapped, abused, robbed, injured is just astronomical." His list was an inventory I was all too familiar with. Most people then, including me, felt that based on the violence we experienced on the street, it was not possible for there to be one sole killer on the loose, but that there must be many.

Years earlier, Kines had been tipped off about another place women and girls were going missing and being murdered: along the Highway of Tears. In December 1995, he flew up to Prince George and travelled along Highway 16, interviewing families and police investigators for a 1,400-word newspaper piece about the murders and disappearances of young Indigenous women in the area. Kines says at that time three murders and two disappearances were publicly known. Racial identity was an obvious factor in the Highway 16 story, he says, because all of the missing or murdered women and girls were Indigenous. There were also allegations of racism on the part of the police and the public. But the demographics were different in the stories Kines reported from the Downtown Eastside. "I knew that some of the missing women, including Janet Henry, were Indigenous, but not all. The early stories tended to highlight the fact that the missing women were all involved in drugs or the sex trade, and less on their heritage."

While it is often claimed in media reports that most of Robert Pickton's victims were Indigenous, this is not true. Indigenous women made up just over 30 percent of the twenty-six victims Pickton was charged with murdering or whose DNA was found on his farm. Some journalists may have been looking at the number of victims Pickton was officially convicted of murdering (six counts of second-degree murder), of which more than half were Indigenous women. Either way, since Indigenous people make up less than 2.5 percent of the population in Vancouver, Indigenous women are significantly overrepresented in those that Pickton murdered. Seeing those disproportionate numbers, Indigenous family members and advocates were the first to bring concerns to light about the large number of missing and murdered women in the Downtown Eastside.

Kines recalls that in the beginning, stories about MMIWG did not get prominent placement. Most of his early stories ran in the B section or even further back in the newspaper. But it didn't stop him. "I was motivated by the families and friends of the women who stayed in touch with me and wanted answers. I think it was their telephone calls that prodded me to keep digging and searching for answers. They were the source of many tips and leads that allowed me to keep writing stories."

In early 1999, the *Vancouver Sun* devoted a two-page spread to the issue, which included photos of all the missing women and a full-page profile Kines wrote on de Vries. The *Sun* also permitted journalists Kim Bolan, Lori Culbert, and Kines to spend about three months digging into the bigger picture of missing and murdered women and girls in B.C. The trio published two series of stories in late 2001, about four months before serial killer Robert Pickton's arrest. The first revealed that the number of missing women from the Downtown Eastside was much higher than police had stated, and the second exposed that the original Vancouver police investigation was deeply flawed. Those failings are described in great detail by former Vancouver police detective Lorimer Shenher in his 2015 book, *That Lonely Section of Hell: The Botched Investigation of a Serial Killer Who Almost Got Away*. With deep respect for the women, he outlines their tragic deaths but also takes personal responsibility for the systemic flaws that hampered the investigation of Pickton and allowed more victims to fall prey to the serial killer.

In the late 1990s, Tahltan leader Terri Brown was working with the National Action Committee on the Status of Women in Vancouver. As part of her work there, she was digging for answers about the high numbers of women disappearing from the Downtown Eastside. "We set up talking circles and women would come and say, 'What is going on, my niece or my sister has gone missing.' It was dumbfounding because nobody knew what to do," Brown told me in 2015.

In 1997, Robert Pickton was charged with forcible confinement and the attempted murder of a sex worker after he stabbed her multiple times on his Port Coquitlam pig farm. She was badly injured and nearly died in the hospital, but survived. The charge was stayed in early 1998. In 2012, at what would later become known as the Pickton inquiry (formally the Missing Women Commission of Inquiry), Crown prosecutor Randi Connor told the public inquiry that she stayed the charges because the woman was substance addicted and incoherent when she was interviewed by the Crown a week before the trial. According to a CBC article from 2012, "after the charges were stayed, 19 women later connected to Pickton's farm in Port Coquitlam disappeared."

At the time, in the late 1990s, family members and advocates were frustrated at what seemed like a lack of action and a deep indifference to the dozens of women who were missing from one small neighbourhood. "The police and the RCMP were not listening to the families of the missing and murdered women," Terri Brown said. She and others wanted police to take the growing concerns of family members seriously and to step up their investigation to stop women from going missing and being murdered.

Terri's youngest sister, Ada Elaine Brown, was found dead in a Prince George hotel room in 2001. Even though the postmortem mentioned previous assaults and noted that Brown had two black eyes when she died, the coroner's office determined that "this death is classified as undetermined." Her sister became one of the many Indigenous women whose deaths near the infamous Highways of Tears were shrouded in mystery. Terri Brown's grief and anger at the lack of justice for her sister and so many other Indigenous women missing or murdered in B.C. spurred her into action. That same year, when she was elected president of the Native Women's Association of Canada, she began to speak out about the disturbing number of Indigenous women—then, at least five hundred—who were missing and murdered in Canada. She underscored how limited investigations were, and how widespread impunity was for crimes against Indigenous women and girls. In 2014, I interviewed Michèle Audette (who became a commissioner for the National Inquiry into Missing and Murdered Indigenous Women and Girls in 2016) and she told me, "I was the interim president when Terri Brown was elected in 2000–2001. She was the one who had the courage to bring the issue to the board, who made it a national issue."

In early 2002, Terri, other family members, leaders, and Elders held a pipe ceremony on the Pickton farm, praying for answers, for a resolution to whatever was happening there. "Family members had told us horror stories and concerns about Robert Pickton's pig farm and so we decided to have a ceremony there," Brown told me in 2015. Not long after, on February 1, 2002, a Coquitlam RCMP officer conducted a Canadian Police Information Centre query on Pickton, unrelated to the missing women, in preparing a warrant for a weapons search. When rookie constable Nathan Wells carried out the investigation on Pickton's property on February 5, he and another officer, Cpl. Howard Lew, uncovered an inhaler belonging to Sereena Abotsway, one of the missing women. Within hours, the largest crime scene search in Canadian history began.

Kines says once the search began on Pickton's farm, there was a media frenzy around it. "Everybody was writing about the case at that point. We had already written extensively about the women, so we shifted our focus to Pickton and why he had not been arrested sooner, given that he had surfaced as a suspect early on in the investigation." On February 22, Pickton was charged with the first-degree murders of two women. In the years following, many more charges were laid.

Police found bodily remains and trace DNA evidence of thirty-three missing women on the pig farm. From 2002 to 2005, Pickton was charged with twenty-six counts of first-degree murder. As Shenher says in his book, after years of treating scores of missing women as unrelated cold cases, "they'd been there all along."

After a year-long trial that stretched from January to December 2007, a jury found Pickton guilty of six counts of second-degree murder. The remaining twenty charges of first-degree murder became mired in a legal standstill, something I find difficult to grasp. From what I do understand, the remaining charges were stayed because the Crown felt a second trial would be too difficult and lengthy to prosecute. The lifting of a publication ban in 2010 allowed the public to see why Mr. Justice James Williams of the B.C. Supreme Court decided to split Pickton's trial into two, and why the first was based on only six murder charges. He reasoned that the process was needed in order to successfully and efficiently put Pickton away, since even proving some of the twenty women were not alive could mean calling up to sixty witnesses per case and would still not guarantee a conviction. While it seems unimaginable, Pickton did not face those additional charges. However, with six life sentences, there is almost zero chance that Pickton will ever be freed from prison.

The judge and the lawyers may have done what was legally the most practical to ensure that Pickton was charged and that the family members were not further traumatized by another lengthy trial. Still, there are mixed feelings among some family members I've spoken to, with some comforted that the serial killer will never be released, and others feeling a lack of resolution.

THE AFTERMATH OF THE PICKTON TRIAL left a mixed legacy. Some policy changes and programs stuck, while others were cut. Placating words that came from reports and politicians about the devastating fiasco didn't always translate into action. At the time, leaders with the Native Women's Association of Canada said the changing of power from the Liberals to the Conservatives under Prime Minister Stephen Harper felt like a door being slammed. While he slashed funding for Sisters in Spirit, the Native Women's Association continued to support families of MMIWG via support groups, family gatherings, vigils, and education through projects that received modest federal funding.

As funding to Canada's leading organization that tackled MMIWG dwindled, pressure was on for law enforcement to explain how they had failed Indigenous women who were murdered by a serial killer, and their families who were ignored by police. In a 2011 Vancouver Police Department report titled *The Tragedy of Missing and Murdered Aboriginal Women in Canada: We Can Do Better*, perpetrator Robert Pickton was deemed Canada's worst serial killer. The report says police could have better protected the vulnerable women in the Downtown Eastside. "Pickton should have been apprehended sooner and the police investigations were initially inadequate," the report reads. It states that the murder risk for sex trade workers is approximately 60 to 120 times that of the general female population. And in a 115-page statement given to the RCMP, the former spokesperson for the Missing Women Task Force, Catherine Galliford, explains that the Mounties' top brass had "enough evidence for a search warrant" for Robert Pickton's farm in 1999. From that year to 2002, fourteen women were brutally murdered by Pickton.

In 2011, the Missing Women Commission of Inquiry investigated police handling of the murders. One of the key recommendations made by the commission in its 2012 report is the establishment of regional police forces in B.C. to replace the hodgepodge of municipal departments, like the Vancouver Police Department and RCMP detachment in Coquitlam, that still exist today. Lindsay Kines has strong feelings about this structure. "It's an absurd system that was instrumental in Pickton slipping through the cracks, and nothing has been done to fix it. I find that particularly frustrating, especially since we were writing about the problems back in 2001, months before Pickton was even arrested and it was learned that he could have been caught years earlier," Kines said.

I asked him how he feels about being credited with breaking the story of what is now an internationally recognized hashtag, MMIWG. His answer is humble. "I'd prefer to give the credit to the families and friends of the missing women for pushing the story forward. They kept insisting that something bad had happened to their loved ones, and their prodding kept me digging. Sadly, they were right all along."

Lorimer Shenher and I visited the former Pickton farm together in 2016 while I was doing a radio documentary called *The Story She Carries* about family member and advocate Lorelei Williams, whose missing cousin Tanya Holyk's remains were found there. When we arrived at the site, the farm was no more: it was merely a fenced-in grassy area filled with large mounds of dirt, and oddly encircled by a trendy-looking neighbourhood filled with moms and joggers who smiled as they passed. But the energy was unequivocal—this was a place where something terrible and violent had happened, and it was like the property had a cellular memory that could never be erased. I put down some sacred tobacco and offered prayers for the lives that had been so brutally taken there. But when I left on a plane the next day back to where I was living in Winnipeg, I felt as though those brutalized souls had stayed with me. I asked one of my

Elders for prayers and guidance, but the haunting feeling, or maybe my own terrified energy, clung to me for many days.

That spiritual connection to the women lost in such traumatic ways is critical to many Indigenous people, and one that family members of women who were murdered at the farm and elsewhere have shared with me. That recognition of spirit is also a deeper part of so many Indigenous cultures. Some of us pray to our ancestors, others to the spirit in the trees and the water, others to the Great Spirit, others to the four directions, and many of us to all of those. When I am close to where a woman has died, I pray to her and for her safe journey to the spirit world. And years before police were paying attention, despite the desperate calls of loved ones to investigate the farm, family members and Indigenous leaders were saying prayers of their own, pleading with the ancestors to help them find justice.

AFTER MY STINT at Vancouver Co-op Radio and after I'd graduated grade twelve in my early 20s, I started to think about what I wanted to do with my life. I was realizing my strengths and envisioning the goals I wanted to conquer. I had done a lot in the last few years since leaving the streets. While I had already gone to the British Columbia Institute of Technology for carpentry, worked in concrete, travelled Europe, done a radio show, and was hardened in many ways by life, I wanted to challenge myself intellectually. I also wanted a connection to my dad's side of the family, something that had always been sparse as I was growing up and remained so as I became an adult. The University of Northern British Columbia (UNBC) was the only university I applied to at the time. It was based in Prince George, the small northern interior city that many of my Sterritt family members lived in. It was a way to test the academic waters many people my age had already treaded. I would become the first person in my immediate family to attend and graduate university and with something, a degree in political science, that would set the tone for much of my life.

Right as I started to settle into Prince George, stories started to surface, word of mouth, about Indigenous women and girls going missing along the Highway of Tears. "There's bad things going on on that highway up there, Ange," Gitxsan and Wet'suwet'en activist Gladys Radek told me in 2003 on one of my visits to Vancouver from Prince George.

At the time, Gladys was fighting a human rights case against the Tinseltown mall in the Downtown Eastside. She had been harassed by the security company at the mall on a number of occasions, at one time even being asked to leave the mall while she was on her way to Starbucks to buy a coffee. She accused Henderson Development and Securiguard Services of denying her access to the facilities because of her race, colour, and disability. Gladys has a prosthetic leg and walks with a limp. She also claimed that her treatment was part of a larger pattern of discrimination against Native people and the disabled. After she won, I wrote a story about it in the newspaper *Windspeaker*, one of the many media outlets I freelanced for over the years. She was granted the highest award ever given for injury to dignity in B.C. at the time. When I interviewed Gladys for the story, we talked at her home—a small, tidy social housing unit across the street from the mall.

"What kinds of things?" I pressed when she mentioned the highway.

The reporter me, the nosy me, is what makes me a good journalist. It's a fearless me that can make a conversation a little jarring. But Gladys was keen to share. "People goin' missing, and murdered, maybe by bikers, who knows," she said. "Mostly Native girls," she added. She also pointed to what she believed was a justice system that was not just indifferent to but complicit in the violence. It was then that I started to pay more attention, to listen more and ask more questions.

As she shared the concerns she'd heard from family members of Indigenous women and girls who'd gone missing, she was piecing together a picture for me, showing that what she described were not individual cases of violence, but in some ways an entire system. She was analyzing the justice system and peeling back the layers of what seemed like a rotting onion. Just as Kines had learned from the family and friends of Janet Henry, I would learn that Gladys Radek was also right all along.

4

Nilhchuk-un, *those who take us away*

THOSE WHO TAKE US AWAY

THE RICH SOIL of the rugged riverbanks collides with the mighty blue ribbon of water known as the Nechako. The cliffs are iconic Prince George landmarks and are burned beautifully into my memories of the city. The people from these waters and lands are the Lheidli T'enneh or "people of the confluence of the rivers." The Dakelh or "people who travel upon water" refer to the broader area as Lheidli Keyoh, the territory where the Nichakoh converges with the Lhtakoh, known in English as the Nechako and the Fraser Rivers.

When I was a chatty 20-year-old, I'd sit on the dramatic banks with my nephews, telling them about my travels around North America and Europe while listening to their stories of growing up in this town, also called B.C.'s "northern capital," which while beautiful also has its rough patches. I have pictures of me with those nephews, both just moving into their teens, the three of us jumping off a picnic table onto the grass with the spruce-lined lazy riverside as our backdrop. These lands have held space for me and are now filled with good memories: of my aunty who broke into my house and filled my cupboards with food and my living room with two loveseats; the time I spent laughing with students at the UNBC First Nations Centre; my gig hosting a campus radio show about Indigenous politics and culture; the drama from a basketball player I was dating. A lot of us students from that time, some Dakelh, some Gitxsan, some Wet'suwet'en, and some Cree, are still really close. Years later, I asked one of them, Gitxsan artist Trevor Angus, as one of the healthier men I know, to be godfather to my son.

I split time three ways between being a student; developing a youth strategy for Carrier Sekani Family Services, an organization that runs social, health, and legal programs for Dakelh (Carrier) communities; and working with youth at a shelter and drop-in centre called Reconnect. At the centre, working with many vulnerable youth, mainly girls, I often heard rumours from them about sexual exploitation and violence against them by prominent men in Prince George, which included allegations about abuses of authority within the justice system. It was always hush-hush, because the girls who shared their experiences were terrified of retaliation. Many of the youth I worked with were extremely vulnerable and susceptible to further exploitation. Some were teen moms, some were addicted to substances, and most were involved in the sex trade. Many would work on Queensway, a street about a block away from where I lived in a basement suite below my cousin, behind my aunty's house and down the road from an uncle. But when the news broke in that summer of 2002 that a judge had been violently sexually assaulting Indigenous girls—one as young as 12—for years in Prince George, it dropped like a bomb in the city. It galvanized suspicions held by many local Indigenous people, especially social and youth workers, that the town was embroiled in serious nefarious activity conducted by those who were supposed to administer justice. It was a horrifying reality to take in and process.

All the girls I worked with were far away from their families, most of whom lived in communities along Highway 16 between Prince George and Smithers. In my interactions with them they were like any kids, but they had gone through so much. Many of us workers were close with them and even referred to them as "our kids." Avril (not her real name) was a 15-year-old girl with concave cheeks and hollow bags under her eyes that made her look skeletal. On one occasion after I'd known her for about eight months, she arrived at the shelter, her head freshly shaved bald, looking for food before heading out to do sex work again. She was trying to earn enough cash to pay off a debt so that she didn't get a finger cut off. She said her head had been shaved by drug dealers' collectors. She was often beaten up. It was awful to see her black eyes or witness her hobbling from being kicked. When I could, I would take her and the other girls to their home territory to visit family, even just for a day, to reconnect and get out of the city. I still remember all their names, nicknames, personalities, and the communities they were from.

I don't think many non-Indigenous people understood then (or understand even now) the coping mechanisms that some Indigenous people, like Avril, developed to survive the intergenerational trauma of residential schools, dislocation, systemic sexual abuse, cultural genocide, and starvation. Even I, like many of my young Indigenous friends, was just learning about the severity of colonial violence through university classes, from many Indigenous professors with lived experiences. Regardless, I can say that most people I worked with at the shelter and family services agency, Indigenous or not, really cared about the youth who came in from the streets looking for food, a warm place to stay, and someone who genuinely cared about them. Just as important was that we *believed them* when they shared their experiences of harm done to them.

Shortly before I moved to Prince George, I was part of a crew of Vancouver Indigenous youth (some I met through the radio show and a Native youth magazine, *Redwire*, I worked with) who produced hip-hop shows and workshops about colonization and Indigenous empowerment. Looking through some of my pictures from the time, I always had a video or still camera in hand and was always documenting everything, sometimes creating indie radio or video documentaries. We took some of our shows on the road and travelled to Los Angeles, rural South Dakota, and Winnipeg. In Winnipeg I even bought a nine-seater van for many of us to travel back home in when our other drivers changed paths. So it was only natural for me to bring those skills to the youth I was now working with in Prince George. I started a month-long program at Reconnect where the youth could learn about some of the elements of hip-hop: break dancing, DJing, emceeing or rapping, graffiti, and beatboxing. Since so many of them were in survival mode, with lives embroiled in emotional and physical trauma, I thought no one would show up, but it was packed. They eagerly participated in each session, learning not just how to make a hip-hop show but also how to promote it, making art and designing posters on the centre's computers. At the end of the program, they performed at the Prince George Native Friendship Centre with two well-known Indigenous emcees I'd promoted in my previous work: Eekwol, whom I brought up from Saskatchewan, and Manik from Vancouver. Three other local Indigenous rappers also performed along with the youth from Reconnect. Seeing them produce, promote, and perform the show was awe-inspiring. I was proud of all of us who believed in the youth and, more so, those youth who believed in themselves.

Even though I trusted and believed everything the youth told me, before the news about Judge David William Ramsay became public, some of the stories the girls shared with me could have sounded like conspiracy theories. A judge, police officers, and an entire justice system were all somehow colluding against them—paying them for sex, beating them, abusing them, then later judging *them* for it? But, having grown up on the street myself, I knew that these stories, while they sounded extreme, were plausible. I knew how simple it was to exploit vulnerable young people and cover up crimes against them. Many of us living on the street were estranged from our families or didn't have a safe family home to return to. We had no fixed address, and some of us would even change our names and pretend we were older so that we would not be picked up by social workers and taken into foster care. We were also targets for unsavoury men. I can't count the number of times I was panhandling and men offered me a warm place to sleep—in exchange for sex. And I always heard stories from sex workers about police buying sex from girls and then stealing their money or roughing them up in other ways. But that was all in Vancouver. In Prince George, the rumours were circulating among a much smaller, more insular crowd, but the themes were the same—powerful men using their power to abuse vulnerable girls and women. These men were supposed to dispense justice to them but were doing anything but.

JUDGE DAVID WILLIAM RAMSAY was appointed to the Provincial Court of British Columbia in 1991, and after only a year in the role he began to exploit and assault Indigenous girls. Court documents recount how from 1992 to 2001 he paid Indigenous teenage girls—all living on the street—for sex; he would then commit acts of violence against them, often driving them to rural areas in his truck to do so. In 2004, Ramsay pleaded guilty to five charges including buying sex from minors, sexual assault causing bodily harm, and breach of trust. He resigned from his position after his crimes were brought to the attention of authorities. One of his victims that he was found guilty of sexually assaulting and causing bodily harm to was "J.," as she was called at Ramsay's sentencing, a 16-year-old Indigenous girl he abused from October 1999 until February 2000. In one incident, Ramsay agreed to pay J. $150 for sex. He drove her in his truck 6 kilometres out of town and into the woods. She took off her clothes, and when she reached for a condom, Ramsay smashed her head against the dashboard. After a struggle, she made it out of the truck, forehead bleeding, but Ramsay caught up to her, pinned her on the ground, and raped her as she cried. As the judge who sentenced Ramsay recalled in court, "He got up, threw her clothes out of the truck and left. No money changed hands. She made her way back to the highway and hitchhiked back to town." Over a year later, J. found out that Ramsay was presiding over a case concerning custody of her son.

Ramsay was also convicted of assaulting another girl. He picked up 12-year-old "H." off a street in Prince George and paid her $80 for oral sex and intercourse. About three months later, then 13 years old, she appeared in front of the court for various offences and Ramsay learned in an official capacity not only her age, but also about her vulnerabilities and trauma she experienced as a younger child growing up. About a month later he picked up H. again and in conversation made references to her court appearance. He paid her $150 to, as the court indictment puts it, "simulate aggressive sex." According to the judge's summary of what happened, "the two got involved in a physical confrontation with respect to the transaction. Ultimately H. pushed the accused away and escaped out of the vehicle. He told her no one would believe her if she reported what had happened."

Another Indigenous girl, referred to as "A." in court records, was 14 years old when Ramsay paid her $80 on about four to six occasions for oral sex. During the time of these encounters A. appeared before Ramsay several times, and he was made aware of her background, including her fragile mental state, low self-esteem, and history with abusive adults. In one of the earlier encounters with A., Ramsay told her he could "let her off sentences" if she kept silent about what he was doing with her. The teen appeared before Ramsay eight times in court.

Yet another Indigenous girl, a 15-year-old referred to as "C.," had appeared in court in front of Ramsay to be removed from the care of her parents and be made a ward of the state, with her consent. Several months later, Ramsay paid her $60 for oral sex. After it was over, he grabbed her by the hair and demanded the money back, but she managed to get away. Before Ramsay sped off, leaving her naked on the highway with no other option but to hitchhike back to town, he threatened to have her killed if she told anyone. About six years after Ramsay pleaded guilty, C.'s dad, Bob Sandbach, went public with her name, explaining that she'd passed away at only 22 years of age from a violent illness related to drugs. In a *Prince George Citizen* news article from 2010, he says she suffered from trauma and smoked crack cocaine as young as 8 years old. In a 2013 Human Rights Watch report, *Those Who Take Us Away: Abusive Policing and Failures in Protection of Indigenous Women and Girls in Northern British Columbia, Canada,* her father claims she was also sexually exploited by police officers. A CBC article from 2008 explains that two officers were the focus of a "sex crime investigation involving underage prostitutes" but were never charged. In 2010, Sandbach was pushing for more mental health supports for those, like his daughter, who are struggling with addictions.

After a decade of getting away with assaulting girls while serving as a provincial court judge, Ramsay finally met his fate during a May 2002 custody case. One of the victims he had violently assaulted had cleaned up her life at rehab and was trying to regain custody of her son. Ramsay was presiding over one of her court proceedings, and though he granted her the return of her child, she broke down outside the courthouse. She then disclosed to social workers what he'd done to her, and they pursued the allegations. More women and girls came forward following her bravery. The ensuing investigation of David Ramsay, then age 59, went on for months until he was indicted in 2003.

According to the court documents, the Crown and defence agreed on the facts laid out by the judge, and on the sentencing of three to five years' imprisonment. In an unusual move, Associate Chief Justice Patrick Dohm gravely disagreed with the proposed sentence. In his sentencing remarks in 2004, he said, "The accused's conduct was utterly reprehensible. He freely engaged in sexual activity, including violence, with young women who were highly vulnerable because of youth, disadvantaged backgrounds and addiction... For the administration of justice and for these young women a greater tragedy is difficult to imagine." He sentenced Ramsay to seven years in prison, a length of time many Indigenous scholars and lawyers considered still far too low given the enormity of his crimes and the harm he caused.

I WISH I COULD SAY I WAS SHOCKED upon learning about Ramsay's crimes, but like Kines learning of the horrors of Pickton's crimes, I too thought: these girls, exploited as children, teens, and women, were telling the truth all along—there were nefarious things going on in Prince George, and Indigenous girls were the target. And more rumours were emerging. From the youth I worked with, from people at the bars I went to as a student, and from those I hung out with at the First Nations Centre at university, I started to hear about more breaches of trust in the justice system in Prince George and the rest of the northern interior and northwestern B.C. They told me that police were also involved in abuses and exploitation of Indigenous girls.

Many of the stories of police violence against Indigenous girls in Prince George never became public because women feared retribution, but some involving men and boys did. In 2003, a Métis man named Clayton Willey was arrested by police in Prince George after someone reported him for carrying a knife, although police later discovered he was unarmed. When Willey refused to lie down in his handcuffs, police knocked him to the ground, hog-tied him, kicked him in the chest (police said this was to gain compliance when he resisted arrest), pepper sprayed him, and used a Taser on him repeatedly. He died of a heart attack several hours after. The arresting officers were cleared of any wrongdoing. In 2004, a video of the incident was entered in evidence in a coroner's inquest, which did not find fault with the police officers. However, the Civilian Review and Complaints Commission for the RCMP stated that "the RCMP must nonetheless take responsibility for the mistreatment of Mr. Willey while he was in its custody."

Five years later, Leonard Cler-Cunningham, a writer researching Indigenous deaths in custody, brought the video to the attention of Grand Chief Stewart Phillip, a renowned Indigenous leader who has served as president of the Union of British Columbia Indian Chiefs. Speaking to media at the time, Phillip said, "I had an opportunity to see an edited version of the video and I can tell you it was sickening, it was very, very difficult to watch and it stirred a deep anger within myself." Cler-Cunningham said the beating and tasing of Willey met the standard of torture. In an email, Staff Sergeant Janelle Shoihet provided me with a summary of the incident that ended as follows: "In 2009, due in part to the initiation of the Public Interest Inquiry, Code of Conduct processes were initiated against two RCMP officers for 'negligence in the care and handling of a prisoner.' Ultimately, the allegations were not established."

The Human Rights Watch report *Those Who Take Us Away* conveys the stories of fifty Indigenous women from B.C.'s northern regions dating back to the 1950s and running up until 2013. The title of the report comes from the literal translation of the word *police* in the Dakelh language, which is Nilhchuk-un, meaning "those who take us away." The word reflects the RCMP's role in the early residential school era when they forcibly removed Indigenous children from their parents and transported them to the schools. This history, and subsequent negative interactions, built a reputation the RCMP will be hard pressed to shake over the next hundred years, particularly since changing their image would require a daunting internal culture shift that may be hard for the force to swing.

A 2011 report authored by the RCMP, called *The Role of the Royal Canadian Mounted Police During the Indian Residential School System*, looked at data from the 1880s to 1990s and found that "the police were not perceived as a source for help but rather as an authority figure who takes members of the community away from the reserve or makes arrests for wrong-doing." According to their report, a loving and concerned parent could be arrested for trying to keep their children from being forcibly removed from their homes by the RCMP to attend residential school, or for their child running away. The report describes how one mother, who had tried to rescue her child from residential school, was fined two dollars for the crime, but since she could not pay, was sentenced to ten days' imprisonment. A search of the word *runaway* in the report brings up more than three hundred instances. The examples show how it was common practice for RCMP to return runaways, sometimes by force, to residential schools in handcuffs. Some of the children were placed in jail for as long as fifteen days for running away. The report states that there was an urgency to find runaways since some cases ended tragically, with children dying from exposure, drowning, or other dangers. It is a heartbreaking read. Some kids would jump trains, others hid in the bush, some would follow the train tracks, just trying to get far away from the torture of residential school, trying to make their way back to their families.

The RCMP report also chronicles cases of men in positions of power within the residential school system, including principals, teachers, and priests, who raped Indigenous girls. They were often not charged by the RCMP, and if they were, it wasn't until decades later. The RCMP report admits that the force was aware of cases of abuse in the residential school system at the time. In another case in 1967–69, a dormitory supervisor was accused of sexually assaulting students (termed "indecent assault" in the report). After a lengthy investigation in which forty students were contacted, he was charged and sentenced to thirty months' incarceration, with two of the charges stayed.

In many of the RCMP's historical logs quoted in the report—written or typed records of incidents at residential schools that detail the abuse of Indigenous girls and boys by authority figures—the children were not believed and the abusers were allowed to stay and continue to abuse, some with extreme violence.

Reading about the residential school era and how much chaos and violence it caused in Indigenous people's lives and homes is gut-wrenching. It's also eerie how similar the historical RCMP logs of officers' interactions with Indigenous children and parents are to more recent social workers' accounts of their interactions with Indigenous children, documents that I have obtained through freedom of information requests. The social workers' logs I have seen are handwritten accounts of assessments of Indigenous parents, their parenting, and why their children were taken into foster care from the 2000s up to as recently as 2018. The contents often show social workers passing harsh judgments on parents and blaming them for their circumstances without awareness of the colonial and paternalistic practices the social workers themselves operate within.

As a former street kid, I remember how intertwined police and social workers were. They had a joint unit with cars that would pluck us from the street and bring us to foster care. The Vancouver Police Department today still shares a unit with the Ministry of Children and Family Development called Youth Community Response, operating several cars and teams that are set up to provide services to Vancouver youth. Two types of cars would pick us up off the streets in Vancouver. The first was a unit called Yankee 20, formerly Car Y177, described by the police as a "high-risk youth/street youth intervention team" for youth ages 12 to 18, comprising an outreach social worker from the ministry and a police officer. The vehicles were not marked but looked like undercover police cars (which I can still spot from a mile away). Teenagers I was acquainted with at the time were afraid of these cars, since we didn't want to end up back in a dysfunctional child-welfare system. To ensure we were not picked up, we had a warning system that would be passed up the street by word of mouth when the cars were spotted. Still, I was picked up by Car Y177 two times, and in both cases I was questioned, ID'd, and taken to a group home.

Our distrust of police and social workers ran deep. We would rather sleep in a dilapidated abandoned building than be carted off by police to a foster or group home where there was no assurance we would be safe from abuse, violence, and neglect. There was nowhere we could lodge a complaint and no guarantee we'd be believed when we wanted to report how we were treated. Things are not much better today: we see government and advocacy groups releasing report after report about foster kids being neglected—or even dying—in foster care. From June 2017 to March 2018, ninety-eight children and youth died in B.C. while in government care or while receiving supports. Thirty-five were Indigenous.

In 2020, I wrote an awful and traumatic story about a 17-year-old Cree youth named Traevon Chalifoux-Desjarlais who died in his Abbotsford, B.C., group home run by Rees Family Services. Rees was contracted out by a delegated Aboriginal agency called Xyolhemeylh that is operated under the Ministry of Children and Family Development. I filed several freedom of information requests to the ministry about the agency responsible for the group home and any reports into his death and was told they could release nothing, citing privacy concerns, even though I made it clear I was not in search of names of children, youth, or even social workers.

More people are becoming aware of the serious systemic failures within child-welfare systems in Canada, just as there is growing awareness of the flaws of policing when it comes to Black and Indigenous people in this country.

According to the Human Rights Watch report *Those Who Take Us Away*, Indigenous people's lack of trust in police is not only tied to historical abuses but also results from modern-day, recent interactions between the RCMP and Indigenous women and girls. In ten towns across northern B.C., the organization talked to dozens of people—including advocates, victims, and former and current RCMP officers—and documented flaws in police protection of Indigenous women and girls. At the beginning of the report, there are a number of unnerving photographs. One is of a woman, her back to the camera, wearing a T-shirt bearing the slogan "Prince George, the Home of Police Brutality." The next few are a jarring series that shows, from seven different angles, the badly bruised and beaten face of an Indigenous woman. Looking at these photos fills me with anxiety, anger, and sadness. I remember how I felt the first time I saw those same pictures as I was scrolling on Facebook.

When I shared the post, my cousin commented, "Well, what did she do to make police do that to her?" It shocked me, but it shouldn't have. When Indigenous women experience violence, people often blame the victim.

More proof of that appeared in my inbox in May of 2019, when I received an email from a source saying they were about to send me a series of videos that I might be interested in reporting on. When I played the videos I was horrified, as were the seventy thousand Canadians who later read my story on CBC's main page.

The one video out of the series that I shared in my online story was the most shocking. Recorded in 2012 in a police interrogation room in Kelowna, B.C., it shows an RCMP officer sitting across from a 17-year-old Cree girl who is reporting being sexually assaulted the previous night. Rather than sensitively taking her report, he cross-examines her. He asks if she was subconsciously "turned on at all" during the rape and says, "You understand that when a guy tries to have sex with a female and the female is completely unwilling, it's very difficult, right?" He also asks if she understands the implications of reporting the crime, saying she could destroy her rapist's life.

The victim later went public with their name, Aden Withers. In 2019, Aden's lawyer told me that the accused was never questioned nor charged. In a telephone interview that same year, Aden tells me how first the rape and then the interrogation by police who didn't believe them ruined their life. I share with Aden that I had seen a video online from a few years earlier of them drumming and singing a Cree song their grandparents had imparted. Through tears Aden tells me that they are no longer that person, that the shame of the assault had crushed them and they had not sung a traditional song since. Aden had called me from a hospital room that they had checked into out of fear they would self-harm. Talking about the incident to media had resurfaced wounds and brought back all the trauma that Aden was now reliving.

The video had come out of a court case that saw Aden and several other teens, many First Nations, file claims against Robert Riley Saunders, a former Ministry of Children and Family Development social worker accused of siphoning money from vulnerable children and youth. One of the claimants accused Saunders of moving her from a stable home into an independent living situation, where he, as her social worker, was able to collect money from the Ministry of Children and Family Development. The ministry admitted to fraud and negligence by Saunders and said it led to a review of their contracting and payment processes. In January of 2020, after a legal fight with the Kelowna RCMP, Aden settled their civil suit against the force. In a *Kelowna Capital News* story, Aden stands with a red hand print across their face (the symbol Indigenous people wear to raise the alarm about violence against Indigenous women and girls), beating a drum and singing. It reminded me of what Aden had said before, that they felt the assault had taken their pride away and they could no longer drum or sing. Now here they stood, taking up a fight for all of those who experience violence, reclaiming something they felt was once taken away.

After the videos of the police interrogation of Aden were made public, Canada's minister of public safety denounced the RCMP's actions, saying "No survivor of sexual assault should ever fear that his or her case will not be taken seriously or that he or she will be re-victimized in the process." In a statement at the time, the RCMP told me they were working to change their investigation process, including looking into a new, advanced course for sexual assault investigators, with training around cultural competency and "trauma-informed investigations." In 2021, nine years after the RCMP interrogated Aden, the force announced a mandatory cultural competency training course to address unconscious bias among RCMP employees. It also said it was still developing training for RCMP employees to be trauma informed and to update sexual assault investigations.

If those commitments had been genuine and made years before, they could have helped those women and girls who brought forth allegations against Judge Ramsay before he was convicted. Or perhaps the Indigenous teens I worked with in Prince George would have been listened to and believed when they shared that Ramsay was not the only person in the justice system buying sex from and abusing them.

During the investigation into David Ramsay, more allegations of exploitation and abuse of teen girls by authorities in Prince George resurfaced. Top RCMP officials in B.C. at the time admitted that even though they had heard that several officers were potentially involved in misconduct, and seen victim statements from exploited teens prior to 2002, they didn't believe the girls then.

But in 2006, the RCMP's adjudication board held a hearing to determine whether one of the accused officers, Constable Justin Harris, should be disciplined for serious misconduct, including six allegations of sexual exploitation (involving at least one Indigenous girl) and breach of trust. The RCMP's deputy commissioner, Bev Busson, and assistant commissioner, Gary Bass, said after Ramsay pleaded guilty in 2004, the allegations about other members of the justice system potentially abusing girls were taken more seriously. Women and girls claimed Harris and other RCMP officers were paying to have sex with underage girls and using excessive force. Harris was suspended with pay in September 2004 because of the investigation, but the case against him was shut down in late 2006, after a panel found the RCMP failed to follow proper guidelines by waiting too long to launch the hearing. In 2007 Harris was reinstated on paper, but he did not return to duties.

A 2021 *Vice* article about Harris states he "segued from a paid suspension to paid sick leave for psychological issues he directly links to the force's handling of the allegations." It adds that Harris's lawsuit against the RCMP has stalled while the force attempts to medically discharge him, more than seventeen years later. In an emailed statement, Harris confirmed that he was never criminally charged and is still being paid by the RCMP. He also confirmed that underage sex workers in Prince George alleged he and other officers paid for sex with underage girls and that there were allegations of excessive force. He confirmed he faced a disciplinary hearing stemming from the accusations, but the case was dismissed in late 2006 because too much time had elapsed since the RCMP became aware of the allegations. In his email he also added, "While it certainly is tragic many Indigenous woman across Canada have been subjected to violence in one form or another, that definitely is not the case with respect to the accusers and their allegations as they concern me... The fact is the Indigenous girls who accused me are liars. Their allegations against me are complete lies."

THE VULNERABILITY OF INDIGENOUS GIRLS in this region to abuse from the police, judges, and other powerful people who can avoid scrutiny has been compounded by the lack of safe ways to get from place to place while living in geographical isolation.

During a call-in news program I hosted for the CBC in 2018 about missing and murdered Indigenous women and girls (MMIWG), a caller tried to get on air by telling my producer that it was only "the Natives hitchhiking along the highway" and rhetorically asking why there were no white girls hitchhiking. While he was echoing a familiar narrative, that Indigenous women and girls are somehow responsible for crimes against them, it made me think: If I'd had the patience, how would I have answered that question if my producer had patched him through? I would most likely have started with the basic facts. For one, there's a large Indigenous population along the highway with close to thirty First Nations villages and reserves along the route just from Prince George to Prince Rupert and at least thirty more on the two other highways the RCMP associate with the Highway of Tears. I'd also have reminded him that Indigenous people didn't choose their circumstances of being removed from their traditional territories and isolated on racially segregated and often far-flung reserves created by the colonials through the Indian Act. I would have shared that between the 1850s and 1860s, reserves in Canada alienated and economically devastated Indigenous people. The outcome—poverty—is part of the reason we see so many Indigenous women hitchhiking along a dangerous highway. But I would most likely have had to pause to answer more questions about reserves because their existence, as part and parcel of the Indian Act, provides answers as to why so many of the missing and murdered along the Highway of Tears are Indigenous (though in fact white girls and women do also hitchhike in the area and are among the missing and murdered).

An Indian reserve is defined in the Indian Act as "a tract of land, the legal title to which is vested in Her Majesty, that has been set apart by Her Majesty for the use and benefit of a band." Indigenous people have the right to occupy reserve land, but not the right to sell, transfer, or mortgage it, unless sold or transferred to the Crown, in the vast majority of cases. Reserves were created as a key instrument of colonization. In 1885, the Department of Indian Affairs was concerned about Indigenous people leaving the reserves and getting too close to settler society. Indigenous people's existence became essentially a threat to white settlement. In order to prevent Indigenous people from gathering in groups to protest their lands being stolen or their cultural practices being outlawed, the Department of Indian Affairs under Prime Minister John A. Macdonald instituted a federal "pass system." Indigenous people who wanted to leave the reserve would need a pass from Indian agents. If caught without a pass, an Indigenous person could face a ten-dollar fine, a lot at a time when wages were around fifty cents a day. While this was hard to enforce in regions with many reserves and limited Indian agents, when it was enforced, it made it difficult to go into town to work or start businesses. And the push to make room and amenities for settlers meant removing Indigenous people from their traditional economies.

By 1904 the federal government began a concerted effort to ban Northwest Coast Indigenous technologies like the fish weir from the headwaters of the Skeena River, saying it would have a negative impact on commercial fishing. In 1933, Indigenous people were also fined for hunting for game in season. But many Indigenous people continued to hunt and fish by their custom. In one instance a "local Indian" running a mill in the Skeena region was charged for having moose meat in the camp. While the colonials permitted Indigenous people on reserves to farm, reserve land was often unviable. If the land was fertile, Indigenous people could not sell what was grown on their land by law since it was federal land, meaning they could not make a living in agriculture on reserves. The poverty experienced by Indigenous people on reserves has deep roots in these policies that made it incredibly difficult for them to thrive or even survive.

If we had put him on air, the gentleman who phoned in might have asked why they didn't leave the reserves if life on them was so deplorable. Many Indigenous people, like my grandparents, did move to towns and cities for work to make money so they could buy the permits needed to hunt and fish or buy food and supplies, in line with the colonials' hope for them to assimilate to the white man's ways. In some cases, like with my grandfather and his brothers, Indigenous people integrated well into settler life and made a good living at it, even though it meant removing themselves, by law, from their communities, traditional way of life, and culture. Others, though, didn't have the same experience.

Many who worked for settlers in the farming, logging, fishing, and fur industries faced discrimination, with lower wages and fewer opportunities for jobs and entrepreneurship than white people. While the colonials asserted that reserves were created to protect Indigenous people from the settlers, the exclusion of Indigenous people from civil society, including being denied the right to vote until 1960, accentuated the reality that they did not belong. In 1927, the *Interior News* reported that the village of Smithers ordered that the "natives are to be given strict application of every by-law, rule, regulation and resolution in an effort to keep them from the more thickly settled parts of town." More famously among Indigenous people, signs were placed on restaurant windows in Smithers in the 1950s saying "No Indians allowed."

When I'm speaking to anyone (not just hypothetically imagining what I would say to an ignorant caller for a current affairs segment) about why Indigenous women and girls are overrepresented among the missing and murdered, it is impossible not to explain how the colonials enforced patriarchy in law and controlled and marginalized Indigenous women in particular.

In 1869, through section 6 of the Gradual Enfranchisement Act, and later, through sections 12 and 14 of the 1951 Indian Act, the federal government ordered the removal of Indian status from an Indigenous woman who married a non-Indigenous man, and forced an Indigenous woman who married an Indigenous man who was a member of another band to lose membership in her own band and to become a member of her husband's Indian band instead. The 1951 act applied this loss of band membership even to an Indigenous woman who married an Indigenous man, if the husband was not himself a member of another band. The 1869 act also removed inheritance rights from Indigenous wives and enfranchised these rights with their husbands. The loss of Indian status meant a woman was forced to disassociate from her community, lose her home on the reserve, and give up any property she might have inherited. Marrying a non-status man also prevented a woman from returning to live with her family on the reserve, even if she was in dire need, very ill, widowed, divorced, or separated. Finally, her family would not be allowed to bury her body on the reserve with her ancestors when she died. The unfair penalties on Indigenous women who "married out" led to long-term effects, including homelessness, poverty, cultural genocide, loss of family connection, and apprehension of their children. Men were able to kick women out of their shared house, as the act gave men sole ownership of property.

In 1923, the B.C. government created the Women's and Girls' Protection Act, which outlawed giving employment or lodging to any "white or Indian woman or girl." It was supposedly created to "protect [women's and girls'] morals" from unruly men. However, it was often used to control Indigenous women, who were under continual pressure from Indian agents, missionaries, and men on reserves to stay out of settler towns. For example, in 1944, a café and rooming house owner in Smithers was charged under the act for allowing an Indian girl in a room. Outlawing Indigenous women's occupation of public space on their own made them more vulnerable, as they were forced to rely more on men—namely white men—who did not face the same exclusionary rules.

In 1970, a Wolastoqiyik woman named Sandra Lovelace married a non-Indigenous man, moved off reserve, and had a son. When she divorced him and returned to the reserve with her child, she discovered that she was no longer entitled to Indian status nor rights to housing and therefore had to sleep in a tent in her home community in the middle of winter. In 1977, Lovelace took her case to the United Nations Human Rights Committee, arguing that the discriminatory measures in the Indian Act violated international law. Her efforts, along with those of Mary Two-Axe Earley, Yvonne Bedard, and Jeannette Corbiere Lavell, led to amendments to the Indian Act in 1985 that removed gender discrimination. The act no longer forces Indigenous women to follow their husbands into or out of status. Still, the discrimination had a lasting effect.

Some call what happened in Indigenous communities across Canada via the Indian Act legislated racialized poverty. Sadly, that same economic inequality, segregation, and racism is a legacy that Indigenous Nations share today. There is no mistaking the difference between often poverty-stricken Indian reserves and the well-serviced white towns that sometimes sit side by side.

That disparity has affected generations of Indigenous people and their children. In today's child-welfare system, Indigenous children are sometimes shipped to foster homes hundreds of kilometres away from their parents. In many cases, Indigenous children are removed from their homes for poverty-related reasons—for example, parents unable to properly feed or clothe their children. Former social workers have shared heart-wrenching stories with me about non-Indigenous social workers having no idea how difficult it is for their Indigenous clients to make it from the reserve and into town for meetings, when workers refuse to meet them even halfway or cover transportation costs. Poverty, and the lack of a reliable and affordable transportation system along the Highway of Tears, has not only meant high rates of MMIWG—it is also part of why Indigenous children are put in care.

Canadians are becoming more aware of how trauma from residential school has affected outcomes for Indigenous people. However, the non-Indigenous public often doesn't hear of the very serious ramifications of systemic racial segregation and economic and land dispossession, as it's rarely discussed in the media or by politicians.

IN 2006, TWO YEARS AFTER Judge Ramsay's sentencing and a year following the allegations of police misconduct in Prince George, a Wet'suwet'en woman named Florence Naziel, whose cousin Tamara Chipman went missing while hitchhiking along Highway 16, organized a walk from Prince Rupert to Terrace to raise awareness about the scores of Indigenous women and girls who were missing from the area. Florence was the first person known to use "Highway of Tears" to describe the length of highway from Prince George to Prince Rupert. At the same time, Gladys Radek, Tamara's aunt, was headed to Prince George to speak at the Highway of Tears Symposium, and convinced Florence to continue her walk from Terrace all the way to Prince George. The pair, along with Ramona Wilson's mother, Matilda, worked together to organize the walk to the historic symposium. "That walk was the one that set the template for me to move forward with the Walk4Justice that would eventually take us across Canada," Gladys tells me during a phone interview. But it was a very difficult journey. "We could feel the spirits of those women along the highway," she says. At the same time, that's what kept them going: "We are thinking about those women that we are walking for and always wishing that we could find somebody, that we could see something in those bushes other than little crosses."

While I wasn't on the walk, I was there at the CN Centre where the symposium was held. Five hundred people attended, including family members, Indigenous leaders, advocates,

RCMP officers, B.C.'s solicitor general, and members of the legislative assembly. They sat at round tables and listened to powerful speakers—family members and advocates—from across B.C. It was monumental. "Out of all the roundtables, out of all the meetings and all the gatherings that I have been to since then, that symposium was the best one, because you knew at the end of the three days that it was definitely for the families, and those recommendations were heartfelt and done by the families," Gladys says.

Three months later, the *Highway of Tears Symposium Recommendations Report* came out. Thirty-three recommendations were listed, with the first being that a "shuttle bus transportation system be established between each town and city located along the entire length of Highway 16, defined as the Highway of Tears." It also suggested RCMP patrols, safe homes, emergency phone booths, and educational billboards along Highway 16. Another recommendation that stood out was the one calling for cell service along the highway. Given the long distances between towns, cities, and Indigenous communities, with many areas along the highway without service, recommendation 8 advised that "Telus Mobility should be approached to look into the feasibility of increasing cell phone coverage along the entire length of the highway thus minimizing or eliminating no signal areas." This, the report said, could allow a potential victim to call for help.

But it would not be until more than a decade later and after a high-profile political scandal that some of the recommendations would be implemented.

In May of 2015, B.C.'s information and privacy commissioner, Elizabeth Denham, launched an investigation and penned a report into allegations about the destruction of records pertaining to the Highway of Tears. A whistleblower—Tim Duncan, a former executive assistant to B.C.'s minister of transportation and infrastructure—said his former supervisor, George Gretes, had triple deleted documents about the B.C. government's progress on making Highway 16 safer.

The report revealed Gretes lied under oath when he denied that he intentionally deleted emails and records about the Highway of Tears. At the time, Indigenous leaders alleged that more than a dozen of the emails were about meetings with a number of First Nations leaders along the Highway of Tears. Carrier Sekani tribal councillor Mavis Erickson said that she believed "there's a cover-up going on" and that the government just "wants this whole story to go away." Erickson, a lawyer and strong advocate for many of the family members of MMIWG, said the mass email and file deletion was simply a continuation of government efforts to sweep Indigenous people's issues under the rug, as was done following colonization.

Denham's investigation revealed that in late November 2014, the provincial Opposition, the New Democratic Party, filed a freedom of information request seeking "government records that make reference to the issue of missing women along Highway 16/the Highway of Tears and specifically including records related to meetings held by the ministry on this issue" from May 15 to November 19, 2014. The Opposition was curious about the files because Parliamentary Secretary Darryl Plecas had stated in the B.C. legislature that in the summer of 2014, staff at the Ministry of Transportation and Infrastructure had travelled along Highway 16 for face-to-face discussions with leaders in First Nations, municipalities, and regional districts. Journalists have speculated that the meetings took place because the transportation ministry was under pressure to address the growing number of Indigenous women and girls going missing or being murdered while hitchhiking along the Highway of Tears. Indigenous leaders were growing frustrated that the recommendations stemming from the 2006

Highway of Tears Symposium, including that the government set up a shuttle bus service along the route, were not being implemented.

Duncan claimed Gretes had ordered him to "get rid of" all emails related to the Highway of Tears. When he hesitated, Duncan said Gretes grabbed his keyboard and mouse and triple deleted the files himself. Denham's report refers to Duncan, the whistleblower, as saying "he sympathized with the families of the murdered and missing victims on the highway because his own father had been murdered in a domestic incident in 2010." In May of 2015, Duncan told the CBC: "To watch as the government doesn't take it seriously, a lot of staffers think it is a joke and it is repulsive to me. It came to the point where I couldn't stay silent."

Headlines reading "Delete Delete Delete" told the story to the public. Some say that story, coupled with the announcement of a national inquiry, catalyzed the transportation ministry to hold a symposium that November. One month later the ministry announced a $3 million government action plan that included funds to support a transit system along the Highway of Tears. Family members of MMIWG had begged for a plan like this for years and had been met with radio silence; it was only when the erasure of their calls for action became public that anything finally changed.

In early 2017, four transit services began as part of the B.C. government's Highway 16 Transportation Action Plan. Service first started between Smithers and Moricetown, with buses running six days per week at $2.75 per ride, one way. In January of 2019, routes were added between Burns Lake and Prince George, Burns Lake and Smithers, and Terrace and the Hazeltons. In a press release, B.C.'s parliamentary secretary for gender equity stated that "people in the communities along the Highway 16 corridor asked for safe, affordable travel options, and this service is answering their needs." But Indigenous leaders in B.C. said that after more than sixty women and girls from the region had gone missing or been murdered, with multiple killers responsible, this commitment came too late.

It took fifteen years, until 2021, for the B.C. government to announce it was bringing cell service to a 252-kilometre stretch of highway between Smithers and Prince Rupert that before had none. In an interview with me shortly after the announcement, Gladys said sarcastically, "Took you long enough." She had just gotten off the phone with Mike Farnworth, B.C.'s minister of public safety and solicitor general, who was keen to hear her thoughts about the news. While she was elated that it was finally happening (albeit belatedly), she also believed that the service may have been needed by pipeline workers who'd been deployed to work on Coastal GasLink's liquid natural gas lines, rather than being implemented because the government cared about Indigenous women and girls.

While three recommendations laid out by the symposium have been implemented (billboards, like the ones I saw along my drive home in 2016, were also erected in some communities warning women not to hitchhike), Gladys says there are still thirty to go. Still, reflecting on the symposium, she and others see the time period as one of great transformation and a turning point for those who were raising concerns about the high numbers of MMIWG.

The final recommendation in the *Highway of Tears Symposium Recommendations Report* is that the RCMP continue its investigation into the actual number of MMIWG on the Highway of Tears. It says: "This ongoing official RCMP investigation should determine the number of missing women and verify their identities."

While the 2006 symposium brought communities together and showed them their power in numbers, there was also movement within the police, an institution that had for many years been silent on the issue of MMIWG. In 2007, the RCMP expanded its investigation from nine cases of missing or murdered women or girls to eighteen. On their list is a woman whose murder the police say is still unsolved, but one that my investigation has shown to be more of a conspiracy of silence— and one that is not unique to the lands she died in.

The territory Levina called home is a territory I took respite in during a time when I was doing my best to heal from wounds that seemed to stick around far too long.

5

Nucwstimu, quiet

A CONSPIRACY OF SILENCE

I ARRIVED IN YUNESIT'IN as the night fell on a warm summer day in 2003. The willows waved their slender branches in a light, sandy wind as fireplaces glowed from the comfort of wooden homes that speckled the desert hills. As we parked by my Tŝilhqot'in friend's mother's house, I saw wild horses trotting softly on the rolling slopes and through the sagebrush that paints the Tŝilhqot'in landscape. There was a peacefulness there that is hard to describe. It's as if it's part of the DNA of the land, connecting it to the people that originate from the territory. I was in these lands to heal. The past five years had been a lot, personally and politically.

During my time in Prince George, I was still healing myself from wounds left by street life. But I could never seem to shake the toxic masculinity my biological dad imprinted on me, and was continually attracting misogynistic men who treated me with either indifference or disrespect. By 2003, around the time Ramsay was pleading guilty, I was at a serious breaking point in my life and at a fork in the road. I'd been dating an abusive man for about two years, on and off, but we were intertwined in our work of promoting and organizing Indigenous hip-hop shows and workshops. Our friend groups overlapped, so it was hard to get space.

Witnessing the unhealthy road I was on, my close friend Ellen (not her real name) invited me to visit her territory, to get away from him and the scene that drew us together. A choice was upon me, and I knew I had to take care of myself and alter my direction in life. She and I drove from Vancouver, where I was visiting during a summer break from UNBC, to her community of Yunesit'in, also known as Stone or Stoney. The community is about an hour away from Williams Lake in the Cariboo region of B.C.'s interior, about seven to eight hours away from Vancouver, and about four hours away from the start of the Highway of Tears, in Prince George, driving along Highway 97.

The day after we arrived there, we plucked tiny soapberries from bushes on hilly fields, made Indian ice cream, and crafted medicine from tree pitch and moose grease. My friend's family members and the horses were like salve to my wounded heart. I was in awe of how many people were fluent in the Tŝilhqot'in language and how gentle but fierce the people were. For me it was a place of deep healing and learning, where everything slowed down, giving me time to reflect and pay respect to the land, the people, and my own experiences.

I ended up visiting there more than once throughout the years. On one trip, I saw an elderly healer whose brown hands faded sharply to white arms when he gingerly rolled up his sleeves—an elongated farmer tan from being out on the land so often. In a child's room with a pink bedspread, and with my friend by my side, I lay down for the healer to do his work. He sang songs and prayed over me, in a ceremony that felt like the spirits were taking away my pain and filling me with light. It's a memory that still permeates my soul with love. On another visit we rode horses on the bluffs in the day, and at night danced the twist at a local bar. What sets the region apart from where I grew up on the west coast is the cowboy culture and western-frontier personality. When I was a teen, my dad had told me about what it was like on reserves in the interior of B.C., where Natives wore cowboy hats and where going to the bars was like going back in time, with patrons swinging to Chubby Checker and the Beach Boys. I could never quite picture it and thought maybe it was one of his beer-induced imaginings. But as I sat drinking a pitcher with my friends one Friday night in a pub in Riske Creek near Stoney, I couldn't help but remember what he said—it was like I had travelled through a time portal. It was here, among friends and acquaintances, that I learned about Gloria Levina Moody and what happened to her decades earlier, not far away from the predominantly white settler town of Williams Lake.

LEVINA, AS SHE WAS CALLED by her family and Nuxalk community, was 26 years old when she disappeared on October 25, 1969. A mother of two small children aged 4 and 3, she was kind, caring, and deeply loved by all her eight siblings, mom and dad, and extended family, with whom she was very close. Her brother David Moody, who was 21 years old when she died (and who also goes by his middle name, Al), says she was fun loving and was known to joke around with her many friends, but was also a homebody who didn't like crowds. "Oh, and she was a great mom who loved children," he tells me over a crackly phone from Bella Coola. Levina also loved to bake and cook and would experiment with different Chinese dishes a lot, he says. She travelled along the coast to different fish hatcheries, for work, with a group of Nuxalk women and played basketball in her spare time.

I have seen three black-and-white pictures of her. In one she is around 13, hair tied back neatly and wearing a black dress with a wide white collar; she has big dark eyes and a large warm smile. In the second photo, her hair is tied back and worn high. She looks straight into the camera with a tiny smile, little pearl earrings dangling to her cheeks. And in the third, she is smiling ear to ear, her eyes disappearing into her grin, flanked by her two beaming children. It is a picture of pure love.

When I first spoke to Levina's daughter, Vanessa Hans, in 2016, I was curious to learn more about her mom since there is so little written about who she was before she died. But about three minutes into our phone conversation—me in Vancouver, Vanessa in Bella Coola—she tells me she remembers nothing of her mom, since she was only 4 years old when Levina was murdered. I ask Vanessa if, when growing up, she heard stories or memories shared of her mom. She says that while everyone in the community said she looked just like her mom, there was a silence surrounding her. No one spoke of her mom, Vanessa says, perhaps to shield her and other family members from the pain of the loss and the brutal way her mother died. I was just starting to understand why there was so little published about Levina. It is often just too hard for the family to speak about, even more than fifty years later. Bringing levity to a hard conversation, Vanessa chuckles, thinking back to being a young girl and wondering why she didn't look much like her "mom" until learning, at 12 years old, that she was actually being raised by her maternal grandmother, Daisy, and grandfather, David. Vanessa's eldest daughter's name is a combination of her grandparents' and her mom's names: Devina. As we end the first of many long phone conversations, Vanessa tells me her mother came from a high-ranking Chief's family. David and Daisy had one of the more culturally active families in the Bella Coola Valley, and they managed to keep their kids out of residential school. When the potlatch was banned, her family continued to practise it to keep that part of their culture alive. Vanessa's final words to me in that first call are "Thank you for seeing her." It would be the first of dozens of times I'd "see" her mom, her story, and her horrific murder, through Vanessa's eyes.

Vanessa's Nuxalk community in Bella Coola rests on an inlet of the Pacific Ocean about six hours west of Williams Lake. With towering coastal mountains and rushing glacial rivers, the area is the gateway to the Great Bear Rainforest. I've done a number of stories about the Nuxalk community and people over the years. I've joked to many of the people I've spoken with that I can barely hear their voices over the phone because they are so soft-spoken. Vanessa laughs when I tell her this, saying, "It's true." It stands in contrast to their strong spirits, their humour, and their brilliance—characteristics that thunder in many ways. During interviews with Nuxalk women, I've appreciated their gentle, thoughtful but steadfast nature as they bravely speak up about injustices they've experienced. This land, this community, is where the Moody family has lived since time immemorial.

In the late fall of 1969, Levina Moody went on a family trip with her mom, Daisy; her dad, David; and her brother David (whom the family calls Al). They headed to Williams Lake to do some Christmas shopping and get out of Bella Coola for a couple of days. The Lake, as it is called by locals, is the nearest centre larger than Bella Coola, and many travel there to pick up items not available in their home community (which in 1969 had roughly two thousand people).

On their way from Bella Coola the family stopped at a café and bar in Anahim Lake called the Frontier Inn, at the time several hours away from Williams Lake. "Levina was teaching me how to play shuffleboard," Al says. While they played the game, the family noticed a man was ogling Levina, and that it was making her uncomfortable. She became so ill at ease that her brother Al asked the man why he was staring, to which he replied that it was because Levina was so beautiful. Her dad told her that she should feel flattered, but she felt anything but. They eventually left, and when the family arrived in Williams Lake later that day they checked into the Ranch Hotel for the weekend.

On Saturday, on the last night of their stay in the Lake, Levina and her brother went out to the Lakeview pub to relax and grab a drink. Newspaper reports from the time mention that it was a "pay weekend" as there was a big livestock sale in town, with hotels and bars packed. This part of the story is difficult to recall details of, David says, in part because of the drinks the family consumed that made everything blurrier, and in part because of the trauma of how the night ended. It is a night no one wants to remember. I am mindful, writing this now, that I have dredged up some brutal memories that will haunt the family for the rest of their lives.

Levina Moody failed to return to the hotel that night. The family notified the RCMP that she had gone missing that same night, but before a report could even be properly filed, they discovered the worst. The next morning, on Sunday, hunters found Levina's naked body on a trail about 7 miles west of Williams Lake, according to an RCMP report from the time. She had last been seen wearing a navy blue coat and a yellow shift dress with green and blue flowers. The report goes on to say she was brutally murdered and bled to death after being beaten, tortured, and sexually assaulted—in part with a tree branch. She is said to have died from that injury. It is one of the most brutal and heinous murders I have ever investigated in my life. The report from 1969 lists her as a victim of second-degree murder.

Vanessa says years later, when she and her brother, Dan, were in their 20s, RCMP investigators shared a box of photographs and records of their mother's death with them. She still doesn't know why. Over the phone, Vanessa tells me that when the officers told them they could look inside, she was in disbelief and wondered why they would permit them to do that, knowing how traumatic it would be. She warned her brother not to look at the documents, but he did. When Vanessa saw one of the images of her deceased mom, she ran out of the station to the river and fainted from the extreme trauma and shock. Seeing the images drove her kid brother to turn to alcohol to cope with the trauma, she says, which eventually led to his demise. Earlier, as a teenager trying to make sense of why her mother had been murdered and how there had been no justice for her, Vanessa had also turned to drugs and alcohol to cope. Now in her 50s, she has been sober for more than thirty years and is a respected cultural teacher and genealogist in her community.

According to current RCMP officers whom Vanessa and I have spoken with, Moody's murder remains open and unsolved. Her case, like Ramona Wilson's, is now among the investigations of the RCMP's Project E-PANA, a task force dedicated to unsolved murders connected to Highways 16, 97, and 5. Few of the women's cases have been solved, but police tell me that all of them remain open in case they uncover new evidence related to them, despite family members' concerns that the unit has faded out because of a lack of new funding since 2016.

Levina Moody, whom the police refer to by her first name, Gloria, is on the list as one of the first known Indigenous women to be murdered along the infamous network of highways. Levina's family believes people are withholding the truth about her case. As with other cases of missing and murdered Indigenous women and girls (MMIWG) that I have covered, the investigation into Moody's murder was shoddy, despite strong evidence of there being a known suspect. Understanding why her case is still cold requires untangling the strands of a messy skein of an investigation.

IN 2021, THE RCMP TOLD ME via email that Moody's case is considered open "until such time that it has been settled through the judicial system, i.e. someone has been charged." According to Staff Sergeant Janelle Shoihet, "It is my understanding that there was at one time someone of interest in this case, however that person died before they could be charged, thus the file cannot be closed, given there has been no judicial decision rendered." In 1999, Vanessa says, officers at the Williams Lake RCMP detachment told her family there was strong evidence, including witness reports, that helped them identify suspects. She says officers told her family that they had identified a suspect named Al Blohm, alongside two other suspects—all of whom by then were deceased. In two hundred pages of documents I obtained via an Access to Information and Privacy request, numerous RCMP reports from 1970, through the 1990s, and up until 2010 identify suspects in the murder—at times even given a polygraph test—but the names are always redacted. In several reports, officers state that the suspects are all now deceased.

A 1999 *Coast Mountain News* article written by Angela Hall is titled "The Final Chapter in a Brutal Murder." The lede reads: "The savage murder that shocked the valley 30 years ago and devastated the family forever has finally come to a close." The article says that the case is still officially unsolved, but that detective John Pilszek from the Special Crime Division in Williams Lake came to the valley and spoke to the family to explain that he knew who was responsible for Levina's murder. The names of the suspects could not be released, or the file ever completely closed, according to Hall, because the three Williams Lake suspects were all dead.

The early police investigation of the Moody murder is unclear at best. The RCMP tell me one of their members had a contact with information about who was involved with Levina's murder. Vanessa says the RCMP's Project E-PANA task force requested to meet with her family in October of 2012. But she was miffed because she had already been told by RCMP officer Pilszek in 1999 that the case was (unofficially) solved. Thirteen years later E-PANA RCMP officers were telling the family they knew nothing of those earlier details and asked for DNA samples from the family (which the family provided). Vanessa says she and her family shared all the information they had been given previously by other RCMP officers but that no one got back to her about it.

A former Mountie, Mel McIntosh, who was on Levina's case in the late 1980s, says that he was aware of Blohm, but that the Moody investigation was a disaster. During a phone interview he tells me that when he transferred to the Williams Lake detachment in April of 1988 and was in charge of general investigations, management told him there were no outstanding homicide investigations. But in October of that year, he got an alert through the internal RCMP information communications system, pointing him to an "outstanding diary date" with a file number and the name Gloria Levina Moody on it. When he inquired, "the records guy" told him the file was in the bottom of a drawer. "So I take the entire drawer, and the file is in absolute disarray," McIntosh tells me from his home in Abbotsford, B.C. "There were probably ten pads of foolscap with what would appear to be the start of a statement, but I don't recall any of them indicating who gave the statement or any identifiers of the statement taker nor the statement giver," he adds. He said the statement would start off legibly but then it would just go into scribbles. "Wavy lines on a piece of paper," he says. The papers were not dated and were loose in the drawer, so McIntosh tried to put them together based on their dog ears. Later he asked an investigator on the Moody case about who had taken the statements. The investigator replied that it was "a couple of [other investigators] who were sent out west and that they probably spent more time drinking than they did taking statements." McIntosh then asked who had taken some of the other notes that appeared as a "to-do list." The former investigator reluctantly admitted that it was him, McIntosh says. And he says that file was not the only part of the investigation that seemed to be ignored.

Another RCMP member at the time told McIntosh that there were bullets left by Moody's deceased body, and evidence of an expensive matching rifle that a potential suspect had recently got rid of. But when McIntosh asked to see his records, the officer said he was never instructed to keep notes.

McIntosh says that the disregard for Moody's file was not because of her race but a sign of the times, reflecting the level of disorganization within the detachment. RCMP officers were less educated and more like gunslinging cowboys back then, especially in backcountry areas, he told me. However, he did share that one of the investigators had "jaundiced attitudes" toward the Native officers in the detachment, a racist view which he felt spilled over into his dealings with Indigenous civilians. In a later conversation he added, "[His] attitude is something that will stay with me forever. He was racist, bigoted, you name it."

McIntosh did have leads into the murder of Levina Moody from 1988 until 1990. He says he learned that an RCMP colleague interviewed a woman who was the mother of a female employee at the detachment; the mother claimed to be a former common-law spouse to the now deceased Al Blohm. She said Blohm had written a letter implying that he had murdered Levina Moody. McIntosh says her name was Toni Brecknock and that she was so scared Blohm would kill her that she waited until he died to come forward. She said that Blohm was extremely violent and committed "demented" sexually violent acts on her. McIntosh says that in 1969, the year Moody was killed, Blohm may have worked as a bartender at a local Williams Lake pub, and was rumoured to ply women with alcohol, take them home, and sexually assault them. None of the accusations about Blohm have been tested in court, and he was never charged.

When I express my shock at how messy the investigation seemed to be even while so much evidence appeared to point at a suspect, McIntosh says, "The things that happened up in Williams Lake would have to be best described as a den of iniquity, who was doing who and who was doing what."

According to McIntosh, an RCMP officer, Murray Neufeld, told him in 1994 that Moody's case was solved: one of the suspects had made a deathbed confession to his brother and sister, under the condition that they could not divulge it to the police until their parents had died, which they now had. McIntosh says as far as the police were concerned, they had enough information, including a confession and a witness, to prove that Al Blohm was involved. He tells me Blohm was one of those guys the police at the time would have called "beyond reproach," as he was liked and seen as friendly by the detachment when he was alive.

As I was working on this book in the summer of 2019, I was contacted by another former RCMP officer on the case, John Brecknock. He is originally from Alexis Creek, a town about an hour and a half west of Williams Lake. He says he joined the RCMP at the age of 19 in 1967 and was stationed in Alberta, where he continues to live today. He retired from the force in 1999. During my interview with him over the phone in 2019, he tells me a suspect, now dead, is in part responsible for the rape and murder of Gloria Levina Moody.

According to Brecknock, in the fall of 1998 while he was working as an RCMP officer in Alberta, he got a call from a potential witness from his hometown of Alexis Creek. The caller trusted him, Brecknock believes, because he had a lot of family and friends in the area. Though the man had not witnessed the murder, he had information about it and told Brecknock that he believed he could go to jail for not divulging it for twenty-nine years. Brecknock's meeting with this man led to interviews with other people, from which he established the names of three men who were involved in the murder of Gloria Levina Moody. "Two of them died with self-inflicted gunshot wounds and another one drank himself to death," he told me. This corroborates Angela Hall's 1999 newspaper article, which states that "one of the suspects killed himself in 1972, and the second died a few years later in what was a form of suicide, death from alcohol… apparently the third man was with him constantly hovering over his death bed in what appeared to be an effort to curtail any last minute confession. The third suspect committed suicide in the 1980s leaving the family to wonder if guilt, nightmares, and shame wrought the justice that the law could not." Vanessa says when the RCMP detectives met with her and her brother in 1999, they shared these same details with the family and also named the three men. Al Blohm's death certificate states he died by suicide by a self-inflicted gunshot wound. Someone named Toni Blohm signed the death certificate.

Brecknock says the suspects' identities can never be disclosed because they were not charged before they died, something he called "bittersweet"—a word that seems strange to me given that denying a family closure and justice isn't sweet at all. Brecknock says he is satisfied, though, that these three men are the ones who committed the murder. The Moody family, he says, "can be assured that I am 110 percent sure that three men were involved in the sexual assault and murder of Gloria Levina." When I ask him about Al Blohm and another name I was given and query whether they had anything to do with Moody's murder, he robotically repeats, "I can neither confirm nor deny the identity of the suspects since they are all passed away now and there is no way that they can be brought to justice." At the end of our conversation Brecknock says that one of the reasons he is not naming the suspects is because the liability could be immense: "Look at the lawsuits against the mounted police now."

While it is frowned upon by the RCMP when former cops speak out about the inner workings of their investigations, it does happen. So it surprised me that Brecknock would go out of his way to speak to a journalist about details of the investigation but stop at sharing a piece of information that could actually provide closure to a family that has been tormented for decades.

My work on Levina's story, up late nights speaking with Vanessa, combing through archives, filing arduous Access to Information and Privacy requests and then sifting through the documents, or looking for former officers who would talk, has taken many unexpected twists and turns along the way. One of those bends has made me feel particularly uneasy.

The day before Brecknock reached out to me via email, Vanessa messaged me a poem that she had told me about before, one she found online years earlier while trying to investigate the murder of her mother. It was written by a woman, writing under the initials "G.T.B.," whose intent seemed to be to honour Levina's life and death. In speaking to several locals in Williams Lake, Vanessa learned that the same initials mark the poet's gravestone—"G. Toni Brecknock," or Georgia Toni Brecknock. According to her 2007 obituary printed in the Williams Lake Tribune, she grew up in Alexis Creek and is survived by her siblings, including John Brecknock.

As one of my formal questions, I ask John if he knew who Toni Brecknock was, and without hesitation he admits that she was his sister. I ask what her connection to Gloria Levina Moody was and he says, "I do have information with respect to that but can't disclose that either because we are getting close to the witnesses and so forth." It is a tense part of the interview and he is stumbling a bit, and listening again to the tape I can tell I'm trying to make light of it and sound cheery, but he is clearly uncomfortable. He then asks where I got the poem, and in return I ask if he'd heard about the motive of the killers. He says he truly believes "that evil lurks in the hearts of some people."

In the middle of our hour-long conversation, I ask him how it feels to have all this information about the murder but not be able to share it with the family to provide them closure. He tells me that the family should feel comforted that there was remorse, given that the killers "did themselves in."

Our conversation was frustrating and I wondered, as I do right now, what his motive was in speaking with me. The interview ends with me once again asking him about the killers' motive, trying my best to find answers for the family; he tells me he believes there are still serial killers that operate on the highways, but "when you're up to your ass in alligators it's hard to remember your job was to drain the swamp."

Vanessa and I began to research the Brecknock family more after that interview. Based on the lengthy obituary of Toni Brecknock we'd found, we did deep dives into friend and family connections of the Brecknock and Blohm families on their public Facebook pages. We then looked at publicly available genealogy records at sites such as Ancestry.com. Through cross-referencing of the public records, we discovered that Toni was married to a man named Al Blohm—the same man that the Williams Lake RCMP officer told Vanessa killed Levina in 1969. We found out through our Facebook research that not only is Toni deceased, but so is her daughter, Dana Blohm, who passed away in 2017.

And then my investigation took another strange turn.

One day after my interview with Brecknock, he reached out to Vanessa via Facebook. It was the first time he had done so, and I immediately felt guilty for mentioning her name in my interview with him. Brecknock's message to her was blank but contained a link to a *Williams Lake Tribune* article that he also emailed to me, supporting the theory that three white men raped and killed Levina Moody. This random message from a stranger, who was also an RCMP officer who had worked on her mother's case twenty-two to twenty-three years ago, disturbed Vanessa.

As I gather information about the killers of Levina Moody, I am disturbed too. But I know it's nothing compared to the fear that Vanessa feels. I have not experienced the racism she and her mother have experienced, nor am I privy to all the information the police, reporters, and strangers have provided her over the years. Maybe I should feel more scared, but I know how racism works. Statistics around lesser charges and sentencing of those who kill Indigenous women and girls versus non-Indigenous, and the discrepancies in media coverage between the two groups, show that people who kill Indigenous women may feel that they will get away with it because the legal system, the judicial system, the media, and the public care far less if an Indigenous woman goes missing or is murdered than they do if the woman is white. And while I am an Indigenous woman, I am also lighter and can pass as white, and I work for a large corporation that, I hope at least, would shine a light on my death if something happened to me. Then again, working for the media for several years, I too have often felt "less than" or unwelcome by white reporters due to their comments and complaints against me. So, really, should I feel scared?

Looking through the Access to Information and Privacy documents, half of which are newspaper articles, I think about how the way Levina's murder was reported was so different from what we see in the headlines today. In so many stories about her that I have read, there are omissions about who she was, how she was killed, and how this could have happened in such a small town where everyone knows each other. Her death was mired in a deep and hollow silence, and as a result her case has lain dormant for more than fifty years. No one has ever been arrested, charged, or convicted. Al and Vanessa tell me that many people from Williams Lake have told them it was widely known who murdered Moody, but no one was prepared to come forward—perhaps because they wanted to protect the men, but also perhaps because they feared that they could face harm or retaliation for revealing the truth.

Testimony at the National Inquiry into Missing and Murdered Indigenous Women and Girls outlined how Indigenous women are easier targets for murder and other violence since there is a widespread notion that we do not matter as much as other Canadians. That idea is reinforced by the silence around cases like Moody's. The length of time that has passed without any progress into bringing her killer or killers to justice supports the idea that murdering an Indigenous woman is easier to get away with in Canada.

Not knowing who killed Levina has meant great suffering for the family. Shortly after the murder, Levina's brother Ron (whom Vanessa grew up also knowing as her brother, since her grandparents raised her, but who was actually her uncle) went to Williams Lake, where he spent time trying to investigate his sister's murder. He was unable to prove anything yet felt he had come very close to the truth. Like Vanessa, Ron had self-medicated, trying to soothe the pain of losing a sister so violently and without any semblance of justice. Years later he too was the victim of murder.

The sorrow and pain of family members who have not seen justice for their murdered loved ones was heard loudly and clearly at the national inquiry. The agony of never receiving closure is yet another layer of injustice and betrayal on top of the systemic violence their families have endured, and with that comes heartache that is impossible to relieve. Masking it with painkillers—drugs or alcohol—can seem like the only solution, especially when access to and funding for healing, like counselling and health care, has been almost nonexistent. Many family members I have spoken with, including the Moodys and the Wilsons, have struggled over the years with their mental health.

As I was wrapping up this chapter in 2021, Vanessa called me with some distressing news. A man, first posing as a female journalist on Facebook, started calling her repeatedly, claiming to be investigating the murder of her mother. The man, who on the phone identified himself as "Phil the trucker," called her several times, saying he knew more about the murder than most others. In one call, Vanessa said he made crude accusations about her mom; in another, he talked about the bar her mom was at before she was murdered. Vanessa said she was so stunned at some of the things the man was saying that she felt paralyzed, unable to hang up the phone. Despite feeling terrified and deeply disturbed, she kept picking up the phone because she felt she was getting more information about who killed her mother, a horrible task she has felt committed to almost her entire life.

The man called several times in 2021, and I often wonder who this person is and why he appears to be trying to scare and hurt the daughter of a woman who was so brutally murdered. The thought haunts me.

While I did the best I could to help ease Vanessa's mind about who may have been responsible for her mother's murder, there will most likely never be charges against the man or men who were involved. I feel deep guilt knowing that I have not brought her the closure she deserves. And part of me wonders if I have just dug up more memories and caused more harm than good.

In 2019, I asked Mel McIntosh and John Brecknock, who had worked on Moody's case in different years, if they felt the file was tainted by racism. While McIntosh stated that discrimination may have played a role, Brecknock wholeheartedly asserted that it did not have any bearing on her murder or how it was investigated. He also stated that he didn't believe racism was alive in the region in 1969 nor today.

For me, it is very clear how deep-seated racism could have been a factor not just in the murder of Levina and the shoddy investigation into it, but in the silence that surrounded it—a silence that has permeated this region and this country when it comes to the treatment of Indigenous people.

IN TRYING TO UNDERSTAND why Levina Moody's vicious, unimaginable murder could have been left without any semblance of justice—with no arrest, no thorough investigation, and scant media reporting—I've thought long and hard about the political climate of the twentieth century, one that gave rise to blatant and violent racism that continues to live on today. In the 1950s, for example, "Indians" from or visiting Williams Lake were banned from businesses and dance halls, as the town enforced segregation. The white people even built an open-air dance hall they called "Squaw Hall" on the stampede grounds so Indians would be separated from the whites.

All my research confirms what every Indigenous person from the Cariboo knows: racism and racial violence are nothing new here, and the disturbing string of violent acts settlers left behind them all across Canada is well documented. In addition to the violence related to land theft in the Cariboo, Indigenous children were targeted with denigration and violence. Four days after a group of British men signed documents to create the Dominion of Canada, the Roman Catholic Church opened St. Joseph's Mission a few miles from the head of Williams Lake. In 1891, it became a residential school, known as St. Joseph's Indian Residential School or Cariboo Indian Residential School. Kids were forcibly taken from their parents and confined at the school for ten months out of the year.

In 1955, at 6 years old, Rose Roper, a Secwepemc and Tŝilhqot'in child from Alkali Lake, began at St. Joseph's and was assigned the number 133. Like other students, she was subjected to starvation and was frequently struck over the head and knuckles with a wooden ruler. Her grandmother, among the last in Rose's family to speak her traditional language, had been poked in the tongue with needles by nuns for speaking her language. Priests and nuns tried to beat the language, culture, and spirit out of Indigenous children in an attempt to "kill the Indian in the child." While he didn't utter that exact quote, the sentiment has been attributed to a deputy superintendent of Indian Affairs in Canada, Duncan Campbell Scott, who mandated residential school attendance in 1920. It was then that he said, "Our objective is to continue until there is not a single Indian in Canada that has not been absorbed into the body politic."

Abuse was rampant at St. Joseph's. In 1989, Roman Catholic priest Harold McIntee, who taught at the school, pleaded guilty to seventeen counts of sexual assault against thirteen Indigenous boys, most aged 10 to 12. In 1996, former St. Joseph's priest Hubert O'Connor was convicted of committing rape and indecent assault against two Indigenous girls in the 1960s. And then there were the children that never came home, who died at residential school. According to the National Centre for Truth and Reconciliation, more than 4,100 children who attended residential school are either named or unnamed in death records. In 1902, an 8-year-old boy, Duncan Sticks, ran away from St. Joseph's and died by a roadside in freezing weather 12 kilometres away from the school. In 1920, another Indigenous boy who was around 9, Augustine Allen, killed himself by ingesting poisonous roots.

Residential schools, in their heyday, were celebrated rather than questioned. Cemented in the colonial rhetoric of the day was the idea that Indigenous people were not human. The institution of residential school reinforced the perception that Indigenous people needed to assimilate into white Canadian life to be treated as human beings. Canadians are only now, in the 2020s, in the early stages of understanding the intergenerational racism and trauma that residential schools harboured, inflicted, and sustained. And few people know that it was only twenty-five years ago that the last residential school, the Gordon's Indian Residential School in Saskatchewan, was closed, in 1996.

Despite what Canadians have learned through the reports in 2015 of the Truth and Reconciliation Commission and in 2019 of the National Inquiry into Missing and Murdered Indigenous Women and Girls, many non-Indigenous Canadians still struggle with the relationship between residential school and the large number of MMIWG in this country.

At a hearing in Richmond, B.C., for the national inquiry in April of 2018, I listened to countless family members and survivors relay devasting accounts of how residential schools affected them and their families and how those experiences set the stage for how their loved ones would go missing or be murdered. Residential schools were the primary tool that the Canadian government and churches used to devastate and fragment Indigenous families. Parents and grandparents who lost their children were also facing Indian agents on reserves, who were swift to bar them from their traditional territories and prevent them from leaving the reserve. Some women and men ended up homeless; some turned to alcohol and addictions to escape the horrific reality they had been subjected to for years. When teens and young adults returned home, they often arrived to a torn-apart community. Even after hearing about many experiences like Rose Roper's—whose family endured three generations of residential school—many Canadians looked the other way.

Healing for Indigenous people has been slow, since we have mostly been forced to mend our wounds unaided. To put it in perspective, organizations like the First Nations Health Authority in British Columbia only started to provide easy-to-access

free counselling for registered Status Indians around 2018 (the
FNHA told me they didn't have the data to keep track of it).
Before that, I, like other Indigenous people facing intergenerational trauma or even firsthand trauma, had to prove—filling
out form after form after form—that I was in the middle of an
extremely severe life-altering crisis to even get four therapy
sessions a year. And before that, throughout most of the twentieth century, many survivors tell me there was nothing. It was
only in 2018 that I started hearing about the mainstream understanding of how addictions were most often a result of trauma.
Before that, it seemed to be a little-acknowledged idea.

Rose Roper, her parents, and her grandparents all survived
residential school. Her father, as a result of his trauma, became
a heavy drinker and in turn was extremely abusive and violent—physically, emotionally, mentally, and sexually—to all her
siblings, her mother, and other women. When Rose's father beat
her mother to death, teenage Rose returned home so she could
take care of her siblings, trying to protect them from further
abuse. Rose worked at St. Joseph's as an older teen from 1965
to 1967. To escape the pain of the abuses she experienced, Rose
began drinking as a teen. One night, at 17 years old, she went out
drinking in Williams Lake, as many teenagers did and do, then
and today. When the night was over she attempted to hitchhike
to her aunty's home in Lac la Hache. She was picked up by three
white men from Williams Lake.

It is hard to figure out exactly what took place because the
accounts of what happened from witnesses and the accused
contradict each other. According to the author of *Carnal Crimes*,
Constance Backhouse, while there was enough evidence,
including a partial confession, to prove that Rose was sexually
assaulted, nobody was convicted of the rape. Rose was left
naked, face down in the snow, with a broken neck and multiple abrasions and bruises on her body and face, on a deserted

logging road near 126 Mile House. According to the police she died of exposure. Shortly after the incident, police investigating the death arrested three white men in their 20s, Alfred William Kohnke, Stephen Arthur Croft, and Robert Leslie Wilson. Police charged them with manslaughter and assault. Newspaper reports show that Kohnke was found not guilty and discharged from custody. Croft and Wilson were found guilty of common assault. The judge fined each $200.

The press coverage from the time of Rose Roper's murder is telling. Much of it reports on the men's unblemished reputations and how they are outstanding members of the community. In newspaper articles from 1967, journalists describe the white men as "steadily employed" and say that "their friends and relatives crowded the courtroom." In contrast, Backhouse says, "on 12 April 1967, the front page coverage of the *Williams Lake Tribune* reported that Rose had been convicted of intoxication in a public place the night before her death." Another article quotes white witnesses who said Rose looked like she was "feeling pretty good" and had gone "roaming from table to table" at a pub that Saturday night. The press also state that Roper tried to sell herself to the men for $500—the equivalent today of about $4,000, which is an unlikely sum to ask three working-class youth to pay. The press make a point to note that she was not a virgin—an opinion of the doctor who conducted her autopsy.

During the trial, the white prosecutor referred to Rose Roper as "a bit of Indian trash" and a "drunken native girl." They also questioned her morals and manners. Even though she had bruises and abrasions all over her body and her neck had been broken, the medical examiner determined that she may have broken her neck herself by falling down.

The two pictures I have seen of Roper are striking. One published in a newspaper alongside an article on the trial shows her dark eyes peeking out of a black pixie cut, looking straight at the camera while shyly covering her mouth with the sleeve of her sweater. Another photo, from residential school, depicts a younger Rose. Her hair is in a bowl cut and she barely smiles. It's hard when I look at her innocent face, knowing everything she had been through at that age and how she died so violently as a teen.

Learning about the history of this region, about the brutal death of Rose Roper and the way she was treated by the judicial system and the media even after her death, makes it hard to fathom how anyone could believe there was no racism in Williams Lake in the 1960s.

FOR THE MOODY FAMILY, the murder of the person who was their mother, sister, aunty, and daughter has haunted their dreams and tinged their memories with sadness ever since. Spiritual and community leaders have held two ceremonies for Levina over the years—one in 1994 in Alkali Lake, and another in Bella Coola in 1999, where family members held rocks from the river and shared and released memories to purify themselves from the pain. It was their own form of closure, but sadly it was not the end.

Despite the fact that it's been more than fifty years, with media coverage faded and with initiatives like Project E-PANA that seem to have forgotten her, the Moody family is still holding out hope for naming Levina's killer or killers within their lifetimes. As Elders in their family pass on, Vanessa says it's a constant reminder that many are dying without having the closure they deserve. With each generation that passes, there is a reminder of the intergenerational trauma caused by the murder and the lack of care that has seemed to surround it.

I follow the Moodys on Facebook and we keep in contact by phone and email. It's incredible after all they have been through to see a new generation of the family thrive and blaze new ground. The healing work the Moody family has done must be tremendous.

In 2018, a story out of Bella Coola on the CBC website caught my eye. A photo in the article is of Levina's granddaughter Jalissa Moody. She is wearing a grey, white, and black knitted Cowichan sweater and smiling proudly while pointing out a row of simple wooden tiny homes. The article explains how she, as an asset management assistant for the band, had noticed a demographic of single men who were unable to find housing, and she had found a solution to fill the gap. It reminded me that like so many family members whose paths I have witnessed, there is hope, there is strength, and there is an amazing ability to thrive.

Despite the Moody family's incredible resilience, they still have something they need to fight against and overcome, a question they reckon with every day: Why was Levina taken from them so young, and why didn't anyone but her family and their Nuxalk community seem to want justice for her? Unfortunately, it would take many more families yearning for answers before the problem of MMIWG finally received a fraction of the attention it deserves.

6

Gidi guutxwdiit seegidit, *caught a killer*

TO CATCH A SERIAL KILLER

WHILE I MISSED MY COMMUNITY and the ocean breeze of the west coast after a year in the northern interior, I took my time to enjoy Lheidli T'enneh territory. I was taking in those rich fall forests, the majestic dancing northern lights, and the misty creeks I'd walk past each day. During one of my many long walks to the university, on the side of a mountain along a lush bush trail, I realized the wild I was in. I braced myself, seeing cougar droppings infused with mouse fur and reading signs tacked on trees warning hikers to be mindful when moose cows had babies. In what is now UNBC legend, I was chased for almost ten minutes straight up that hill by a huge mother moose. I arrived with my shirt completely soaked in sweat and my sweater around my waist and was the laughingstock of the First Nations Centre. I still think it's hilarious and feel no shame. I was and am what many of us call a "city Indian," after all.

At the end of 2003, I wondered if UNBC and Prince George were where I was supposed to be and began to think about returning to Vancouver to finish my degree at UBC. I was feeling on the outs with my Sterritt family, who had on occasion suggested I thought I was "too good for them" because at the time I didn't drink and was not interested in late-night calls to discuss family drama. While I loved them, I was starting to feel that I didn't fit in. But I took my time to make a decision, and while I tinkered with the idea of moving back to the big city, I was offered a dream job as an on-air researcher at CBC Prince George in 2004, producing radio for a mainstream audience. I was proud of the work I did then, including putting Gitxsan Elders like renowned artist Judith Morgan and Knowledge Keeper Yvonne Lattie on air, but there was little interest then in Indigenous stories, and my pitches were entertained only occasionally. At the same time, after campaigning, I won a seat as an elected member of UNBC's student council. It was a monumental year, as a Cree student also became president.

But I, like others, also sensed the city was on edge. Concerns about police brutality and misconduct were coming to a head, and not long after, Prince George judge David Ramsay was convicted of sexually assaulting and causing bodily harm to several Indigenous girls. In the same year, I was accepted into the political science program at UBC and started to transition my life back to Vancouver. I regretfully told UNBC that I could not fulfill my role and returned to my old city as someone very different. I had left as somewhat of a lost person on a mission to find my way, and returned as a student who had worked hard to heal myself. I now spent my days with my head in books about Aristotle and Socrates, and my nights working on papers about political theory. While I was on the street, I had briefly taken up martial arts as a way to balance my energy and defend myself if need be. Now I was a gym rat, spending hours on the treadmill with a book propped up on the console. And while in some ways my old Native hip-hop scene followed me into the dorm where I now lived, I was slowly breaking away.

While studying at a computer lab at UBC, I met a kind and bright Tsimshian man. He brought me to Indigenous student group meetings where we fought for our tiny presence and space at the university. At the time, the Alma Mater Society refused to give us the same standing as an international student group that was able to vote in elections. I remember being dumbfounded at how still, in 2005, we were being treated as if we were not equal citizens. (In 2018, UBC's Alma Mater Society president Marium Hamid expressed a "profound regret" for not making "serious efforts to advance reconciliation or recognize Indigenous rights" over the course of [the society's] 100 plus year history.")

I spent a lot of time feeling alienated from the largely non-Indigenous population on campus, as well as from the academic readings and lectures mainly by white people that often stood in opposition to Indigenous Peoples' world views, our politics, and even just our presence. In an international studies class, I argued with a white professor that Indigenous Peoples were also victims of genocide, something she never acknowledged. Another white professor—along with the entire class—refused to believe that Indigenous Peoples were not conquered at the time of colonization.

That Tsimshian man I dated, and ended up engaged to, treated me well. Commiserating about our similar shitty experiences at UBC, sharing lofty ideas, and eating traditional foods like oolichan grease, black cod, and smoked fish kept me afloat. Though that time in my life was transformative and abundant, it was hard not to turn my mind back to Prince George as investigations into the Highway of Tears murders started to finally ramp up.

IN THE SAME YEAR I was starting my new life in Vancouver at UBC, in 2005, the RCMP in B.C. started Project E-PANA, their task force dedicated to unsolved murders connected to

Highways 16, 97, and 5. While many Indigenous women, like me, felt deeply skeptical about it, it did seem like change was finally coming.

Project E-PANA was created when the RCMP's "E" Division Criminal Operations ordered an investigation of the murders along the Highway of Tears, as pressure mounted from Indigenous family members and advocacy groups. The goal of the task force was ultimately to determine if a serial killer or killers were responsible for the dozens of murders. "E" represents the RCMP's British Columbia division; pana is an Inuktitut word, which according to the Project E-PANA website means "spirit goddess that looks after the souls just before they go to heaven or were reincarnated" (although many Inuit friends have told me it has several meanings, including "knife that kills a whale" or a "snow knife"). At the time, the RCMP's Provincial Unsolved Homicide Unit was looking into what behavioural science profilers believed were the linked homicides of Alishia Germaine, age 15; Roxanne Thiara, also age 15; and Ramona Wilson, who was 16 when she disappeared—all Indigenous teenage girls who are still on E-PANA's list. The task force, however, didn't focus on Indigenous women and girls, but those of any background.

In 2006, E-PANA began investigations into nine cases of missing and murdered women and girls, including Levina Moody. The year after, it doubled its investigation to eighteen unsolved cases—thirteen homicide investigations and five missing person investigations dating from 1969 to 2006. As noted earlier, little progress has been made on the cases, particularly since 2016, though they all remain open.

While countless media reports cite E-PANA's eighteen cases as the official number of women and girls missing or murdered along that network of highways, that is not correct. The actual number is more than four times that. The RCMP's list is static, meaning that if another woman is murdered, she is not added to the list. If a woman on the list is found or if her case is solved, she is not taken off the list. In 2016, I spoke to former RCMP staff sergeant Wayne Cleary, who was once the lead investigator of Project E-PANA. In the telephone interview he admits he doesn't know why names are not added to or taken off the list. "When this project was put together it was an historical investigation, meaning if other files came up we would not be investigating those. They set their parameters for what they were going to do back in 2006 and stuck to that," he says. The real number of women and girls missing or murdered on the network of highways at the time (in 2006), Cleary tells me, was closer to sixty. "They looked through fifty-eight or fifty-nine cases, before settling on the eighteen. Some were murders that were solved, and of course that person could have been responsible for others, so we looked at all that," he adds.

According to Staff Sergeant Janelle Shoihet of the RCMP, "Through investigation it has since been determined that more than one person is responsible but a single person may be responsible for more than one woman's death." She said the criteria for a case to be selected for Project E-PANA were strict and included the following: it was a stranger-to-stranger crime; the crime occurred on or close to Highway 16, 97, or 5; the victim was female and believed to be participating in a high-risk lifestyle or activities; and the case was unsolved. But some Indigenous women and scholars are critical of the term "high risk" since it can essentially blame victims for a crime that was perpetrated against them. They say that pegging a woman or girl as "high risk" places some of the responsibility of the abuse or violence she faced on her own behaviour or actions. At any rate, some of the women on the E-PANA list were not engaging in what most people would consider high-risk behaviour. For example, Monica Jack was just a 12-year-old girl riding her bike. Levina Moody was just out with her family on a weekend trip. Neither was hitchhiking or involved in the sex trade, which is what the RCMP considered high-risk behaviour, according to then staff sergeant Bruce Hulan and other earlier E-PANA investigators, who spoke to the media about this as late as 2010. But following the Pickton inquiry, it seems as though the definition of "high risk" has changed, at least for some police forces.

In *Forsaken: The Report of the Missing Women Commission of Inquiry* (the commission also known as the Pickton inquiry), Commissioner Wally Oppal advises that "it is wrong to attribute the women's vulnerability to predation to their 'high-risk lifestyle.' This narrow view cannot explain the disappearance of so many women over a sustained period of time." He adds, "Often they were treated not as persons at all, but as 'subhumans' diminished in the eyes of many by their 'high-risk lifestyle.' Like poor women across Canada and around the world, their devalued social status made them the target of predators."

I reached out to the RCMP to ask if their definition of "high risk" had changed since 2010. An RCMP communications representative pointed me to B.C.'s provincial policing standards website. A document on it states that a woman's Aboriginal identity should be taken into consideration when determining if she is high risk, but the checklist to determine if a woman is at a higher risk does not list race as a factor. The checklist does, however, list being a sex worker as contributing to a women's vulnerability. The document also states that if a missing person is considered high risk, "appropriate resources are immediately assigned" and a senior officer is notified, but there are no statistics or anecdotes of how often this happens or if these actions are mandatory or if there are even checks and balances.

Other urban police forces have heeded Oppal's call for change in more concrete ways. In 2020, Victoria Police Department spokesperson Bowen Osoko told a reporter with *Vancouver Island Free Daily* that protocols around naming a person "high risk" changed following the *Forsaken* report. "In the past people might hear that Jane Doe was missing, and learn that she was a sex trade worker and think that of course she was missing because she led a transient life," Osoko says in the article. "In reality, she might have been on Pickton's farm." The Victoria Police Department's definition of a high-risk missing person investigation has widened to include if the person is under 18, female, Indigenous, suffers from mental or physical health issues or from drug addiction, is involved in high-risk trafficking, has a medical diagnosis of Alzheimer's or dementia, and if going missing is uncharacteristic. Anyone who fits some (or sometimes one) of the criteria of being "high risk" prompts an immediate missing-person call out, Osoko says. This is the opposite of what was often done in the past, and even recently, when it comes to those who are, for example, Indigenous and involved in street life. I've seen many examples where police may have actually not put out a missing report if there was an indication of a woman or girl being "high risk" because it may have been assumed that she was "on a binge" or "travelling around."

When I ask other RCMP officials if being Indigenous alone makes a person high risk, I am told no. But clearly some detachments' criteria make clear that a woman's Indigeneity does make her more vulnerable, or at a higher risk of going missing or being murdered. The SisterWatch committee, a project of the Vancouver Police Department and Downtown Eastside community groups, also has stated that Indigenous women face unique risks. The group aims to eliminate violence against women and girls in the Downtown Eastside and provides information about violence against women. It also operates a twenty-four-hour tip line to receive information about crimes against women, or any other matter affecting the safety of those in the neighbourhood.

STATISTICS ALSO BACK UP the reality that Indigenous women face an elevated risk of violence. Here's another grim fact: in Canada, Indigenous women are about seven times as likely as non-Indigenous women to be killed by serial killers. The RCMP uses the FBI's definition of serial murder as "the unlawful killing of two or more victims by the same offender(s), in separate events." A *Globe and Mail* analysis found that at least eighteen Indigenous women died at the hands of convicted serial killers from 1980 until 2015. Most were killed by non-Indigenous men. When the scope of the analysis broadened to include cases with a probable suspect, like those connected to Robert Pickton through stayed charges or DNA found on his farm, the number of Indigenous women murdered by a serial killer grew to about thirty-five. And living or being along a highway seems to make the likelihood all the greater. A 2019 *Atlantic* article quotes an FBI press release from 2016 that states: "If there is such a thing as an ideal profession for a serial killer, it may well be as a long-haul truck driver." Through its Highway Serial Killings Initiative, the FBI has investigated more than 750 murder victims found near highways in the United States and identified about 450 potential suspects, including a disproportionate number of truck drivers.

At least five serial killers have operated or have been suspected of operating along the network of highways associated with the Highway of Tears—Cody Legebokoff, Garry Handlen, Bobby Fowler, Edward Isaac, and Brian Arp. Along the interlinked B.C. highways, by my count, at least five Indigenous women and at least seven non-Indigenous women have been killed by serial killers from 1969 to 2019.

In 2014, Cody Legebokoff, a white 24-year-old from Fort St. James who was living in Prince George, was sentenced to life in prison after he was found guilty of the first-degree murder of four women. All of the murders took place within miles of the Highway of Tears. His victims were Jill Stuchenko, who was 35; Cynthia Maas, who was 35, Indigenous, and had a disability; Natasha Montgomery, who was 23 and Indigenous; and

Loren Leslie, who was 15, had mental health issues, and was legally blind. The first three worked in the street sex trade and were addicted to drugs when Legebokoff picked them up. Maas in particular was extremely vulnerable, having been traumatized twice by the child-welfare system, and having a disability. Between 2009 and 2010, he brutally beat and then murdered these women. None of the cases were documented on Project E-PANA's list before they were solved, because again, it only covers the time period from 1969 to 2006, and new cases are not added.

Judging by the RCMP's 2015 update on its *Missing and Murdered Aboriginal Women* report, all four women would be classified as "knowing their killer" since, in the eyes of the RCMP, they were acquaintances of Legebokoff. In court, Legebokoff said he only met Stuchenko once at a party, where she told him she was a sex worker, the night he murdered her. He also said he met both Maas and Montgomery on the nights he murdered them. The Crown told the court that Legebokoff used the women to access cocaine. The 2015 RCMP report states that in 2013 and 2014, thirty-two Indigenous women were homicide victims, and in 100 percent of the solved cases, they knew their killer. CBC journalist Andrew Kurjata wrote an analysis of the report, stating that "the police classification that these murdered women 'knew their killer' does not mean that these women knew their killer well or intimately." In fact, when you look into the categories more closely, he said, the odds of family being involved actually decrease if the victim is Aboriginal. Between 1980 and 2012, 30 percent of Aboriginal female homicides involved what RCMP characterize as "acquaintances," which is defined as "close friends, neighbours, authority figures, business relationships, criminal relationships and casual acquaintances." In other words, a broad group of people that includes neighbours you might see taking out the trash, a grocery store clerk you might see on a weekly basis, and, as was pointed out during an RCMP news conference about their report, johns you "know" if you're a sex worker.

In a 2015 letter to Grand Chief Bernice Martial of the Confederacy of Treaty Six First Nations (who was concerned about the way the RCMP statistics were being interpreted), then RCMP commissioner Bob Paulson states that since 70 percent of murdered Indigenous women and girls were killed by someone they knew, 70 percent of the offenders were then Aboriginal men. However, Paulson was unable to say where the statistics were extrapolated from, explain how they were retrieved, or even supply the data sets he was referring to, citing an update to come. Commissioners of the National Inquiry into Missing and Murdered Indigenous Women and Girls debunked that finding in their 2019 report. In the data I have collected, out of the solved cases along the three highways in British Columbia, nine of the murders were by white serial killers (four different men) and three of the murders were by an Indigenous serial killer (one man).

In sentencing white serial killer Cody Legebokoff, Justice Glen Parrett of the B.C. Supreme Court was emotional, his voice cracking. He noted that while there had been calls for a national inquiry, E-PANA's budget had been reduced by 84 percent. "It is a mistake, in my view, to limit the seriousness of this issue," he said.

In 2019, an Access to Information and Privacy document I obtained revealed that E-PANA lost 99 percent of its annual budget between 2009/10 and 2017/18—from a high of $5.5 million in 2009/10 to just $30,000 in 2015/16, where it has remained for all periods reported since. At the height of the task force, it had seventy officers and support staff, but the document shows that it was down to eleven employees in 2017/18. When I asked former RCMP staff sergeant Wayne Cleary about it in 2016, he told me that E-PANA was "winding down" and said there were about ten to twelve officers and support workers remaining. He explained that as there is less to do, more resources get withdrawn.

Trying to get answers about how investigations were conducted along the Highway of Tears has been difficult. Until 2016, the RCMP had never granted me an interview about E-PANA investigations, despite my asking several times over the years. They provided me boilerplate statements or comments via email but would not answer specific questions—hence my filing of the Access to Information and Privacy request on the budget. Before providing that information, RCMP officers simply told me that the unit was still looking into the unsolved cases. I had asked two times, unsuccessfully, in late 2015 and early 2016, for an interview about E-PANA's work on Levina Moody's case. I wanted to know why she was on the list when it is clear that information that could have solved the case has been in the hands of police since at least 1998. After my third request for an interview, specifically asking for a general operation update—querying if E-PANA was no longer operational, how many cases were solved, how many officers were currently working on the unit, and why some cases were on the list when we knew through court records and police files that the killer was in jail—an RCMP representative told me to look at the Project E-PANA website for answers to those questions. But since I started this investigation in 2015, the website has remained unchanged—simply a list of eighteen women's names, a description of what E-PANA does, and pictures of each woman, and that's it.

Finally, after numerous interview requests via telephone and email, I submitted my fourth request: an earnest query about why the unit was called E-PANA. In addition to my questions about the name's meaning—I understood "pana" to mean "knife," among other meanings in Inuktitut—I thought it strange that the RCMP would use an Inuktitut word for a project focused on a region nowhere close to Canada's Arctic. It was this question that finally got me the interview with Cleary.

Cleary says the quantity of evidence E-PANA was dealing with was mammoth. With just those eighteen cases alone, there were more than 1,400 persons of interest, 1,000 polygraph reports, 750 DNA samples, 3,100 interviews, and 275,000 documents. Lots of it, he says, was historical evidence, but they were adding to it. He informed me they constantly followed up on tips, suggesting the force was bogged down with the mountains of evidence.

But some family members have worried that evidence and information they've shared with police that could have helped to solve cases on the E-PANA list fell to the wayside. Some say they know the police never followed up on the tips they provided, or that they never received calls back to further investigate. Maybe it was the sheer volume of evidence the unit collected and the reality that it was not well funded that made it difficult to investigate every single piece of evidence that came in.

The RCMP's Provincial Unsolved Homicide Unit and local detachments assert they never close a case until there are convictions, and always accept tips and evidence. Cleary says that even when a woman's or girl's case has been solved, they keep the file open and keep following up on tips "because all cases are technically always being investigated and the 'solving' part is not the be-all end-all." He also explained that police still need to ensure an arrest and sentencing are adequately followed through.

CLEARY'S EXPLANATION IS TRUE for at least one girl on the list: Monica Jack. Jack, a 12-year-old Nlaka'pamux girl, went missing near Merritt, B.C., in 1978. I've seen pictures of her wearing a brown western-styled shirt, holding her baby nephew, with her two younger sisters and her mom alongside her. Jack was kidnapped while she rode her new bicycle, then raped and killed in a trailer. Her body was found on June 2, 1995—seventeen years after she was murdered. Garry Handlen was arrested and charged in relation to her death after he confessed to the murder in 2014 during an undercover operation.

I covered the trial in 2018 for CBC Vancouver. Media attention was scant—there were two local reporters and one Canadian Press reporter who came to the B.C. Supreme Court and listened to testimony alongside a jury. Handlen was found guilty of first-degree murder and sentenced to life in prison in late January 2019. After she had testified, Monica's mother, Madeline Lanaro, was present for proceedings at the courthouse in downtown Vancouver, and she seemed distrustful of mainstream media. I had tried to interview her for almost two years, and she finally approached me during the trial. "Are you with the Aboriginal Peoples Television Network?" she asked. When I said no, and explained I was with the CBC, she looked disappointed and walked away. For many reasons, I don't blame her. Mainstream media has been a part of the colonial machine that has perpetuated stereotypes about Indigenous women who are missing or murdered, has blamed victims, and has questioned their right to justice.

At the end of the trial, after days of three reporters, including me, negotiating with Lanaro, she finally decided to hold a press conference in front of the courthouse, flanked by her brother, her daughter, and an advocate. It was devastating. The pain on her face, in her posture, and in her voice was palpable and heart-wrenching as she approached us on a walker. She sobbed through the entire conference as she took questions from reporters.

Handlen is a serial killer who was on the loose for decades, with a record of criminal sexual violence stretching back to 1969. He is suspected of killing at least two other girls—15-year-old Theresa Hildebrandt and 11-year-old Kathryn-Mary

Herbert. In 1979 he received his fourth sexual conviction, for assaulting an Indigenous girl he picked up hitchhiking near Hope, B.C. During the Monica Jack murder trial I spoke to this survivor, now a grown woman, in person at the courthouse, on the phone, and at one point in the front yard of her house. She explained to me how after Handlen picked her up, he stopped the car and repeatedly violently sexually assaulted her. She managed to escape partially dressed and was picked up by another motorist. She told me about how poorly she was treated by the justice system. Handlen was initially sentenced to eighteen years for the brutal assault, but it was reduced to twelve years by the B.C. Court of Appeal. She felt so unprotected and terrified by her experience and of him coming after her again that she legally changed her first and last names. At one point during the trial, she and I were talking in the courthouse parkade when Handlen's lawyer walked by us. Visibly shaken and angry, she asked him how he sleeps at night. His face bright red and his head down, he replied, "I don't."

At the press conference, I asked Madeline Lanaro whether the life sentence for the man who killed her daughter gave her closure. Through tears she told me in a shaking voice that "none of this will ever bring my daughter back."

Nothing will bring back the girls and women, beloved by family members, who were victims of at least four other serial killers who for more than thirty-five years roamed the network of highways that runs through B.C. In September 2012, RCMP investigators announced they believed that U.S. convict Bobby Fowler, by then deceased, had been responsible for killing as many as three women along the three B.C. highways. That year, his DNA was linked to the 1974 death of 16-year-old Colleen MacMillen, who was hitchhiking just a few short kilometres to a friend's house from her own home in Lac la Hache. Police believe Fowler may have also killed 19-year-old Gale Weys and 19-year-old Pamela Darlington, both in 1973. Weys was last seen asking for a ride to her parents' home in Kamloops from the pub she worked at in Clearwater. When she couldn't find a ride, she decided to hitchhike. Her body was found in a ditch about 6 kilometres south of Clearwater. Darlington was last seen leaving a Kamloops pub. Her body was found the next day on a bank of the Thompson River at Pioneer Park. Thinking about these disappearances takes me back to Levina Moody's 1969 murder; she was also travelling through from one interior town to another. Learning of what happened to the two girls hitchhiking is also an eerie reminder of the fate that could have been mine.

Parents who have lost their daughters often speak of being tortured by guilt and pain, asking themselves what they could have done to prevent their violent deaths. My mother, too, told my aunt Mary that she was constantly haunted by me living on the streets in the 1990s, especially since there were no cell phones then, and pay phones were not always convenient. I often think of the stress she faced during the times I was gone, hitching, living rough on the street. She would go weeks without knowing where I was or who I was with, only aware that I was travelling thousands of kilometres across North America. And it was equally terrifying for me. Every time I put my hand on the door handle to get into a car that pulled over, I would rely heavily on my instincts to decide whether or not it was safe. And when it became clear on more than one occasion that it was not a safe ride, I would have to rely on my ability to psychologically navigate dangerous situations. Often, I would have to get inside the mind of a driver who was making lewd or violent remarks. I would agree with him, try to act more like a bro or buddy, and do my best to keep him calm until we got to a gas station where I could grab my bag and run to safety. In one situation, in Maryland in the U.S., a man turned on dark metal music and told me how he liked to rape girls in hot tubs and then beat them. For what seemed like an eternity I just went along with his story and agreed with him, acting like I understood why he would do those things, fear pulsing through my veins that I would be next. Thinking back to all those situations where I held on to heavy objects in case I needed to smash the passenger side window, or prayed to every ancestor, god, or spirit I knew to keep me alive, I feel incredibly grateful and also surprised that I am still alive. Learning about the known serial killers along and around the Highway of Tears always reminds me of what it was like to be a hitchhiker, at the mercy of a driver.

AS I WAS DOING RESEARCH for this book in 2019, I learned of two other serial killers that have murdered women and girls along the network of highways. Brian Peter Arp was initially arrested in 1990 in connection with 18-year-old Marnie Blanchard's murder the year before. He was released because of insufficient evidence but then arrested again after the murder of a 38-year-old Cree woman, Theresa Umphrey, in 1993. He was convicted of both murders and is now in prison. Edward Isaac, a Dakelh man, was charged with first-degree murder in the 1981 killing of 13-year-old Roswitha Fuchsbichler, when he was 23 years old. He pleaded guilty to manslaughter in 1987 and received a life sentence. He was already serving a life sentence after pleading guilty to second-degree murder for the killing of 15-year-old Nina Joseph in 1982. Isaac was also charged with killing 36-year-old Jean Kovacs in 1981. All were killed in Prince George. I asked my former classmates from UNBC if they knew of this man, since some of them might have recognized him from their community of Fort St. James, but almost no one had ever heard of these murders. One woman remembered the man as "Fast Eddie" and told me he had a number of siblings who all struggled with alcoholism and addictions. Another woman, closer to Isaac's age, felt that he was set up and could be innocent.

At the time of my interview with former RCMP staff sergeant Wayne Cleary, I was not familiar with Isaac or Arp so didn't ask him about either. But he told me there are about six murders on the Project E-PANA list, including Monica Jack, Colleen MacMillen, Pamela Darlington, and Gale Weys, that are now solved. He would not disclose two of the solved cases because he says the suspects are no longer alive. In 2021, I followed up with the RCMP about this, since there have been rare cases when a killer can be convicted posthumously. Staff Sergeant Janelle Shoihet said that the RCMP had recently looked at charging Kam McLeod and Bryer Schmegelsky, two men who murdered three people in B.C. in less than a week before killing themselves, but that the B.C. Prosecution Service "was not at all interested in pursuing such a matter." Presumably, that means other posthumous convictions are also unlikely.

Cleary also told me he was not revealing some of the solved cases to me because family members had requested privacy. This is hard for me to believe, considering none of the families I have spoken to have suggested they would not want the public or even the media to know about their loved one's case. From speaking to multiple former RCMP officers, I believe it is likely that the cases he does not want to disclose but that E-PANA considers solved are those of Levina Moody and Tamara Chipman—whose suspected killers are both deceased. Both families have never been told that their loved one's cases are solved, and neither have said that they would want privacy if that was the case. Further, neither family has received a clear message from police. Cleary expressed satisfaction in linking DNA to a potential killer but frustration in learning that a suspect is dead, such as in the case of Bobby Jack Fowler. But I'm still not clear why it's okay to release Fowler's name if he is dead but not the killers of Levina Moody. Perhaps the difference between Levina's murder and the other women's cases is the DNA evidence for the latter. But current and former RCMP officers have not stated whether that played a role in naming a suspect. In an email Staff Sergeant Shoihet told me, "The RCMP constructed a thorough timeline as to Bobby Jack Fowler's activities in Canada and his DNA was scrutinized against all unsolved women's homicides in Canada during the times that he was proven to have been in BC. His DNA has not been linked to any other outstanding homicides, other than of Colleen McMillen [MacMillen]."

At the end of the interview with Cleary, I finally asked my original question about E-PANA. Why did RCMP investigators choose this name? Cleary chuckled; he didn't defend the name but justified it by saying that it's been used since 2006. He told me that no one had made a query about the name until I did. Given the weight of the larger issue of missing and murdered women and girls, the name of the task force is nobody's highest priority. But I find it ironic that that query was what finally gave me access to an interview with E-PANA. When I asked why the name was not in a language of one of the Indigenous Nations along the Highway of Tears, he just said it was one of the investigators' decisions and Cleary never asked about it but felt it was suitable. But I find the disconnect between the project's name and the culture of local Indigenous communities to show a lack of a relationship with the families and what they are fighting for, not to mention with the land from which the women were taken.

Today E-PANA remains a skeleton of what it was, but it is still operational according to the RCMP. In August of 2019, Shoihet told me that "the investigation [E-PANA] is supported by the Special Projects Major Crime Unit and there remain a dedicated group of investigators who continue to review and act upon any new information that is received. At any time, the Officer in Charge of Major Crimes can call upon and allocate investigators to support the E-PANA investigation should the need arise."

I don't know what that means, exactly. I do know that when I cover the story of a family member who has concerns about how their loved one's case is being handled, an officer from E-PANA will reach out and tell them the investigation is "active." Whether that means that E-PANA is looking through more evidence, or talking to community members, or has a dedicated officer assigned to re-examine evidence, or is just open to new leads, I don't know.

IN THE SUMMER OF 2019, a massive manhunt began for Kam McLeod and Bryer Schmegelsky, the suspected killers of a white couple and a white professor who were murdered on highways hundreds of kilometres to the north of the Highway of Tears. The search took centre stage for the RCMP, who coordinated forces across three provinces. The story dominated the news on radio, TV, and the internet until the killers eventually killed themselves in Manitoba. In media reports at the time, Sheila North, then the Grand Chief of Manitoba Keewatinowi Okimakanak, compared the investigation and the coverage to that when an Indigenous woman is murdered. "Families that do their own searches are feeling a little bit let down and not respected in the same way as these other families are," she said.

Very few murdered Indigenous women, even when killed by serial killers, have made international headlines. I have yet to see a manhunt for a killer when the victim is an Indigenous woman. Cody Legebokoff killed four women within a short time span, all in just over a year. There was no manhunt for their serial killer and no media coverage until Legebokoff was caught by luck. A rookie RCMP constable had pulled him over on a remote logging road because, according to a case report written by the officer, the pickup truck was speeding erratically and the officer suspected the driver of poaching in the backwoods. Legebokoff had incriminating materials in his truck and was arrested, but he could easily have continued on his killing spree if it weren't for this officer stumbling across him, since there was no police investigation and no media coverage.

Since Legebokoff's arrest, more than a dozen women and girls have gone missing or been murdered in connection to the Highway of Tears or adjoining highways. "I've stopped counting," says Gladys Radek, renowned Gitxsan and Wet'suwet'en advocate for missing and murdered Indigenous women and girls (MMIWG). She says by 2013 she had counted more than four thousand MMIWG in Canada. "How many more serial killers will we learn about and when are we going to find our women?" she asks. In 2016, Canada's minister for the status of women, Patty Hajdu, repeated the same number as Gladys but said a dearth of hard data makes it impossible to pinpoint an exact figure.

The murders and disappearances of Indigenous women have historically been ignored by the public, the police, and the media. Tamara's case was different.

7

'Et'doonekh,
it might happen

HOPE

CLOAKED IN RED AND BLACK BUTTON BLANKETS waving like flags in the streets, Gladys Radek and other Indigenous matriarchs beat drums in unison, winding like a river down Hastings Street from Main at the annual Valentine's Day Women's Memorial March in Vancouver. As we sing the Women's Warrior Song, the one gifted to all Indigenous women by Martina Pierre, Sawt, of the Lílwat Nation, I feel power surge through me. I'm connected to the rock and the rubble of these streets from my time living near them, from reporting on them, and from seeing the lives that have been violently lost on them.

In 2008, I took a part-time job in the Downtown Eastside as a women's mental health worker. "I want to be down there again, and give back," I told a friend. Every day I worked there I connected with women, including many who were deeply impacted by missing or murdered family members or friends. Working there deepened my connection to the neighbourhood and seeded a resolve in me to shed light on the circumstances that led to the vulnerability Indigenous women there experience every day. It strengthened my yearning to help others have compassion and understanding for those whose trauma is an integral consequence of colonization.

For many years, I'd taken part in the Women's Memorial March to honour the spirits of those whose lives were cut too short. The event started in 1992 in Vancouver after a woman was murdered on Powell Street. While women I spoke to at the time told me that her name was not spoken due to the wishes of family members, in 2017 two family members reached out to me to tell me they were now ready to say her name: Cheryl Ann Joe. Her cousin Melodie Casella called me and shared brutal details of her murder. It was the most gruesome murder I have ever heard of and the details still haunt me today. When I asked Melodie why the family didn't want to speak about her name earlier, she told me, "We didn't want [the women's march] just to be about Cheryl—her mother, Linda Joe, wanted it to be about all of the women whose lives were taken."

Cheryl Ann Joe was a young mother of three small boys from the shíshálh (Sechelt) community on the Sunshine Coast of B.C. A 26-year-old Coast Salish woman with an infectious laugh and a big heart, Cheryl was planning a career as a police officer, to help protect Vancouver's vulnerable. She was murdered on January 20, 1992, her mutilated body found dumped near a warehouse loading dock in East Vancouver. Her killer, Brian Allender, is still in jail and has applied numerous times to work outside the prison. The last time he did, Melodie raised the alarm, stating the danger he posed to the public, and as a result his request was denied.

During one of the marches, as women weaved through the streets flashing abalone shells from their regalia, their cedar hats and hide-wrapped drumsticks popping in and out of the crowds, two Elders asked me to sing with them at the front line of the march. I felt my heart grow to the size of the city. I stood side

by side with two iconic women, Bernie Williams, a Haida matriarch, and Gladys Radek, a Gitxsan and Wet'suwet'en leader. And
behind us, thousands clamoured through the Downtown Eastside streets. Gladys walks with a stature that is unmatched. She's
outspoken and angry, but generous and funny, like so many
aunties of mine back home. She resonates like a heartbeat.

During one of my interviews with her, she tells me she was
never a leader, but says the reason she marched every year is
that the stories of the missing and murdered women are embedded in her heart. She says the women leading the memorial in
the Downtown Eastside gave her a sense of who she was. She
connected with the women and the marches in this neighbourhood while she was looking for her niece Tamara Chipman, putting up posters in centres and on the streets in 2005.

It's hard to hear about Gladys's past. In a matter-of-fact way
she tells me she was "institutionalized since birth." The pain is
visible on her face when she speaks about this time in her life.
She tells me she was hospitalized at the Miller Bay Indian Hospital in Prince Rupert from when she was born until she was
almost 4 years old because she had tuberculosis, a disease that
disproportionately affects Indigenous people due to poverty,
overcrowded and inadequate housing, food insecurity, and
inequitable access to health care.

When Gladys was 5, she says she was put in foster care and
abused by her foster parents. As a teen, she kept running away
from the group home she'd been living in, where she says she
saw the group home "dad" sexually abusing other girls. When
she did return to her mom and stepdad, both were heavy drink-
ers and could become violent.

Though she carries the emotional burden of her childhood,
Gladys is not just a survivor, but a strong-willed fighter who
will not let her past get in the way of her future, or the women's
lives she is fighting for. The women's memorial marches served
as her platform to speak out for others who, like her, had

suffered and survived a history of colonial racism, trauma, and abuse. She says the women leading the marches pulled her onto the front lines and gave her a sense of who her people were.

I remember sitting in the CBC newsroom in 2013, a few years after I had seen Gladys in person at the marches, and seeing her face on *Power and Politics*, one of the CBC's flagship programs. Gladys made it her mission to ensure Tamara's face was seen on posters and screens from coast to coast, pressing reporters and police officers to take notice of not just her, but the growing number of other missing and murdered Indigenous women and girls (MMIWG). And the public started to notice and listen more than they had before as a result of the way police and reporters probed Tamara's case, thanks in part to Gladys's relentless work.

GLADYS RADEK'S NIECE Tamara Chipman was 22 years old when she was last seen. Her dad's friend spotted her hitchhiking near an industrial park about 4 or 5 kilometres away from downtown Prince Rupert on September 21, 2005. It's a detail that Gladys finds painful to think about. They were close.

Tamara had soft golden curls, dyed blond from her natural brown; beamed a contagious smile; and stood a slender 5 feet 10 inches tall, with an elegant walk that radiated confidence. But she was tough. She practised judo, and according to friends, family, and associates her "don't take no guff" attitude had brought her clout at her small high school in Terrace. She was respected—and by all accounts a strong young Indigenous woman.

These descriptions of Tamara linger with me, and I think of her when I'm driving the highway and sense the emotions hanging over it, or interviewing family or friends with beautiful memories to share, or looking at faded photographs. Her spirit sings strength. She could take care of herself. At the CBC town hall on the Highway of Tears in Prince George in the fall of 2016, a member of the audience made a comment during the

Q and A about how women and girls living in communities along the Highway of Tears could benefit from self-defence classes. The notion, while earnest and well intentioned, made my heart drop, because so many of the women missing or murdered in this area were and are like Tamara—strong, independent, and able to take care of themselves. I'm reminded of how often the weight of responsibility for violence is, perhaps unintentionally or out of ignorance, placed squarely on the victims themselves. Another example is the signs I've seen along the highway and in smaller communities that say, "Girls don't hitchhike, killer on the loose." However, without an affordable transit system until recently, people living in poverty and with limited supports were unable to get safely to where they were going. In Tamara's case, with her mother living in Rupert and her father in Terrace, she would sometimes travel by thumb, as many did, simply to get from A to B.

Tamara's dad, Tom Chipman, remembers the day she was born. He was only 19 years old. "It was a pretty emotional experience, my first child—it makes you think about growing up in a hurry when you have a little baby in your arms. It's like, yup: it's adult time," he tells me, in person at his home in Terrace, B.C., the same town where Tamara grew up. He was with his first wife, Corey, Tamara's mother, for sixteen years before they parted company. In October of 1994, just after Tamara's 11th birthday, Tom started a relationship with a woman named Christine Ridler. Tamara was Christine's bridesmaid at their wedding in 2001. Christine and Tom's grandson—Tamara's son—sits with us as we conduct the interview.

One of Tamara's favourite activities, starting from when she was a small child, was fishing with her dad on his gillnetter. "Anytime we were on the boat she was on the boat with us," Tom says. When she was a toddler, Tom put a tiny red life jacket on her and tethered her to the boom so she didn't fall overboard. This story makes my eyes well up; Tom's love of the ocean and of his daughter reminds me of time spent fishing with my stepdad for sockeye and spring salmon in Campbell River. Feeling this connection to Tom's story makes his loss feel personal to me.

When she was 9 or 10 years old, Tamara would help Tom set his fishing lines up and down the coast from Prince Rupert and then on the Fraser River. "She was a great deckhand," Tom says proudly. Summers fishing brought long hours on the ocean, the sun beating down on the aluminum boat loaded with glistening salmon, halibut, black cod, and red snapper.

Tom made a decent living fishing and spoiled Tamara, who was his only child. "We always had money and she always had the best of everything. She was lucky, you could say," Tom says, trailing off. "She loved to ride her ATV and she drove it all through the trails. I remember one time, I came home and she was riding the thing sideways—I thought, 'Oh boy.'" Tom laughs and shakes his head affectionately, looking down at a photocopied colour picture of her with hearts speckled on it. Above her photo are the words "Tamara Chipman, Missing, since 2005."

In every photograph and video I have seen of her, Tamara's dark eyes sparkle like polished black pebbles. Her son has the same wide, warm eyes and gentle smile as his mom. When he holds up a painting that someone gave him of her, he grins, his memories mostly gleaned from these tributes to her. He was only 2 years old when she went missing and says he has only one memory of her. "I remember her carrying me downstairs to a laundry room and washing the clothes," Jaden tells me shyly. His recollection helps *me* to remember that Tamara was like all other moms, who had to balance the joy and responsibility of caring for a small child. But unlike most other moms, her life was taken before her baby was even a boy.

Jaden, who now lives with his dad, is kind, gentle, and respectful. When we spend the day with his grandpa Tom at their home in Terrace, shortly after we walk in the door he helps my 5-year-old son onto a chair and sets up a movie for him. Like his mom, he has a strong work ethic, and while we're there, he spends time helping the neighbours out with yardwork.

He's curious about what I might know about his mom, and he looks worried when I ask questions about the long days his family searched for her. I try as best as I can to tread tenderly on the harder questions, but as a journalist, I know it's also my job to follow up on rumours, to rule them out or corroborate them, and to eventually chip far enough into things to get to the truth—something I take seriously.

I ask Tom why he had waited so long—several weeks—to report Tamara missing. I have to ask this because I had heard others state in articles online that she was not reported missing for so long because she had outstanding warrants and the family didn't want to cause trouble. But I learn quickly that that is not the reason they didn't report her missing immediately. Tom was out on his boat at the time. Tamara had been living between his house in Terrace and her mom's in Rupert. She was also, family members think, in an abusive relationship with her son's dad, who it seemed she was drifting away from. She was in a bit of a transient time in her life. So family, including Tom, her mom, and friends, just thought she was at one place or the other.

It's hard for me to ask him about this. Over the years Tom has been hounded by media, from CBS's 48 Hours in the United States, which did an episode on the Highway of Tears, to local papers, to the CBC. In fact, the only reason he is speaking at length to me is that his story will be part of my book, not a news cycle that can be cutthroat and disrespectful in trying to get the story. "Sometimes it's like they just twist the knife trying to get your tears," Tom tells me. It's a terrible thing to hear about an institution that is run by people who are like family to me, and who have given me a career that has sometimes treated me well, but I know how deep the mistrust of media runs and that the reasons are often justified.

After Tom and Tamara's mom realized she wasn't with either of them, both considered the possibility that she was at her own place in Terrace, or her son's dad's home. When Tom realized she was not at any of the places they'd assumed, he frantically called family and friends back home, telling them to start asking around and looking for his daughter. It had been three to four weeks before they realized she was actually missing and filed a police report.

Tom tells me that talking about Tamara's disappearance is tough for him. I also find it jarring and uncomfortable asking questions that bring up horrible memories. It's easier on Tom to remember her resilient character when she was undoubtedly alive. He chuckles and often refers to her as a firecracker. In her carefree teenage summer days, she'd cruise with Tom in one of his white-striped hot rods. In the powdery winter, she'd drive a snowmobile like the wind. Her wild side didn't scare Tom—he taught her to drive when she was just 13 and she knew what she was doing, he insists. Listening to him talk, it's clear she brought him joy, just like their life on the ocean did. During their blissful days together on the water, he never could have imagined that he would be searching those same seas for his daughter just years later.

In an interview, Eric Stubbs, RCMP operations supervisor at the time of the disappearance, tells me that finding Tamara would have been difficult after all the weeks that had passed before the report was filed in 2005. Like the currents in the ocean, the possibilities of where she could be were endless. Tom also worried that since it had been so long before her disappearance was reported, if she had died, anything could have happened to her body—the killers could have dumped it into the depths of the Skeena River or deep in the forest. Not only that, but possible leads to where she was could have gone cold—an unimaginable situation for any parent.

Search parties of up to three hundred relatives and friends scoured the land and waters for about two months, Tom says, right up until the snow came. Tom and his wife, Christine, spent tireless days and nights searching Terrace and Rupert logging roads, lonely stretches of highway, and even ditches for his only child. During testimony at the national inquiry, a family friend, Arlene Roberts, shared that droves of fishers and firefighters from the Kitsumkalum First Nation took part in the search, starting at four in the morning and going all day, from Terrace to Prince Rupert to Kitsumkalum.

Tom has described the time searching as fruitless and heartbreaking.

Arnie Nagy, a Haida shore worker and millwright in the fish plant and a childhood friend of Tom and his siblings, searched the bush along the Skeena River when he was out hunting. "It was very nerve-racking and scary 'cause I was not sure how I would react if I found her," Nagy tells me from his Prince Rupert home. "I wanted to find her, but at the same time I didn't, if that makes sense." Nagy looked for disturbances in bogs and along creeks, logging slashes, and dirt roads.

Tom and Gladys also searched the Downtown Eastside of Vancouver, in case Tamara had travelled there to visit her aunt Gladys without telling them. And while there had been sightings of women who looked just like Tamara, she was not there.

While some members of Tamara's family feel that the RCMP did not help with the search effort at all in the early days, Stubbs tells me police did conduct a ground search. In 2008, he says, a tip came in. RCMP members focused on a rural stretch of a forest service road and brought in approximately forty ground search and rescue volunteers from Kitimat to search the area.

To this day, no trace of her body has been found. While evidence has been gathered, no suspect has been charged.

Disturbing and hard-to-believe rumours have swirled through Terrace and Prince Rupert for years, but one of the stories carries significant weight, for both Tamara's family and investigators.

Stubbs, who was the RCMP's director general of national criminal operations when I interviewed him in 2016, was dedicated to Tamara's case at the time of her disappearance. He says a theory shared by locals about how Tamara was murdered and who was involved in killing her—people who are all now also dead—is most likely true. "We believe we know what happened and it pains me—for one, that we don't have a charge, and for two, that we do not have Tamara's remains to bring to the family," Stubbs tells me over the phone from Ottawa.

In an era when RCMP are under fire for everything from dismissing Indigenous family members' concerns about missing person cases, to racism, to sexual harassment within the force, Stubbs stands out as an honest and caring officer who is dedicated to fairness and justice. In the dozens of interviews I have conducted with families, advocates, and police on the Highway of Tears, I've never heard anyone utter a pejorative statement about him. In a local newspaper article, there's a photo of Stubbs, in uniform, light brown hair slicked back and eyes a piercing blue, standing between two Indigenous Elders who are gifting him a hide drum and traditional Dene gloves, proud, gentle smiles on all their faces. From my discussions with family members, and from seeing tributes online, it is clear to me that he is considered someone who broke the mould. What shocks me is that he says that all he really did was pay attention, direct an investigation, and take seriously the case of a missing Indigenous woman—things investigators in previous and even more recent investigations haven't done. I ask him about this, and while he resists taking the compliment, he admits that all officers get attached to cases, feel passionate about certain ones, and encounter some they never forget. Tamara's, he said, is one of those cases for him.

"We do believe we know who committed that homicide, but it won't be resolved... I'm trying to be careful with what I say," Stubbs tells me, mindful that he is speaking to a journalist. "We do believe the person responsible for Tamara's death is deceased and that complicates the situation of getting a charge and locating Tamara back to her family. It's very problematic, but there is always that hope that a hunter or person from the public comes forward to help locate her remains," he says.

Stubbs does not say how he knows that Tamara was murdered or how the suspect in her case died. But a retired Prince Rupert pastor named Lloyd Thomas claims he worked with the Prince Rupert RCMP to gather information from a witness who allegedly saw Tamara being killed. The story he tells, unlike Stubbs's, is horrifying and extraordinary.

I haven't met Thomas in person because these days he lives in the United Kingdom, where a number of his family members—he's a great-grandfather—also reside. He was 78 years old when we corresponded about Tamara in 2019 and in his late 60s while ministering in Prince Rupert. In pictures posted on Facebook, he is white, tall, and stocky, with white hair and thin-rimmed square glasses. Among his own posts, some topics are controversial; there's a photo of the flag of Israel burning, since he is critical of the country's historical displacement of Palestinians, and a post about how the Russian president Vladimir Putin spied on him personally. He told me, candidly, "I tend to get in other people's problems." His Facebook content makes me concerned about his credibility. But people that I have spoken to, including Gladys Radek, Tom Chipman, and a former officer, think there may be merit to his theory about how Tamara died.

Thomas says in 2007, while family members, friends, and police were still searching for clues into Tamara's disappearance, a friend of his asked him to come to the Prince Rupert Regional Hospital to speak with a "drug-addicted" patient who was having violent flashbacks.

Thomas was told that the patient was haunted and terrorized by memories of a murder she either witnessed or participated in but was not willing to speak to the police about since she did not trust police. In an interview in 2016, Ray Michalko, who in 2007 was a former RCMP officer and private investigator probing the Highway of Tears murders, told me he helped Thomas set up an interview with the potential witness using RCMP recording equipment.

According to Michalko, Thomas's theory is based on what the woman recounted in their interview: that the woman was driving the car of a Terrace drug dealer who sat in the passenger seat, when they picked up Tamara. It is not clear if they had heard about her searching for a ride earlier or if they randomly came across her. Once they were out of town, the man allegedly jumped into the back seat with Tamara, brutally beat her, and then strangled her to death. It is a horrific possible end to a beautiful and strong Indigenous woman's life. But it is just one theory.

Thomas alleges that in his conversation with her, the woman identified where Tamara's body was disposed of—in a wooded area near Highway 16. Thomas says he later took Tom Chipman to the site, something Tom confirmed to me. But on July 11, 2007, Thomas says, the RCMP told him they were no longer pursuing inquiries about the potential witness to Tamara's death but would not say why. According to Tom Chipman and Lloyd Thomas, the officers searched the area but no evidence was uncovered.

Thomas says in the spring of 2010 he was informed the woman had died of natural causes. The man allegedly involved had also died, according to Thomas, and RCMP officers have said they believe everyone who was involved in Tamara's death is now dead. I looked up both the possible witness and the drug dealer in B.C.'s online court system and saw that her appearances in court, mostly on drug possession and theft charges, stopped in August of 2009. His appearances, mostly on drug trafficking charges, ended in December of 2006. On several occasions both were summoned to court on charges they obtained together.

In 2021, I spoke to the woman's brother, who wanted to set the record straight, saying she had no responsibility in the murder of Tamara. Despite being very close with his sister, he told me, she never shared anything about what Lloyd Thomas alleges—that she was a witness to, or a participant in, Tamara's murder.

Many years later, he is still frustrated that some newspapers printed commentary at the time that he feels blamed his sister for the murder. "She probably had PTSD from the cops coming down on her, the press coming down on her, and everyone pointing fingers at her; it probably ripped her right apart," he says. He tells me she died of liver and kidney damage in 2010 in a Vancouver hospital.

At the beginning of 2022, I give Tamara's dad, Tom Chipman, a call to check in and he tells me something that I never expected: there is potentially a new piece of evidence that the police are now investigating.

He says Jaden's dad found a letter in his garage while cleaning. Eighteen pages later, Tom says, Jaden's dad realized the anonymous note could possibly provide leads to solve Tamara's murder. Tom says the RCMP are in possession of the letter and have said they are taking it seriously and making their way toward Terrace to reopen the investigation. In an email the RCMP tell me, "Tamara Chipman's investigation has always been open, at no point has it been cold or closed. Investigators have continued to investigate any and all tips and continue to seek additional information that relates to the investigation."

Tom took days to even think about reading the letter. "I guess it's time to take my head out of the sand and read it," he says. "I just hope it's not another wild goose chase... It just brings everything back up again." It could be a tiny sliver of hope that ends in another roller coaster of emotions with no closure and no justice for Tamara. I can't even imagine the pain this new development, and the potential reality that Lloyd's theory was just a theory, has caused.

Tamara's case has always made me uneasy, physically, mentally, and spiritually. My head is pounding as I write this part of my book. And I am unsure why I feel this way when the other murders are equally brutal. Sometimes it is almost like I can hear Tamara saying "Stop, stop searching." But then I will get a message that tells me to keep going. All the death, violence, and pain that has been left behind is a lot to unpack.

In my 2016 interview with Michalko, he said he thought he had solved Tamara's murder. He implied that he had further information to corroborate Thomas's theory, something he shares in his own book, *Obstruction of Justice*. In a second interview with him the following year at a Tim Hortons in Delta, B.C., he told me he had heard that Tamara's killers were motivated by jealousy, anger, and Tamara's brash words shared at a party. But it's still not clear what happened to her, and we may never know.

SADLY, RAY MICHALKO DIED in 2017 of unknown causes, so, as I come to the end of my investigation of Tamara's death, I'm unable to ask him further questions. One of the ways Michalko helped my investigations into the Highway of Tears was by deepening my understanding of the so-called underbelly of the northwest, particularly Prince George and Prince Rupert. In our meetings on the phone or in person he would tell me about how crime and criminals are familiar residents in the part of central and northwestern B.C. where the highway is nestled.

Like a wayward soul, the region has often been laden with darkness. It can be rough. Michalko had investigated numerous types of files in the area and had a battery of stories that would blow most urbanites' minds. While he was investigating an insurance case in Prince George, for example, he told me how one of his clients, who was mingling with the wrong crowd, was robbed and locked in the trunk of a car for being in the wrong place at the wrong time.

When I moved to Prince George in 2002, stabbings were not uncommon at hockey games or nightclubs. To those who haven't spent time in the area, the stories locals tell about violence might seem unbelievable or inflated, but the incidents they describe are as mundane as the sawmills, the rough vernacular, the rivers, and the long, dark stretches of highway. One time, a Tsimshian friend from Vancouver was visiting and a group of us went out to a club called the Generator. I warned him, "Be careful, this is a rough town," but he just laughed—he probably thought I was exaggerating and that he had seen worse. But he ended up looking too hard at and maybe flirting too much on the dance floor with a woman whose boyfriend was watching. My friend was chased out of the bar by the knife-wielding boyfriend and hid under a car for most of the night until the coast was clear to escape in my van.

In 2011, *Maclean's* ranked Prince George as Canada's most dangerous city—gang wars, high levels of drug abuse, and one or more serial killers landed it the number one spot. That same year, a string of nine murders rocked the community of just 74,000. Vancouver recorded forty-three homicides in the same year, with a population of 603,500, or eight times the population of Prince George. The city thus had a murder rate almost double that of Vancouver's. In 2012, Prince George and its sister city, Prince Rupert—what some think of as the end point of the Highway of Tears—were ranked among the worst places to live in Canada. Over the years, the crime stats have improved in both cities, as they have elsewhere in Canada, but there are still murders and disappearances along the highway, including a disproportionate number of Indigenous women and girls.

At a small dinner I attended at Arnie Nagy's home in Prince Rupert to honour the work of family members of MMIWG along the Highway of Tears, Tom Chipman expressed frustration that anyone who knew anything about his daughter's disappearance had apparently also vanished into thin air. "No one will ever know [what happened]," Tom told me in his usual measured tone. Today he acknowledges that she was likely murdered, but without her remains, there's no resolution.

According to Gladys, the investigation into Tamara's possible murder seemed to drag on without any answers. From the several people I've spoken to about the case, it was also a bit messy internally. Yet the Chipmans and Gladys also praise the RCMP for taking steps to do more than what was then the status quo. Tom says Eric Stubbs of the RCMP took it upon himself to hold press conferences with media on the highway and to implore the public for new information. Tom himself used the press conferences to get the word out about his missing daughter to news outlets and reporters. Tamara's is one of the first cases in at least thirty years where RCMP and media raised the profile of the disproportionate number of MMIWG along the Highway of Tears.

While many resources went into Tamara's case and several people—Ray Michalko included—believe her case has been solved, it's unclear whether Project E-PANA agrees.

In the Tim Hortons in Delta, B.C., Michalko thumbed his fingers as he counted the cases he thought may have been solved. "Well, there's Nicole Hoar, Alberta Williams, and Tamara Chipman's—I think I have figured out how they were murdered," he said. But he didn't want to provide details to me, still clinging to the idea that he might have hypothetically caught a killer, and seemingly wanting to be the one who solved it.

TAMARA'S TRAGIC UNSOLVED DISAPPEARANCE is not isolated. Even though Indigenous women make up only 4 percent
of the female population in Canada, they represent 10 percent
of the total population of women missing for at least thirty days,
according to the RCMP's report *Missing and Murdered Aboriginal Women: 2015 Update to the National Operational Overview*. Of
these, 64 percent were identified as missing due to "unknown"
circumstances or suspected foul play. Since Tamara went missing, many more women have vanished from the network of
highways associated with the Highway of Tears, some in circumstances bearing a chilling resemblance to hers.

In the early hours of 2011, Madison Scott, 20, went missing
from a party at Hogsback Lake in the Vanderhoof area, about an
hour west of Prince George. She, alongside Tamara, was featured
on the U.S.-based CBS crime investigative program *48 Hours*, in
a 2016 episode called "The Highway of Tears." In the same year,
as I drove along Highway 16 speaking to family members for
this book, I saw multiple billboards lining the highway with
Scott's pictures and the words "Help find Madison Scott," along
with similar posters at gas stations. She is non-Indigenous but
her backstory, of growing up in the sawdust belt, riding snow-
mobiles and driving pickup trucks, is much like Tamara's.

Immaculate (Mackie) Basil, a young woman of the Tl'azt'en
Nation, disappeared in an eerily similar way to Scott. She went
missing on June 14, 2013, when she was 26 years old. She vanished into the night, leaving behind only a couple of clues—that
she was seen with her cousin and another man leaving a house
party, and a truck driver spotted her hitchhiking alone in the
Leo Creek area, north of the Tache reserve. Like Tamara, she was
a strong Indigenous woman. In 2016, her family put together a
$20,000 award for information leading to finding her. As with
Tamara, many tips that have come in point toward a suspect,
but with little to no reliable physical or even circumstantial

evidence, it's difficult for the family and the police to corroborate leads.

As an Indigenous woman myself and as someone responsible for gauging public interest, I constantly grapple with why
and how most cases of MMIWG seem to go unnoticed by the
public. Do Indigenous women mean less to the wider public?
To the media? Tamara's case cut through the apathy. Her mysterious disappearance sparked a ripple of care in the flatlining
interest in the issue of MMIWG along the Highway of Tears.
At the time, hers was one of the most high-profile cases of a
missing Indigenous woman. Eric Stubbs and Tom Chipman
attribute the breakthrough publicity of Tamara's case partly
to the "loud" and very physical presence of Gladys Radek: her
car plastered with images of missing women and girls; her several walks for justice; and her ability to clearly describe racism,
sexism, and violence on TV screens and radio waves across the
country. Stubbs says it was also Tom's relatable, measured tone,
his "dad-next-door" manner, and, despite his shyness, his passion to find his only daughter. Gladys and Tom assert it was also
Stubbs, the lone cop who finally spoke out about MMIWG on
the Highway of Tears. But together, they were like a constellation of stars, acting together to illuminate Tamara: a mother, a
young woman, a fighter, a wild woman, and someone who still
had her best moments ahead of her.

When I spoke to Gladys in late 2015, she was holding out
hope that authorities would acknowledge all the recommendations from the Highway of Tears Symposium report. She
was also hoping a national inquiry would lead to action. "For
this government to fund every organization out there to protect our women: we need shelters, housing, rape centres, sexual
assault centres, support [for] healing and wellness; there is so
much, all the organizations they've been cutting the funding
from," Gladys said.

While the inquiry was and is a focal point of many grass-roots, national, and international organizations, many women, particularly in the north, wanted more, including shelters and housing for Indigenous women (especially in remote communities where there are few to none), healing centres, and adequate funding for trauma counselling. They wanted institutions to address systemic anti-Indigenous racism. They felt what was needed to mitigate violence against Indigenous women and to help them flee brutality could not be solved by a single national inquiry.

But according to the dozens of family members I spoke to for this book, in order to even start having conversations about all the reasons Indigenous women go missing or are murdered, we needed an inquiry.

8

Nin̓chím̓s,
to question someone

THE INQUIRIES

THERE IS A SAYING my Kwakwaka'wakw friend from Alert Bay used to repeat all the time: "All sickness comes from the spirit world." When you are sick, he'd say, there's a teaching that your ancestors are trying to convey. This came to me over and over again at the end of 2009 as I struggled with a physical illness that had me bedridden for weeks and very sick for almost a year. But it was that dramatic illness that would propel me to get back to who I was destined to be.

While I was still working in the Downtown Eastside, I felt as if I was being pulled away, like my ancestors could tell I had strayed too far off my path. I was not telling stories, I was not shining a light into darkness. While it was necessary work to help people in crisis, I often felt I was just putting Band-Aids on people's trauma. While I was trying to help, I was just swimming and sometimes drowning in a giant pool of pain.

The descent of this leg of my journey came while I was helping a woman with mental illness, who was also a pretty extreme hoarder, clean up her home to save her from eviction. While cleaning her little apartment, I accidently inhaled chlorine gas (for four hours). The next day, when I woke up, I felt like my lungs were completely charred. It felt like I had smoked a minimum of five packs of cigarettes. I spent the days after that making daily visits to the hospital, on Ventolin and oxygen, with severely damaged lungs. Because I was coughing nonstop, with breaks sometimes for only two or three minutes, doctors put me on various levels of steroids. I broke three ribs from the constant hacking. But my employers gave me no time off and no accommodation for my injury, even though it happened at work. Eventually I ended my employment there, with a tiny monetary settlement my union negotiated.

But as the months went by, some days unable to lift myself up off my pillow due to the broken ribs and struggling to breathe or eat, I started to panic. Ironically, my Elder offered to do a pipe ceremony with me, which I clearly could not do. I was alone in my East Van home, feeling desperate. Thinking back to what my Kwakwaka'wakw friend said, I began to pray all day and night, asking my ancestors for help, just like I had done when I was in dangerous rides while hitchhiking and when sleeping rough on the street. During my prayers, in a vision, I saw a powder-blue imaginary sky striped with a royal-blue banner boldly printed with the word *journalism* rippling across it. It brought me to a screeching halt as I started to remember what and who I was. Yes, I liked to help people and try to create change, but I was a storyteller. Telling stories was in my DNA and had carried me through many times in my life, from the Downtown Eastside to Prince George to Vancouver. And here, my ancestors had my back. "You've got this," they said. "You will get through this." From the end of my bed, on my cell phone and my old-school Apple desktop, I started to reach out to contacts I had at CBC when I did casual work in radio in Vancouver a few years earlier, while I was attending university.

As my cough lessened and I regained my health, I started to apply for jobs at the CBC. A recruiter there contacted me, saying there was a project opening for me in Winnipeg. Not long after, I was off to produce radio segments for a program called *ReVision Quest* with a team of Indigenous producers, including Wab Kinew, Waubgeshig Rice, and host Darrell Dennis. I kept in contact with a boyfriend I'd been seeing since the fall of 2009, and it wasn't the healthiest relationship. But a trip back to Vancouver would set us on a new path that would connect us for many years to come.

After we produced the series, CBC Winnipeg's newsroom executives asked if I wanted to come back and work on a project about poverty. I agreed, but before starting, I went back to Vancouver to visit loved ones. While there, I spent time with friends in the Sḵwx̱wú7mesh mountains. Before reaching our destination, at one of the peaks, we stopped at a waterfall cascading through jagged rocks before plunging into a pool of mountain water. Elders had told me that moving water is one of the places where it is easier to connect to spirits and ancestors. After singing a Sḵwx̱wú7mesh song, my friend told me she saw an Elder Sḵwx̱wú7mesh spirit beside me in full regalia, holding up her hands, saying "unity." I felt the power of the moment and embraced it. It felt like water crystals and sparkles were shooting out from the falls, sharing a message with me: *magic is coming.* Before I returned to Winnipeg, I hung out with my boyfriend one last time, and then he drove me to the airport the next morning.

After only a few months back in Winnipeg, I started experiencing strange symptoms—an aversion to meat and exercise. On a gut feeling, I bought a pregnancy test. "I am ecstatic, my girl," the boyfriend said when I called and told him the stick had turned the colours that meant "pregnant." His joy was short lived as his trauma about becoming a father unfolded, and from then on I was mostly alone in pregnancy, birth, and child-rearing.

I freelanced all through my pregnancy, writing for magazines and online news sites, doing casual radio work at CBC, and working with youth at an art studio. My thirty-six-hour labour started on November 28, 2010, and ended with a traumatic emergency C-section that became badly infected. I remained in hospital, tended to by racist nurses, for several days until my staples could come out. To give him credit, my son's dad was there to cut the cord, to see our baby's eyes for the first time, and to stay with me in the hospital. But he was not there so much as I wobbled with a newborn after surgery, trying to figure out my meds and food, and breastfeeding and changing diapers, alone. It was treacherous, but it is amazing how quickly you can learn.

I wanted to give my son a name that would inspire him to lead a life where he didn't need to fight. To honour his Anishinaabe heritage, I called him Namawan, meaning "fair wind." His middle name, Lax Ha, is Gitxsan and means "sky" or "heaven"; his other middle name, Sha'gota, meaning "winter dance," came from my friend, Lílwat Elder Seis'lom, who gave him the name because he was born after the first snow.

Two months before my son was born, the provincial government had ordered the Missing Women Commission of Inquiry to look into the Pickton murders. On maternity leave I chose to keep working, focused on telling the stories of missing and murdered Indigenous women and girls (MMIWG); I knew first-hand from the women I worked with just how important it was to have these stories heard, read, and seen in the news. CBC was not interested in my freelance work on this, so I went to other outlets—like the Georgia Straight, The Tyee, Briarpatch, and community papers—that were willing and eager to publish those stories.

Between trying to get my son to latch, changing diapers, and cleaning spit-up, I reported on what would become widely known as the "Oppal inquiry," also known as the "Pickton inquiry." Family members were emailing, calling, and texting me, telling me that they were furious about it.

WALLY OPPAL WAS NAMED the commissioner of the inquiry to investigate police handling of the murders committed by serial killer Robert Pickton. His appointment was marred with discord from the get-go. The former attorney general of British Columbia had overseen the controversial staying of twenty of Pickton's charges—a move that upset many family members but made sense to some working in Canada's legal system.

The aim of the Missing Women Commission hearings was not to examine Pickton's convictions, but to investigate the police handling of the missing women cases from the Downtown Eastside of Vancouver between January 23, 1997, and February 5, 2002. It looked into the 1998 decision to stay the charges against Pickton of attempted murder, assault with a weapon, forcible confinement, and aggravated assault. And the commission's goal was to recommend changes in how missing women cases are conducted and changes to improve inter-institutional cooperation.

It was also a chance for family members to finally voice their concerns about years of silence around and lack of justice for their loved ones. But just a month before the commission was set to begin, in September 2011, advocates and family members grew concerned that none of the Aboriginal or community groups provided standing at the inquiry would be afforded legal representation. "Standing" is a legal principle that outlines who is entitled to bring a case before the court for a decision. At the time, I interviewed Kasari Govender, then of the West Coast Legal Education and Action Fund (or West Coast LEAF). Govender is someone I have interviewed numerous times over the years, as she is always keen, highly informed, and balanced. In 2019, she became B.C.'s first independent human rights commissioner. West Coast LEAF was granted standing at the commission with its coalition partner, the Ending Violence Association of B.C. She told me then that her organization pulled out of the inquiry in August because they felt the commission had reached a point where it no longer "represented a meaningful exercise." She added, "With its denial to fund legal counsel to Aboriginal and community groups we feel it greatly compromises the inquiry and many groups are feeling pushed out."

Eight of the other groups granted standing at the commission also withdrew from the proceedings after the B.C. government announced it couldn't afford to pay the legal fees for groups participating in the Pickton inquiry. The relatives of the serial killer's victims, however, were provided funding for legal counsel, albeit for one lawyer for many families. Jeannette Corbiere Lavell, then president of the Native Women's Association of Canada, said Indigenous women were caught off guard and insulted when they found out there could be only one independent counsel to ask questions on behalf of all family members. "To us it appears discriminatory and it boils down to the fact that racism and sexism continue to lead the investigation," she told me for a 2011 article.

One lawyer was provided for the attorney general of B.C., three lawyers for the Department of Justice Canada, nine lawyers for the commission counsel, two lawyers for the Vancouver Police Department (VPD), one lawyer for Kim Rossmo (a former VPD criminologist), two lawyers for the Criminal Justice Branch (prosecutors), and one lawyer for the Vancouver Police Union.

Wally Oppal was also frustrated with the decision and what seemed like further bias against some of the most vulnerable members of society. "It would be the height of unfairness to require unrepresented individuals to cross-examine police who are represented by highly qualified counsel," Oppal wrote in an eight-page letter to then attorney general Barry Penner in June of 2011. In it he urged Penner to fund the groups representing the issues and needs of the missing and murdered women.

David Eby, then of the B.C. Civil Liberties Association, was also troubled by what he saw as a lack of parity at the commission. "The government's decision means some of the best lawyers in Vancouver will be working on a limitless retainer to destroy the credibility of Aboriginal women, sex trade workers, and other vulnerable witnesses if they dare criticize the police, and these witnesses won't have their own lawyers to defend them. It's outrageous," he said to me during a phone interview.

In August of 2011, Barry Penner announced his resignation as attorney general. Before his departure, he gave me a statement in an email exchange: "These continue to be challenging economic times, and there are limits to how many millions of taxpayer dollars we can provide to lawyers representing advocacy groups. Funding lawyers for all the participants would add an additional 12 legal teams, effectively tripling the number of taxpayer-funded lawyers at the inquiry."

On his blog, Eby wrote, "In the big picture, setting aside the petty fault-finding exercise, this commission is supposed to be about restoring the faith of B.C.'s Indigenous populations who live on- and off-reserve, restoring the faith of B.C.'s marginalized populations including those with addictions and those who are homeless or otherwise on the fringes, and restoring the faith of the population at large that might be on the edge, that if you go missing the police will look for you as aggressively as they look for anybody else."

Before the commission began, the VPD issued a report called the *Missing Women Investigation Review* looking into how Pickton got away with killing so many women over more than a decade—upwards of forty-nine women, if his jailhouse confession is true. The report detailed eight key findings about why the investigation failed, including poor management and leadership, multijurisdictional issues, and a lack of resources, training, and analysis. While the first key finding of the report outlines that the VPD failed to see a serial killer at work and respond appropriately due to management issues, the sixth finding reads that the VPD "did not cause the failure of the investigation into Pickton because the RCMP had responsibility for that investigation while the VPD focused on other investigative avenues." According to the review, the RCMP asserted authority over the investigation in 1999 but then abandoned it. The report allows that if the VPD investigation had been better managed, the VPD could have brought more pressure to bear on the RCMP to pursue Pickton more vigorously.

When I read the report, what stands out starkly is what is not there. The force does not adequately address the implicit and systemic bias against women who are often thought of as not worthy of care in society. Instead the report says that more police attention is given to "women with more conventional lives than sex trade workers... not because the sex trade workers were considered 'second class' citizens, but because the nature of their lives is much more unpredictable and risky than more conventional lifestyles." It then goes on to describe in detail this unconventionality and how sex trade workers have "little day to day accountability to employers, nuclear families, schools and the like, and are constantly exposed to risk of death by disease, drug overdose or at the hands of any one of the numerous violent men who seek to pick up sex trade workers on any given day." It's another vivid example of victim-blaming. To address accusations of bias against these women, the report says, "Some of the allegations of bias were likely fuelled by administrative delays and difficulties faced by families and friends when reporting sex trade workers as missing."

The VPD report lays out how it failed the women in the late 1990s, but the cracks that would cause the fractured, failed investigation appeared earlier. As early as the mid-1990s, many

Indigenous people, family members and friends of MMIWG, felt they needed to do their own investigations, their own media coverage, and their own collection and dissemination of data. At the time, residents of Vancouver's Downtown Eastside alerted Ernie Crey, the acting president of the United Native Nations, to the disappearances of women from the neighbourhood. Then located at 108 Blood Alley in the Downtown Eastside, the United Native Nations represented the needs of Vancouver's urban Aboriginal population. "Folks were coming up and saying that women who live in the neighbourhood—women in the sex trade, women who were dependent on drugs, and women who were mentally ill—were disappearing," Crey told me for a 2011 article. He spoke out when women began vanishing, and he became an even louder voice for victims' families after his sister Dawn Crey disappeared from the Downtown Eastside in November 2000. Another B.C.-based Indigenous group, the First Nations Summit, was also searching for answers. In 1997, Karen Isaac of the Summit provided police with a list of forty-eight women she described as homicide victims believed to be of Indigenous ancestry from the Downtown Eastside.

After earlier requests submitted to the RCMP had yielded no real answers, Indigenous leaders Chief Joe Mathias, Grand Chief Edward John, and Robert Louie from the First Nations Summit escalated their concerns, writing to then attorney general Ujjal Dosanjh, asking for his intervention in what they called an inadequate investigation of "the brutal murders of fifty-five Aboriginal women in the Vancouver area over the last ten years," with a list of names enclosed. Dosanjh responded to the letter with information about the Provincial Unsolved Homicide Unit and urged the Summit to provide information to Sergeant Honeybourn, who was in charge of the unit. A beat officer who worked in the neighbourhood, Constable Dave Dickson, was assigned to the Provincial Unsolved Homicide Unit in 1997 to look into the list, which police had found was even lengthier than fifty-five names, at seventy-one. Within weeks, he was able to account for all but two of the women. However, nineteen of those were women he thought "appeared to have relocated." No one in the force challenged his findings, but family members continued to be skeptical and critical of the way the VPD seemed to be ignoring concerns about missing loved ones.

According to Crey, a police liaison explained the mystery of the missing women to him by saying they were simply part of a transient population—one day in Calgary, the next in Victoria, on a bus to Vancouver the following morning. It is an assumption that is still heard today and that is often made in error.

But inside the cop shop, one officer believed the women's disappearances were far from easily explained. In the summer of 1998, Detective Constable Lorimer Shenher was assigned to the VPD's Missing Persons Unit to investigate the cases of the missing women in the Downtown Eastside. The department's expectation was that he would locate the women, as was assumed to have been done in the past. The VPD report says he made extraordinary efforts to find the missing women, but he couldn't. Instead he recognized that a serial killer could be at work. Within a week on the job Shenher received a Crime Stoppers tip that implored him to look at a man who at the time was referred to as Willie Pickton, a pig farmer in the Vancouver suburb of Port Coquitlam, who apparently bragged to his friends about being able to dispose of bodies on his property. It was then that Shenher's attempts to convince the RCMP, who had jurisdiction over Port Coquitlam, to investigate Pickton began.

In late August 1998, Shenher reported that nearly all of the cases of missing women in the Downtown Eastside were suspicious, connected, and should be treated as such. In the VPD's review and in Shenher's own book, it is clear that a number of personality and political conflicts clouded the investigation. Shenher's name appears 482 times in the police review report, and it is clear he consistently followed up on tips, pursued solid leads, met with witnesses (even ones that were incredibly hard to track down due to mental health issues and addictions), re-interviewed family members and persons of interest, and broke ground in the missing women's cases. It is also clear that he had difficulties trying to coordinate or correspond with the RCMP.

Shenher said he asked for a multijurisdictional task force in 1999. However, he was told he would only be granted a "working group," which he later called Project Amelia (after the famous brave pilot that went missing), also referred to as the Missing Persons Review Team. The focus of it was to find out where the women "might have gone," he said. "Four of us decided that was crap and worked as much on the Pickton tips as we could because he was our most compelling suspect/person of interest by far and the only one with actual, viable tips," he tells me in 2022. He says he and his colleagues were strictly forbidden from calling the working group a task force, because it would mean they were actively investigating with a significant number of detectives, and, he says, that was patently untrue. The word *Persons* in the name, he says, was swapped out eventually in favour of the word *Women* for political reasons for the review because officers knew they had to acknowledge that it was really only women who were missing. "When the VPD brass first insisted in 1999 on calling it the Missing 'Persons' Review Team when it was established, it was because they explicitly said they didn't want to draw more pressure for resources by acknowledging only women were being targeted until we could prove that was the case, even though all of our missing cases associated were women."

Shenher created a "suspect focused" investigative team that identified Pickton as a prime suspect. Their efforts were hampered by the multijurisdictional aspect of the investigation, as well as other organizational and operational obstacles. When

Pickton was finally arrested in February of 2002, the monster jigsaw puzzle came together and the picture revealed for family members and friends that the investigation was nothing short of a mess. In a CTV article from 2010, Lilliane Beaudoin, whose sister Dianne Rock is suspected to have been one of Pickton's last victims, said she was appalled when she learned that the VPD's and the RCMP's failures to share information amid jurisdictional disputes stalled the investigation for years. "They had enough evidence," she said. "They should have at that time followed up on it and arrested him instead of bickering... over jurisdiction."

When the inquiry started to break down, when it became evident that lawyers representing the voices of the sex workers and Indigenous people would not be funded by the province's taxpayers in the same way police lawyers were, Jeannette Corbiere Lavell called for a national inquiry, one that could effectively examine the violence against Indigenous women and girls, and with their full participation—this time including and supporting advocacy groups and family members whose expertise and knowledge could assist its deliberations. "In cases that involve the ongoing genocide of our people, it's so crucial. I can't wait another one or two years to watch more women go," she told me for a 2011 article. "This summer [2011] alone, 30 women have been reported as missing or murdered."

Despite the Pickton inquiry's flaws, it did underscore bias against the sex workers dealing with poverty and addictions in Vancouver's Downtown Eastside, bias that led to Pickton's ability to kill without interference for years. Commissioner Wally Oppal's 1,448-page final report, *Forsaken: The Report of the Missing Women Commission of Inquiry*, chronicled the police mistakes that allowed dozens of women to be murdered. But like the VPD's report, Oppal's refused to admit something that by 2020 was hard to ignore—systemic racism. In his summary, he says, "I also conclude that there is no evidence of widespread institutional bias in the VPD or the RCMP."

While Pickton did not target Indigenous women specifically, they are overrepresented among his victims most likely because of their vulnerability, which Pickton exploited. Indigenous leaders like Corbiere Lavell saw the Pickton inquiry as just the tip of the iceberg in exploring the vulnerabilities Indigenous women face and how their race strongly influences why they are murdered more than other women in Canada.

"As Aboriginal women, we have the role of leading the next generation. Every woman and every girl is our future, as Native people, and this is why the impact [of the inquiry] is so critical," she told me in the 2011 interview. A robust investigation into what was going wrong in Canada with hundreds missing and murdered was a far-off pipe dream then, but hundreds of family members, motivated by a desire for justice and a need for answers, did not back down from fighting for it.

IN EARLY 2011, when my son was 4 months old, I was invited back to work with CBC again, this time on a TV documentary called 8th Fire. It was lauded for involving Indigenous journalists, accurately portraying Indigenous people, and frankly addressing stereotypes often perpetuated by the media. With my baby on my back, I travelled all over Canada—from Edmonton, to Prince Rupert, to Toronto—and interviewed Indigenous people from Saik'uz to Enoch to Gitlaxt'aamiks. It was a meaningful and fulfilling experience that would set the tone for much of my career that followed.

As the shooting of the doc neared an end, I was offered a TV reporting job in Yellowknife. Despite being deeply homesick in a land of strangers, mommying solo, and working full time, I stayed there with my son for almost four long years. It was amazing to witness Indigenous journalists broadcasting in several of their own languages, including a full television program called *Igalaaq*, spoken only in Inuktitut. During my stint there, I covered the Idle No More movement, which was spurred by Prime Minister Stephen Harper's decision to axe water protection laws in Canada under Bill C-45. I did national live hits with a Canada Goose parka on and icicles growing from my eyelashes. It was then I started to see the winds change direction within the media. CBC was covering Idle No More and other Indigenous stories through the eyes of Indigenous reporters interviewing Indigenous people. Instead of the one Chief or the one professor, I was starting to see everyday Indigenous people—students, parents, Elders, lawyers, and activists— being interviewed about the importance of land and water.

In 2014, on the heels of some incredible experiences, I made my way to Toronto, where Massey College had awarded me the prestigious William Southam Journalism Fellowship. I was the first known Indigenous person in Canada to take part in the fellowship in its then fifty-two-year existence. We travelled to Finland, Berlin, and Cuba, attended fancy galas, and frequented private dinner clubs. While it was fun and enlightening, it was also hard. When the college held its annual Sir John A. Macdonald Day celebration, students and fellows stood at a podium and read aloud quotes from the first prime minister of Canada, including those that referred to Indigenous people as savages. The other four journalism fellows, including three white female journalists, were deeply uneducated when it came to Indigenous people in Canada, often asking me harmful questions such as "Why did your people not want to be assimilated?" When we travelled to other countries, the white journalists would tell locals that what I said about my Gitxsan people hunting and fishing did not accurately characterize all of Canada, which minimized my people's experience and made me feel as if I didn't represent the same country they did. The other fellows' lack of understanding about me or about any Indigenous cultures was often painful. Despite the ignorance, I took my studies seriously and learned a lot. But it was hard to focus. The conversations I had in the fellowship were constant reminders of the misunderstanding, indifference, and discrimination that Canadian politicians and the public had toward Indigenous women and girls and the violence we experience.

During my time in the fellowship, at the end of 2014, in a sit-down interview with Peter Mansbridge, Conservative prime minister Stephen Harper was asked about the plausibility of a national inquiry into MMIWG. Mansbridge probed, "There seems to be some indication that your government may be at least considering some form of formal inquest or inquiry or investigation." Harper curtly expressed his feelings. "Um, it, it isn't really high on our radar, to be honest, Peter," Harper answered. "You know, our ministers will continue to dialogue with those who are concerned about this. They're studying it. But we have an awful lot of studies and information on the phenomenon and an awful good indication of what the record is in terms of investigation and prevention of these sorts of things," he added. Harper went on to say that his government had created strong laws to prevent and punish criminal activity, particularly when it came to family violence.

Not long before that interview, in the summer of 2014, in response to 15-year-old Tina Fontaine's slaying and a renewed call for a national inquiry, Harper reiterated his line that, "first and foremost," crimes should be dealt with by police. "I think we should not view this as sociological phenomenon," Harper infamously stated. He was refusing to acknowledge the root or systemic causes of violence against Indigenous women and our marginalization, in large part a result of colonization. He saw violence against us solely as a crime without a historical origin. In fact, at a press conference in Pittsburgh, where it was announced that Canada would be hosting the next G20 meeting in 2010, Harper declared that in Canada "we also have

no history of colonialism." The statement did not land well in
Indigenous country.

Indigenous families across the country were also focused
on crime and policing, but for different reasons than Harper.
Relatives of MMIWG wanted their loved ones' cases thoroughly
investigated, especially in situations where police, investigators,
and the justice system had fallen short. The Missing Women
Commission of Inquiry looked at some of the systemic issues,
such as limited and outdated policing systems and inadequate
resources, and concluded that police had failed the missing
women. Now families wanted more—to find out not just how
and why women were disappearing and being murdered at
alarming rates, but how the people who murdered them were
being left to go free or let off, sometimes without even a slap on
the wrist.

WHEN THE NEW LIBERAL GOVERNMENT was elected in the
fall of 2015, it brought with it promises for a new era, one in
which society would finally address the horrible living conditions for Indigenous people, including the limited access
to safe drinking water in remote communities and an even
more limited access to safety for Indigenous women and girls.
The National Inquiry into Missing and Murdered Indigenous
Women and Girls, first announced by Minister of Indigenous
and Northern Affairs Carolyn Bennett, Minister of Justice Jody
Wilson-Raybould, and Minister of Status of Women Patty
Hajdu in December 2015, was met with shock, emotion, and
much fanfare from media outlets across Canada.

Lorelei Williams, an Indigenous woman whose cousin
Tanya Holyk's DNA was found on the Pickton farm, and whose
aunty Belinda Williams is still missing forty-five years after she
disappeared, expressed her joy about the inquiry on CBC TV
after the announcement. "I feel emotional, I can't believe this is
actually happening," she said, wiping the tears from her face.

In August of 2016, Ottawa launched the $53.8 million independent inquiry and announced its lead commissioner, former judge Marion Buller, and four other commissioners: Michèle Audette, Brian Eyolfson, Marilyn Poitras, and Qajaq Robinson. Their final task would be to publish a report that outlined the inquiry's findings and recommendations. This process would give family members the chance to heal and be heard, Prime Minister Justin Trudeau told reporters at the time. It was an emotional moment, and a move thousands of family members across the country lauded.

But the lead-up to the national inquiry was rocky. The federal government's Department of Indigenous and Northern Affairs, then led by Minister Carolyn Bennett, held consultation meetings (information sessions) with Indigenous family members across Canada to determine what they wanted from the inquiry. And in many ways, these meetings were problematic.

Even before the meetings, Indigenous women and family members said the inquiry needed to put families first and operate in a trauma-informed and culturally safe way—something they didn't feel was happening at the beginning. Family members also talked about the importance of these meetings being in their own communities, with their Elders, family members, ancestors, and culture present. But in every province, pre-inquiry meetings were held in ballrooms of fancy hotels and government offices rather than in Indigenous community spaces.

Indigenous family members also critiqued these meetings for not being culturally specific. They were either bureaucratic and cultureless, or else "pan-Indian"—treating Indigenous cultures as homogeneous and relying on easy cultural nods such as smudging or using the four directions (which are valued and sacred but not used by all Peoples, especially on the west coast). I was the only journalist invited by family members to three pre-inquiry meetings in Vancouver—one at the Department of Indigenous and Northern Affairs headquarters, another at an upscale hotel, and a third at a massive conference room with Persian rugs and crystal chandeliers. In that one, more than one hundred family members sat in a large circle sharing their stories of how their loved ones disappeared or were murdered and how the loss had impacted them. For family members who were in the city only rarely and who were unused to being put on the spot to share in front of dozens of people, it must have been intimidating and hard, emotionally, mentally, and spiritually. One Elder stood off to the side to help those who were feeling retraumatized. He brushed them with cedar boughs if they asked and took them to a room so they could decompress after unearthing such big emotions. I shuddered at the number of times family members left in tears, shaken from telling their stories. Carolyn Bennett criss-crossed the country for numerous meetings like this, from Nunavut to Toronto, to hear about the grief, frustration, and hurt of those who had lost daughters, mothers, sisters, aunties, grandmothers, and granddaughters.

In one pre-inquiry meeting at the Pinnacle Hotel on January 13, 2016, I sat quietly on the wall-to-wall red carpet, legs neatly tucked against my chest and with my notebook, computer, and recorder beside me, blogging for CBC about what I was witnessing. To the far left of me sat Jody Wilson-Raybould flanked by Carolyn Bennett and Patty Hajdu. I took a picture of them, feeling awkward, knowing media was not permitted to be there, but knowing since I was invited by women I worked with in the Downtown Eastside who trusted me, I had to take on that responsibility to be a witness and report with integrity on all the facts presented at this event. Directly in front of me were more than one hundred people sitting on plastic folding chairs arranged in a circle, facing one woman in the centre who was there to facilitate the meeting. On a flip chart, she wrote quickly with a felt marker: "When it is done, what do you want the national inquiry to look like?" I took a picture of it, one that I still have and find hard to look at. It seems brash and poorly thought out to put the pressure of determining the inquiry's end goal on a large group of people facing very serious levels of trauma.

And as it turned out, making an inquiry from scratch was not what the family members talked about. They spoke of what they knew best and have spoken about most often—their own stories. It made me think: maybe there was a missed step here. Instead, the burden of creating a national inquiry was placed on people without any support; they had to decipher what would work best within the parameters of a limited budget, without an assistant to create briefings, and without an hourly wage— all things that government representatives would have been provided for the same tasks. It made me wonder if this was a performative exercise rather than a genuine one where family members' perspectives were being heard and put into action. For the family members, who wanted with all their hearts to make sure the inquiry was successful, it was a daunting, anxiety-provoking process. And while the federal government was armed with technical staff, like assistants who were paid a salary to run the inquiry, many family members weren't provided the funding to take time away from work and travel to the city to attend.

As I sat there on the carpet, I thought, well, what *should* the inquiry look like? I assumed the facilitator would provide examples. Would it look like the Royal Commission on Aboriginal Peoples, or the Truth and Reconciliation Commission, or the Aboriginal Justice Inquiry of Manitoba that was based in part on the horrific death of Helen Betty Osborne? But these were not questions the facilitator brought up. Grieving families were simply asked: What should we do? They were not given technical assistance to perform research, nor resources to learn about other inquiries themselves—they were just given a space to contribute based on their own experiences.

When the terms of reference (the scope and limitations) of the inquiry were leaked to the Aboriginal Peoples Television Network in the summer of 2016, weeks before they were officially released, families spoke to reporters about their fears of how the inquiry would unfold, some expressing outrage that they were not included in the design process. Many were furious that the final terms of reference did not include the words "police," "policing," or "justice system." They feared that this inquiry would mimic the Oppal inquiry, the one that many family members and their lawyers had walked out of in protest, in essence repeating history for them. As this new inquiry was kicking off, many of the recommendations of the Oppal inquiry had still not been implemented.

The failure of Oppal's Missing Women Commission of Inquiry is one reason some questioned the validity and purpose of a federal inquiry into the almost 1,200 known MMIWG in Canada. Many say the commission failed to get to the bottom of the question it was meant to answer: Why and how did a serial killer manage to operate freely without fear of repercussions for over a decade? The new question could be: Could a national inquiry do any better if it was funded by the same federal government—regardless of who was in power—that had neglected the issues for years before?

If the apprehension about the terms of reference was foreshadowing how the inquiry would play out, it was almost doomed. While commissioners touted a "family first" inquiry, family members criticized them for making decisions without their inclusion. Then, staffing issues would put more family members, and the public in general, on edge. First, commissioners fired their communications director just over two months after he was hired. Michael Hutchinson, a Cree man and a former anchor with the Aboriginal Peoples Television Network, with an impressive CV related to similar commissions, let the public know of his departure from his role via a cheeky-yet-forlorn Facebook post: "Is it ironic that I found my missing cousin one weekend, and then lost my job at the Missing Women and Girls Inquiry the next? Lol." While Hutchinson and I had many off-the-record conversations about why he left, I respected his request not to report what he told me. He did say, on record, that he was told if he spoke to the media it could lead to his being sued for defamation by those at the national inquiry. Then, four months later, the interim communications director, Sue Montgomery, resigned. In Twitter messages, the former *Montreal Gazette* reporter described to me her frustration with the lack of transparency in the inquiry. These first two departures were a preview of the journey the inquiry would take over the short term, and they were followed by several others, including high-profile Indigenous leader and manager of community relations Tanya Kappo, director of operations Chantale Courcy, and the inquiry's first executive director, Michèle Moreau. None of them were able to talk publicly about their departures.

From its start until it wrapped up, the inquiry lost at least twenty people from firings, layoffs, and resignations. Included in the resignations was one of the commissioners, Métis lawyer Marilyn Poitras. In her public statement and in interviews, she pointed to what she called a "colonial" process.

One of the few press conferences by Chief Commissioner Marion Buller was held at UBC's First Nations House of Learning. It is a twenty-five-minute drive or an hour-long bus ride from Vancouver's Downtown Eastside. While it is a beautiful building, I found it an odd place to hold a press conference for this inquiry—on a student campus, near Vancouver's most expensive neighbourhoods, and far away from where vulnerable Indigenous women were most likely to go missing. Buller stood in front of a number of mics on a small stage and, after a short comment on the status of the inquiry, took reporters' questions. Grappling with the reality that this inquiry, something I had heard Indigenous women like Buller praise, was now somewhat in shambles, I reluctantly pressed her for answers to why the commission was losing so many people. "What is going on inside the inquiry?" I asked. "We are told there are more troubles brewing, with a tug-of-war between health and legal departments." Buller stiffly answered that she believed that was not true and insisted several times, despite the numerous questions from reporters, that there were no problems internally with leadership.

Not long after the disappointing press conference, family members, advocates, and activists called on the inquiry to "reset," or stop and reconsider whether the right people were in positions of power—something the Truth and Reconciliation Commission had to do when it also started to unravel. In 2008, that commission's original chief commissioner, Justice Harry S. LaForme, resigned, citing a power struggle and unreconcil-able differences regarding the function of the commission. The two other commissioners, Claudette Dumont-Smith and Jane Brewin Morley, resigned in January 2009 citing similar concerns. Less than a year later, Murray Sinclair was appointed to replace LaForme as chief commissioner of the Truth and Reconciliation Commission, with Marie Wilson and Wilton Littlechild to replace commissioners Dumont-Smith and Mor-ley. The move to reset worked strongly in favour of the residen-tial school survivors who wanted to see truth and justice but also healing.

But Buller brushed off those calls to reset and pushed for-ward, letting the public know they were proceeding with the commission at "lightning speed." Despite the apparent dysfunc-tion, it was hard for many, including me, to let go of the hope that the inquiry first promised: to give family members some answers to why their loved ones, Indigenous women and girls, went missing or were murdered far more than non-Indigenous women in Canada, and why little seemed to be done in the courts. So while observers were worried (and angry) about what was going on inside the inquiry, they were still hopeful that it would bring the family members a measure of the justice they had craved and deserved for so long.

On May 30, 2017, I covered the first story heard at the first inquiry hearing, held in Whitehorse, Yukon, on the murder of Mary Johns. At press conferences before the hearing, Buller told us reporters that this would not look like other hearings; that it would look and feel less colonial. When we asked about what that meant, she said the hearings would be held in a tent, which she said was more traditional. Though Buller refuted this, another source told me that, in actuality, the original hearing venue's roof had caved in and the next best option was already booked, so they rented tents in desperation to let the "show go on." Still, as I watched the hearings in Whitehorse for two days, I realized just how powerful the stories people told were. This was an important if not essential event, not just because family members were finally given a space to share their truths, but also because it was a chance for the rest of Canada to listen. Mary Johns's story resonated with me in terms of how it mirrored so many other stories of MMIWG.

Johns's sister-in-law Frances Neumann and Neumann's daughter Tracy Camilleri testified about her murder, telling the heartbreaking story of how the 29-year-old was found dead in serial killer Gilbert Jordan's barbershop in Vancouver in 1982. The "boozing barber" was linked to the deaths of several other women, many of them Indigenous (including Mary Johnson, Barbara Paul, Patricia Thomas, Patricia Andrew, and Vera Harry). The story, like so many others I'd written about, was a slap in the face because of how, for years, Jordan was able to get away with his many murders of Indigenous women. Neumann and Camilleri's telling of Mary's story included the intergenerational effects of her murder on her son, who ended up first in prison, and then living in the Downtown Eastside. This is a story that had received very little media attention, and it was indeed the inquiry that brought it into the public eye. Family members had pinned their hopes for justice on the inquiry, and I could see, at least in this case, just how the inquiry was giving some of them faith in the process—that the truth, buried for years, would finally come out.

But by the summer of 2017, family members' feelings about the inquiry shifted to frustration again as numerous hearing dates were delayed. The communications director at the time, Bernée Bolton, said these alterations were all choices made by the family members, something I was not able to confirm. But as it had done from the start, the inquiry rolled forward, focused on meeting its target to present a final report by 2019.

The next round of hearings for the National Inquiry into Missing and Murdered Indigenous Women and Girls took place in September 2017 in Smithers, B.C., close to the Highway of Tears, where Ramona Wilson, Tamara Chipman, and dozens of other women and girls had gone missing or been murdered. For the hearing, Chipman's aunt Gladys Radek completed what she said would be her seventh and final walk: a 350-kilometre journey from Prince Rupert to Smithers, at the end of which she would testify at the hearings. I asked her if it was her last walk because the inquiry, something she had been fighting for since 2008, was finally happening. "No," she told me. "My health started to fail... osteoporosis and also had quadruple bypass surgery after my heart attack in December 2015." Still, she felt that after years of walks to the House of Commons, up and down the highways, and through the Downtown Eastside, all pushing for this national inquiry—here it finally was. But for Gladys and other family members, the staff issues, delays, and general dysfunction of the inquiry meant that rather than the moment of closure they'd been anticipating, they were experiencing mixed emotions.

What frustrated many family members the most was how long it had taken the federal government to hold the national inquiry. Indigenous family members, advocates, and survivors had been requesting a national inquiry since at least 2006, starting with those organizing the Highway of Tears Symposium. But there were larger issues too. "You can't unravel genocide in two years," Gladys told the CBC as the Smithers hearing was gearing up. She was right: poverty, racism, and hundreds of years of colonialism are challenging issues to articulate, never mind address. It's hard to get non-Indigenous Canadians to even believe that colonial violence exists, let alone act on it to create safety and equality for Indigenous women, girls, and two-spirit people. The inquiry would not be able to solve all the problems that contribute to the oppression of, and denial of rights to, Canada's most vulnerable.

I ATTENDED THE FINAL community hearings held in the Vancouver suburb of Richmond, B.C., in April 2018. I was told by another source inside the inquiry that commissioners waited until later in the process, when there would be less media attention, to hold the hearing in the Vancouver area because they felt it could be "explosive" in terms of any criticism of the process or those in charge of it. This made sense given that family members and advocates of MMIWG had been highly vocal and critical about the national inquiry. Vancouver was the home of the failed Pickton inquiry, the origin of the Women's Memorial March, and the place where women often rallied and spoke about the Highway of Tears—not to mention the largest city in the province with the highest number of missing people in the country. Here, a lot of eyes were on the inquiry, scrutinizing its work. And it turned out to be good strategy because by the time of the Richmond hearings, the dust had settled from the shakeup over staffing issues and critiques around the inquiry's colonial process. But now other issues were slowly surfacing. Family members were reaching out to me and speaking out on social media to say they felt the inquiry was not trauma informed, something I had noticed was lacking at the pre-inquiry meetings. Most of the concerns were about after-care—for example, that counselling funds promised to family members were either not provided, or not provided in a timely manner after what was in some cases hours of gruelling testimony that took apart the most traumatic parts of their lives, section by section, recounting violence and abuse in residential school, by foster parents, and by authorities.

So at the hearing in Richmond, I had this critique on my mind as I scanned the large ballroom lined with plastic chairs on the main floor of the Sheraton Hotel, one of several rooms where hearings were held. As I was listening to testimony, I asked myself questions: Is this trauma informed? Are the family members being cared for? Is this culturally informed? Is this going to lead to what the family members have fought for? I noticed a large number of volunteers in purple T-shirts responding immediately to family members and observers who were visibly upset or triggered by what they were saying or hearing. When a family member or survivor testified, they were surrounded by numerous people—commissioners, someone asking the questions, Elders, and loved ones—and often, nearby, there were spiritual and emotional helpers, tissues, and baskets of sage, cedar, sweetgrass, and other medicines.

When I started then to take note of my own role, my observations were both comforting and uncomfortable. I immediately noticed how close I was to these stories and this community compared to other reporters I saw lounging on couches outside of hearing rooms or frantically taking notes at the back of the room. I sat beside family members, hugged them, listened to them without recording, and put my arm around their shoulders while they cried. These were family members

I had worked with in the Downtown Eastside, who were part of my own Vancouver urban Indigenous community, Elders I respected and had close relationships with, and local cultural leaders I had learned from throughout my entire life—not just as a journalist, but as a co-worker or friend. As an Indigenous journalist, throughout my career I'd often seen other journalists so removed from Indigenous communities that there was no way for them to fully understand the correlation between colonization and violence against Indigenous women today. I heard journalists sharing victim narratives about Indigenous women, insinuating that they were benefiting monetarily from sharing their stories, and rejecting the notion that any institution in Canada had worked to destroy Indigenous people, their culture, and their rights. All this was going through my mind as I saw and listened to Indigenous women sharing their heart-wrenching stories at the hearing of the national inquiry. I was also reflecting on all that had unfolded that year as I reported on the inquiry from the beginning—all the follies, and all the mistakes and mishaps.

I listened as a Mi'kmaq, Métis, and Cree two-spirit grandmother named Blu told her story. Beside her sat a commissioner, and another statement gatherer gently asked her sensitive questions about her life and the impacts of systemic racism and violence, often during very tender years as a child, teen, and young woman. Much of her testimony was about how the child-welfare system tore apart her family and led to the vulnerability she experienced as a young person. I sat beside a Gitxsan Elder I knew, who said she didn't recognize me at first. My look had changed since my ponytailed, makeupless days when we worked together in the Downtown Eastside. She started to cry as she listened to the testimony, and then she quietly disclosed to me that she was a survivor of Robert Pickton but was too ashamed to tell anyone. My heart felt as if someone had pulled the plug on it; my throat closed and my stomach churned. She said she felt stupid that she had gone with Pickton in the first place, and because of her shame she had never told anyone until that moment. I just wanted to hug her forever. Over the years she'd taught me about what it means to be a good Gitxsan Elder, to be kind, patient, and loving. Now, hearing of this extreme violence she'd hid for so long, I could feel the heaviness of her pain.

The full weight of the hearings hit me then. They were not just about addressing the hundreds or thousands of missing and murdered Indigenous women in Canada, but an opportunity for the truth to finally be heard and for survivors and family members to feel believed and validated. In turn, the blame could shift away from the victims to those who committed the violence. This was a place where Indigenous women and girls who were normally too afraid and too ashamed to speak out could sit in a safe space—their stories would not be questioned in a way that suggested they were exaggerated or untrue, but rather, they would be acknowledged as their truth. This may not seem huge to some, but as an Indigenous woman who has shared my own truth and spent decades not being believed, and who has reported on others in similar situations, it's incredible progress to be able to tell our truth on the public record. It is so very healing to be seen.

And the hearings at the national inquiry were just as important to non-Indigenous people witnessing or covering them. One of my non-Indigenous camera operators told me about his experience being the videographer for the hearing. While he had accompanied me to many interviews with Indigenous people on similar topics, he told me witnessing the stories shared in this format was "life changing." "I had no idea about any of this, Ange," he told me back at the office. "No idea." Hearing this made me realize the inquiry was allowing non-Indigenous people to really grasp the impacts of colonial violence by learning from the people who were hit the hardest by it.

During the hearing, my own separate worlds often collided, and sometimes it was uncomfortable. I saw Indigenous women I had worked with in the Downtown Eastside who seemed disappointed to see my media badge hanging around my neck. It was a reminder of just how little trust many Indigenous people still have in journalists, even in one they know personally. I also remember having to check behind my back as I hugged a family member, making sure that my colleague who was also covering the hearing would not see me and report me to bosses as being biased. This is something that has happened to me several times, starting in 2016 when I became a more visible CBC personality and continuing often until 2020, when the world started to watch how the media and other institutions treat employees who are Black, Indigenous, and people of colour.

AS THE HEARING came to a close, I could feel my brain pulsating like a living drum, beating and thumping. I left the hotel feeling a tremendous weight, a responsibility to do family members justice with my journalism on a topic the media had failed at as an institution for years, and one it often continues to fail at today. One of the most important achievements of the inquiry for family members like Gladys, and for Chief Commissioner Marion Buller, was that finally the word *genocide* was being used to describe, in part, what has happened to Indigenous people, particularly women and girls, in Canada.

And starkly, it was what many journalists and members of the public criticized. They said that the word *genocide* shouldn't be used in connection with the high rates of MMIWG. According to the United Nations, the definition of genocide includes: killing members of the group; causing serious bodily or mental harm to members of the group; deliberately inflicting on the group conditions of life calculated to bring about its physical destruction in whole or in part; imposing measures intended to prevent births within the group; or forcibly transferring children of the group to another group. Despite the fact that Indigenous children were forced out of their Indigenous communities and involuntarily placed into schools where they could only speak English; despite the fact that at these schools they were beaten, tortured, sexually abused, and even killed; and despite both historical and recent forced or coerced sterilization of Indigenous women, journalists mocked the claim. CBC journalist Evan Dyer's article titled "What Does It Mean to Call Canada's Treatment of Indigenous Women a 'Genocide'?" featured, at length, Roméo Dallaire's and Irwin Cotler's opinions on why *genocide* isn't the right term, and only two sentences from Marion Buller about why it is. It concludes by explaining how using the term *genocide* will be harmful to Canada. It does not read like a neutral article, even though the CBC has defended the article, saying that it "sought to explain the historical and international significance of the word genocide" and that "the piece included multiple perspectives for and against its use." Articles like this were a signal to me and others that the media's habit of silencing and dismissing Indigenous people had not changed.

Still, those who have kept on going, despite the lack of care from the media, governments, police, and the public, give me hope. Gladys is one of those; over the years she has been a teacher, a leader, and an inspiration to many.

She, among hundreds, attended the national inquiry's closing ceremony on June 3, 2019, where commissioners presented their final report. It revealed that persistent and deliberate human and Indigenous rights violations are behind Canada's high rates of violence against Indigenous women, girls, and 2SLGBTQQIA people. It also says that "the thousands of truths shared before the National Inquiry reinforce the existence of acts of genocide against Indigenous women, girls, and 2SLGBTQQIA people." The report was presented to federal officials at the Canadian Museum of History in Gatineau, Quebec. There, Gladys had something to say. She walked up to Prime Minister Justin Trudeau, who held the inquiry's final report, and asked him to come out to see her Toyota hatchback that was parked out front, her "war pony" plastered with photos of the missing and murdered. Trudeau, who was involved in the closing ceremonies, shook his head. He would soon be on his way to catch a flight to Vancouver for a global women's conference. Like times before, Gladys and other Indigenous people would say they felt Trudeau's leadership resembled that of governments of the past: words around "reconciliation" were solely performative. It would have been something to have the prime minister make a more personal acknowledgement of Indigenous women and all their years of fighting. But like so many disappointments Gladys had seen, this one didn't stop her or hundreds of other family members who still continue on their search for justice.

When I followed up with her in 2021 to ask how she felt about the inquiry, two years later, Gladys told me that the staff did the best with what they had. The outcome—that it was able to call what has happened to missing and murdered Indigenous women, girls, and two-spirit people a genocide—was what she'd been fighting for all these years.

9

'Mnsaksit gilelix, *going on top*

RISING ABOVE

IT'S A SUNNY FALL DAY, but unmistakably the winter weaves its way through the wind. The sun is reflected in tiny little sparkles off the muddy Red River in Winnipeg, Manitoba. With this serene view in the distance, a mass of oak leaves under my feet, I am waiting for a group of searchers to arrive.

The land that surrounds this body of water has deep history rooted in Anishinaabe, Cree, Métis, and Dakota cultures, stories, and movements over thousands of years. As Métis author and lawyer Jean Teillet says in her book *The North-West Is Our Mother*, the region "was more of a perspective than a geographic place with fixed boundaries." She speaks of the area once being an "endless stretch of land with delicious food, clean water and rich resources." She says lii vyeu, or "the old ones," left little physical evidence behind as they walked softly on the land and took what they needed to sustain their communities. Just like my Gitxsan people and the Sḵwx̱wú7mesh I grew close to, the Indigenous people of this land used the lakes and rivers as

highways to travel for hunting and fishing, ceremony and feast-
ing. The prairie territory I am standing on was abundant with
great herds of buffalo; the boreal forest also provided shelter,
water, wood, fish, and meat. And like other Indigenous lands, the
land the Red River flows through is thick with a colonial history and rife with rebellion and battles that are spoken keenly
of today. Just like my Gitxsan people in our lands, the Anishinaabe, the Cree, the Métis, and the Dakota are still here, rich in
culture and resistance.

It was a foreign land to me, far from the mountains and the
ocean, the salmon, and the teachings I grew up with. Still, I was
back where I first found out I'd be a mom, where I'd shift from
a transient young adult to someone who was on an unmistak-
able trajectory: to tell stories of Indigenous people with all the
care and love they deserved. That new path meshed inextricably
with motherhood as I strived to share with my little boy that
we as Indigenous people matter, that Indigenous women like
his mom are loved, and that we will never give up. And it was
my son (and the accident that affected my lungs) that landed
me smack on this track. I now had more than myself to take
care of. My responsibility to set an example for future generations was inescapable now. And Namawan was now witness to
everything I was trying to accomplish.

My managing editor at CBC Yellowknife was kind enough to
let me transfer the last bit of my contract to the Winnipeg loca-
tion as I waited for work to open up in Vancouver, after I completed my fellowship. I'd had a rough go in Yellowknife, and at
least in Winnipeg, my son could have the comfort of his paternal family. Still, moving from Toronto, the largest, most metropolitan city in Canada, to a much smaller city that had been
called the country's "homicide capital" and the "most racist city
in Canada" was another hard turn. My son was entering kin-
dergarten for the second time, since the starting age differed
between the two provinces, and I would go back to television

reporting in a busy (and known to be dramatic) newsroom. But there in Winnipeg, in late 2015, I met some of the most creative, determined, and unwavering family members of missing and murdered Indigenous women and girls (MMIWG). One of them was an Anishinaabe and Métis woman named Bernadette Smith, who, disillusioned by police efforts to find her sister and horrified when the body of 15-year-old Tina Fontaine was pulled out of the Red River, took matters into her own hands. In hopes of finding justice for her own family and others who were devastated by not knowing what happened to their loved ones, she cofounded Drag the Red, a group that coordinates volunteers searching the Red River for the remains of missing people.

Smith's sister Claudette Osborne-Tyo was a 21-year-old mother of four when she vanished. She was last seen at Winnipeg's Lincoln Motor Hotel, now called Four Crowns Inn, on McPhillips Street, and after making a number of calls on various pay phones, made her last call at Selkirk Avenue and King Street on July 25, 2008. Fifteen days earlier she'd given birth to her fourth child. Smith says she was disappointed with how police handled her sister's disappearance. It was ten days before they even started to investigate. Osborne-Tyo had made a call had made a call on July 24 to her sister Tina Osborne and left a message saying she needed a ride home because she was in bad company. But Tina didn't get the message until she added minutes to her phone, two days later. Even after that evidence, Smith says, she needed to get political and put pressure on police to act. "My sister had a criminal record, she was on the street, she was Aboriginal, and she was a woman. She had all these things against her," she tells me in an interview in Winnipeg for a 2015 article. Osborne-Tyo's body has never been found. "My sister has been missing for years. We have no answers," Smith says. The Winnipeg Police Service's Project Devote—an integrated task force made up of Winnipeg police and the RCMP—was investigating the case, and she says she spoke to its officers about once a month, but the family had heard of no new information since 2010.

Project Devote launched in 2011 and was responsible for twenty-eight cold cases: eight missing persons and twenty homicide victims. However, it didn't have much success and in nine years closed only one case—that of Myrna Letandre, whose remains took years to be discovered in 2013 in a rooming house in Winnipeg after she went missing (in spite of family's attempts at the time of the disappearance to alert the police to the person who was eventually convicted). In the spring of 2020, Winnipeg police announced it was shutting down Project Devote and starting a new project. It would operate more like a community centre, with the aim of finding vulnerable people who they said had "high-risk lifestyles" before they went missing. Investigators would work closely with grassroots community groups that provided services to Indigenous women and youth.

Bernadette Smith and other Indigenous women welcomed the project, noting that a focus on working in collaboration with Indigenous families to "ensure vulnerable Indigenous women and girls are not exploited is incredibly important," as she told the CBC in 2020. "These are all good steps towards reconciliation, building relationships and hopefully bringing answers to families. There is more work to do, but this is a move in the right direction."

Smith, like many others across Canada, was stunned by the news in 2014 that 15-year-old Tina Fontaine's body had been found at the bottom of the Red River, wrapped in a duvet cover and plastic and weighted down by rocks. Learning about her death while I was in Toronto terrified me. Tina's death reignited calls for a national inquiry, calls that were instrumental in finally making it happen. But when I moved to Winnipeg, the reality of this little girl, discarded into the river, became all the more devastating.

On one of my walks through our North End Winnipeg neighbourhood near the Alexander Docks, I came across a striking memorial. Directly in front of me was draped red cloth curling around a square alcove in a chain-link fence. White wooden chairs with pillows sat carefully placed around cement blocks that worked as shelves for a stuffed yellow Minion, a Barbie doll, and rocks painted green and purple with the words *family*, *joy*, *play*, *home*, and *live* on them. Reading the word *live* made my stomach sink as I realized it was a memorial for Tina Fontaine, the girl who was barely beginning her youth when she died. I also knew that this little girl may have been related to my son—his dad's family are, like Tina, from the Sagkeeng community and related to the Fontaines. It was another reminder of how connected so many of us Indigenous people in Canada are to each other, and how much more cutting these brutal deaths are to us.

Tina was in and out of government care from the time she was an infant as her parents struggled with trauma. Her young mother also grew up in foster care. While Tina had a period of stability with her great-aunt Thelma Favel in Powerview–Pine Falls (next to Sagkeeng First Nation), all of that changed for her in 2011, at 12 years old, when she learned that her father had been beaten to death by two men. Tina's life started to fall apart: she skipped school and frequently ran away from home as her aunt pleaded with her to get help. A 2019 report authored by the Manitoba Advocate for Children and Youth said victim services failed to set up the counselling that Tina needed. "In the nearly three years of involvement since the homicide death of Tina's father, victim services neither met directly with Tina nor did they arrange a single counselling session for her to help her manage her loss and grief," the report says. In April 2014, concerned that Tina was experimenting with drugs and speaking with adult men on the internet, Favel asked Manitoba's Child and Family Services to help. The only options available were hotels and temporary shelters. In the three weeks before she disappeared on August 8, Tina was reported missing four times.

Outrage over her death rippled across the country. As I refresh my memory with her story now, looking at all the murals of her, thinking about the memorials and all the online tributes that have been posted, I can't help but think: Where was all that support, all that love, all that care, all that attention for her, before she died? When we see an Indigenous girl struggling in the school system, on the street, and in other public spaces, what goes through our minds? Rarely do people know how to help. And a large part of the problem is the lack of resources available—including counselling (and help setting it up and getting to it), support for parents who are struggling (including income support, housing, and counselling), and adequate supportive housing for teens and young adults. But another part of the problem is the way the public has been trained socially and psychologically to blame Indigenous girls and women for their struggles and deaths, rather than understanding the impact and the depths of colonization.

When Raymond Cormier, 57, was acquitted by a jury of the second-degree murder of Tina in February 2018, there was more than outrage; there was fury, deep sadness, and emptiness. Cormier did not have to answer any questions in court, but seeing him on a CBC segment talking about how he gave her drugs and how Tina suggested to him that she wanted "to play" when she asked him for a place to stay when she was homeless makes me feel sick to my stomach. She was a child facing multiple traumas, she was in government care, she had little family, she was in deep grief, she was extremely vulnerable—yet this man positioned himself as a victim of a child's desire. In 2019, the Winnipeg police told the CBC that while her case is still open, they are not currently pursuing any suspects.

AFTER THE DISCOVERY of Tina's body, family members of MMIWG began searching the river and the shore relentlessly for other remains or any other evidence. Tina's was one of seven bodies that were pulled out of the Red River in 2014. Bernadette Smith believes that Drag the Red efforts contributed to four of them being found.

On that sunny but chilly fall day in 2015, I meet up with Smith on one of her Drag the Red searches. We meet at St. John's Park overlooking the Red River, where she and several others are lifting equipment out of a truck bed, including rakes and poles. Several metal bars with hooks and chains, which they normally drop into the river from their boat to pull up possible remains, stay in the truck. She shows me the contraption, mentioning that the boat they usually use is broken; dragging all kinds of materials from the river is hard on the boat, and the upkeep is expensive. Today will be a ground search, she says, since the boat is out of commission.

As we wait for others to arrive, Smith and I shuffle through brown and yellow leaves in the park and arrive at a sheltered bank of picnic tables where we sit. She tells me how she grew up there, in the North End, explaining how they used to take a piece of cardboard as a float to swim across the river. Like other families, they also used to fish from the Red River for catfish, walleye, and northern pike. My own son's huge Anishinaabe family have all lived in this neighbourhood for years, since they relocated from their Sagkeeng community. It can be a rough neighbourhood, but it can also be a creative hub where people hold workshops on permaculture and food security, paint murals, and teach youth life skills. Some see and experience the North End today as violent and poor. Others, though, including Smith and friends of mine, see and experience it as tight-knit, community oriented, creative, and resilient.

Today the Red River is much different than when Smith's family fished there in the 1970s. Car parts are thrown in the river and strewn along the bank, as are old cell phones, diapers, and, heartbreakingly, sometimes body parts of human beings. When Fontaine's body was found, Smith decided to post on her Facebook that the Red needed to be dragged. "It was really to guilt the police into action, but they never did anything, they said they needed evidence to search and wouldn't do anything until we had evidence." From the picnic table where we are sitting, Smith looks to the east where a fence now runs along the Red, a look of determination on her face. "Neither police nor RCMP responded to my call to drag the red, but Kyle Kematch, whose sister Amber Guiboche disappeared from Winnipeg in 2010 at the age of 20, came forward and said, 'Let's do it ourselves.' After that, a team came together to drag the Red." Another man, Percy Ningewance, came forward to volunteer. He had experience dragging water for bodies in his home community of Lac Seul in Ontario. In 2014, he told the *Winnipeg Free Press* that he'd found the bodies of five drowning victims during searches over the years. Then another man said he could provide a boat. The community members had a couple of meetings, strategized who could do what, and a week later they were mapping out the river, gathering equipment, and organizing volunteers.

Even with qualified people, it hasn't been easy. Smith's husband is a welder and helped to build the bars and the quads—four hooks welded together to drag. But without formal training, they were experimenting with weight and length and lost equipment, hooks, and money. "We were really learning in our first year, and our second year [2015] has been a little different."

Smith says a group of forensic and physical anthropologists, all women from the University of Winnipeg, University of Manitoba, and Brandon University, came forward to help. They began training Drag the Red volunteers on how to identify remains and how to conduct a ground search effectively.

Brandon University's Dr. Emily Holland has been an integral part of Drag the Red ever since. Any time volunteers find any kind of remains, they take a picture and send it to her, and in half an hour or less she responds and lets them know if the remains are human, nonhuman, or unidentifiable. If they are not positively identified, she asks the volunteers to collect the remains and bring them to her.

"It's been really a community effort. We rely heavily on our volunteers. We have two crews—the ground search, and Kyle heads up the water crew. This year we started to fundraise and we have been able to buy a boat," Smith tells me.

As we begin searching the shore in a line, many volunteers, wearing reflector vests and armed with rakes and sticks, start to poke and dig around in the brush and rocks on the shore. I see Kyle Kematch, a tall Anishinaabe man. His teal sweater stands out amid the taupe sand and dirt and the grey stones that hug the river. He and his sister are poking at an object with a stick they've found. It's almost like this process of searching for clues and answers is now part of their cellular body memory. As gulls squeal over our heads, he tells me they are not looking specifically for any one demographic. Drag the Red looks for everybody. But he tells me that Tina was the inspiration for this mission. "She was very young and there are a lot of vulnerable people out there. The fact is this is an easy route to get rid of somebody," Kematch says.

Squinting his eyes toward the river, Kematch tells me this is where his sister Amber Guiboche might be. She disappeared from Winnipeg on November 10, 2010, five days after she turned 20 years old. Kematch believes her case was not seen as a priority because she led a high-risk lifestyle. On August 12, 2014, investigators asked the public for help in identifying someone that may know what happened to her. "She was small like Tina, you know," her brother says. "If she is in there, it's just like, she can't get buried [at a funeral], she can't be pronounced dead or nothing like that." This lack of closure is what so many family members have told me is the most gut-wrenching for them. "If we find some sort of evidence, I don't hope to find her in there, it's just got to be done, we need to find my sister."

Kematch says other grieving families appreciate his work; some can't search on their own because they are hurting too much. "But people have had enough. Like my sister, who was just a kid, these women and girls have their whole lives ahead of them. Everybody who has had kids knows what that could be like. She had loved ones who now feel the pain."

Smith says it's been hard to fulfill Drag the Red's original intention: to get police eyes on missing person and unsolved murder cases. "We've certainly seen that for non-Indigenous people. This summer [2015] a non-Indigenous woman went missing and police set up a command post, they dove in retention ponds. We don't see that type of attention on our cases. We hear from loved ones saying, 'Why don't we get that type of response?'"

Still, their effort has gained traction, and over the years more and more Indigenous people have lent their support to help. In 2016, 18-year-old Kayleen McKay ran from her Métis community of Duck Bay to the western bank of the Red River in Winnipeg—450 kilometres in eleven days—to honour her cousin Shawn Nepinak, who took his own life in the Red River in 2015. She ran about 40 kilometres a day and raised nearly $16,000 for Drag the Red to buy a new boat. She remembered searching the riverbanks as members of her family set out on the water with Drag the Red. After her run, her father told CBC News he was proud of his daughter and said, "I didn't know Kyle, I didn't know Bernadette, but they truly cared. They could feel our pain."

Smith says Drag the Red is not just doing the physical work, but also trying to change policies that seem riddled with racism. "It's very disheartening to know that there is a two-tiered system.

We are all human beings, we all matter, we all have people that love us, and we all want to be treated the same," Smith says.

In our 2015 conversation, despite her frustrations, Smith acknowledges that things have improved. Police now have preventative measures under a strategic unit called Project Return for at-risk youth. She says if a youth goes missing, a report goes out right away instead of waiting forty-eight hours, as was the case before. In Smith's sister's case, the family had to wait two years before they could access the pay phone records. Now one can access phone records immediately with a warrant. She says relationships with police have also changed. "There was not a lot of trust. Police are now more accountable because there are strong voices out there."

WHILE LOBBYING FOR family members of MMIWG to have better access to victim services, Bernadette Smith started campaigning to be the elected official for the neighbourhood she grew up in. She was elected to the Legislative Assembly of Manitoba in the summer of 2017 as a New Democratic Party representative of Point Douglas, in the North End, where we met in 2015. One of the first bills she brought forward, in 2018, was an amendment to Manitoba's Child and Family Services Act, revising it so that a child cannot be seized solely because of poverty. In November of 2018 she told the Canadian Press, "I went through the system myself and had this been in place when I was a child perhaps I wouldn't have had to live in a group home." Smith continued, "Perhaps things would have been different in my family if supports would have been provided to my mom and to me." She called it a game changer, and it is. As I've reported on the stories of MMIWG, including attending the national inquiry hearings, interviewing countless family members, and reading reports into violence against us, it has become clear that child-welfare policies—from residential school to the Sixties Scoop to today's foster care system—are intricately connected to the high rates of MMIWG. Family, community, and cultural fragmentation inevitably leads to trauma, addictions, poverty, and violence.

Poverty, referred to as "neglect" in reports written by social workers as the main reason Indigenous children are apprehended in Canada, is the result of everything from land dispossession to legislated racism to systemic exclusion. Bernadette Smith, like so many other family members of MMIWG, was and is looking at the bigger picture, picking up the pieces left behind after colonization tore apart families, communities, kinships, and our land. Something she and others have pointed to is how implicated the media and the police have been as instruments of colonization—how both have worked to silence Indigenous women's and girls' voices, but also contributed to the larger project of empire building in Canada.

One of the most important parts of countering this silence for me as an Indigenous journalist has been to keep the stories of MMIWG alive. But it's been equally important to me to raise and amplify messages about the beauty and resilience of Indigenous people. That resilience is not about how tough we are, not how much shit we can take, but how we come together in pain and in love, how we support each other in tragedy and in success, how we speak out against wrongs, and how we continue to relearn our languages and reclaim our culture, land, identity, and connections.

While life in Winnipeg had challenges, I found strength in the city that seemed to draw me in. The Indigenous women there taught me about what it means to come together as a community, and to use skill, ingenuity, and determination to find justice for their loved ones. While it was nice for my son to witness this too, of his own Anishinaabe and Métis family, when I got the call from CBC Vancouver about a job opening, I could not wait to get to the city I had come to call home.

10

Hilakanthl ayookhl lixs gyat,
breaker of laws of others

BREAKING THE RULES

THE MOSS IS SO GREEN it flickers off the trees like neon LED lights. The viridescent fuzz hangs like long, dewy Muppet arms edging the trail, and prehistoric boulders hug the path that snakes up the mountain I often climb. Seeing this forest feels religious to me, like an intertwining of the spiritual and super-natural beings that my ancestors and family members spoke of. The conifers and deciduous trees, the lichens and the thick undergrowth take my breath away and bring me back to stories of my grandmothers carrying bentwood boxes on their backs along the mountainous grease trails. Standing on kʷikʷəƛ̓əm (Kwikwetlem) territory—"red fish up the river" in reference to the sockeye salmon that once ran plentiful in the Coquitlam River and Coquitlam Lake—I think about the oolichans and the steelhead that Wiigyet, our trickster, created. I am not in Gitxsan territory, but I feel connected to these lands—and the kʷikʷəƛ̓əm, Sḵwx̱wú7mesh, səlilwətaɬ, xʷməθkʷəy̓əm, and Stó:lō friends I grew close to. Walking around Buntzen Lake, a spiritually important place where səlilwətaɬ oral history says the double-headed serpent Say Nuth Kway perished, I feel grounded and good to be wrapped back in the arms of this land and of my old pals. While this is not my territory, I feel like I am home.

I learned a lot from our adventures in Yellowknife, Toronto, and Winnipeg, but I struggled. I was still paying off my student loan while getting used to paying for diapers, child care, strollers, and swim lessons. It triggered the instinct for frugality I had honed when I lived on the street and learned to make five dollars last a week. But I was no longer a teenager; now I was an adult raising a child, trying to teach him by example and show him that when you put your mind to something you believe in, you can achieve anything. At the start of my parent journey, I was burned out, working protracted days as a reporter and often spending long nights with a baby, grieving the loss of my old life. But five years later, I had grit; I had polished off the dirt and become a strong and confident Indigenous woman who was ready for a change. My dreams were larger than I was: they encompassed my family, my culture, and my community.

After witnessing outright racism in Yellowknife and Winnipeg and seeing high levels of ignorance from privileged white journalists and intellectuals in Toronto, I thought Vancouver would be a place of comfort for me—a place where people were more educated about Indigenous people, especially when it came to missing and murdered Indigenous women and girls (MMIWG). Surely after the province had seen the Pickton inquiry, the Highway of Tears Symposium, the marches organized by family members, and the vocal Indigenous people speaking up about land, people would be more aware. While it was refreshing to be back home with my chosen family on the west coast I'd so missed, as soon as I started the job I was in for a rude awakening.

THE NEWSROOM WAS physically how I remembered it. The big rotunda of TVs broadcasting the twenty-four-hour news cycle was still at the centre of the space, and about 75–85 percent of the journalists were still white, with all of us working in pods of desks. At that time, I was still one of the only openly First Nations employees there. Nonetheless, it felt exciting to be a multiplatform reporter back in the city where I'd spent so many years. I was thrilled to start sinking my teeth into the stories I loved to tell. But even before I began my first day there, one of the newsroom leaders, a white man, questioned the "type of stories I normally did," telling me that I'd not be focused on Indigenous stories here but rather on daily news and whatever the assignment desk deemed important enough to tell. Indigenous stories were often not considered critical enough to tell.

While not all Indigenous reporters want to tell Indigenous stories solely or even primarily, the reality is that many, like me, do want to spotlight our stories that have previously been underreported, neglected, or not respectfully or accurately covered. Many Indigenous journalists have felt silenced when we want to tell Indigenous stories because we have been called biased when we do. In its defence, CBC told me, "Today at CBC there is widespread acknowledgement and recognition that lived experience and cultural insight broadens and deepens our journalism."

When I pitched an in-depth radio documentary on Lorelei Williams (who had lost her cousin to the Pickton farm and had been missing her aunt for forty years), showcasing her push to hold the MMIWG national inquiry that was then gaining momentum, a white woman who was a national producer at the CBC shut it down, saying, "We've already done news stories on Williams." This even though my pitch entailed a close look at Williams's current work preparing for the national inquiry, and the coverage would give us access to all the inquiry's private meetings, something that had obviously never been covered before. I found it strange, considering guest experts make repeat appearances on the same or several different programs regularly. Luckily, another national producer—a woman of colour—championed it, explaining the importance of the national inquiry and Lorelei's story, and fortunately it went forward. But that first rejection and the initial directive to cover what I was told to left me confused and frustrated. I was worried, in particular, about the type of resistance I'd face when I pitched stories about MMIWG, and I wondered how much ingrained and normalized racism I would experience and witness here at the country's national broadcaster. Neglecting or refusing to tell Indigenous stories is an unconscious or conscious attempt to erase us and is part and parcel of the legacy of colonization, something the media has always been complicit in. I felt that everything the family members of and advocates for MMIWG had told me they'd experienced, from the silencing to the dismissal, was what I was observing now from a mainstream media outlet that I respected.

That was the start of many rejections of my story ideas from producers, both local and national, setting a pattern that would remain strong for years. I heard a cascade of excuses from producers, the most common one being "I don't get it." In several news or current affairs meetings, my pitches were declined, laughed off, or described as "advocacy journalism"—a phrase that white journalists often applied (and sometimes still apply) to Black or Indigenous journalists or journalists of colour when we covered stories about our own communities. In one instance, two white journalists took issue with an investigative story I did that focused on Indigenous inmates at a prison, primarily because both felt I was not hard enough on the prisoners themselves. They took it upon themselves to make a complaint against me, accusing me of advocacy journalism. In another instance, a man in upper management said, "What is she, an advocacy journalist?" when I corrected a non-Indigenous host's pronunciation of an Indigenous word. There are many more examples.

Those using the term "advocacy journalist" were implying we Indigenous reporters were "too close to the story" (even if the community was hundreds of kilometres away from ours and a completely different culture) and hence biased, unable to cover a story with balance and integrity. This kind of dismissiveness almost always came from white people, including people I respected, making it all the more disappointing. Even more frustratingly, the exact same pitch by a white journalist would often be picked up, almost immediately. During one TV broadcast, at the last minute, a producer pulled an investigative story I'd done about an Indigenous woman's suspected murder because she "didn't get it," even though I'd worked on it for more than a week (a long time in daily news time). Eventually that story ran after I made an emergency call to a senior national manager in another province, but the incident sent a chill through me as I wondered how much energy and time I would spend defending my journalism on Indigenous people.

I realized quickly that I was being told to blend in, assimilate, and accept the norms there, or leave. But I chose not to. I chose to keep pushing to tell Indigenous stories. I chose my dignity. I chose my Indigeneity. I chose my humanity. But it would end up being a difficult path.

I WAS STILL WORKING HARD to heal the traumas I had experienced as a child and on the street. I was reconnecting with my community and trying to get my footing in a city and an industry that seemed to be at odds in many ways with Indigenous people. On my first week back I witnessed five Vancouver Police Department (VPD) officers on top of a lone young Indigenous woman, and as I tried to intervene, I was told that I could be arrested as well. The city seemed not just cold and unfriendly but often violent toward people like me. And the place where I spent most of my time, in a mainstream media outlet, seemed just as unsympathetic to Indigenous people. I felt like I was experiencing a new trauma, constant racism in the newsroom or from a collective of non-Indigenous people daily.

I realized that on this leg of the journey I needed to use that tool I'd found when I was a youth on the street—my pen would again emerge as an agent of change. And I, along with many other BIPOC journalists, would start to speak publicly about the harm, the racism, the microaggressions, and the differential treatment we were experiencing and witnessing inside our newsrooms, across Canada. This time, I didn't feel so alone. And over time, the tide would begin to turn as the world began to listen to us.

In 2018, for the first time, a white producer approached me in a hallway at CBC and apologized to me for our lacking coverage of MMIWG. "I just want to let you know that I appreciate all the work you've done to cover missing and murdered Indigenous women," an executive producer said. "And I really want to apologize on behalf of CBC for failing to report adequately on missing and murdered Indigenous women and girls over the years." She remains the only person from any media outlet I've ever worked at to express remorse for failing to give Indigenous issues the coverage they merited. Not long after, as part of her commitment to do better, she invited me to do a CBC column on Indigenous affairs.

It was her attempt to change the way our outlet covered Indigenous stories, but I was skeptical. I had developed trauma and some legitimate trust issues with colleagues and white people in general. But she reassured me this would give me a chance to tell stories that would not be dismissed with privileged judgments. I agreed, and together we came up with the name Reconcile THIS. It was a cheeky name meant to reflect the less meaningful and more performative steps taken by institutions across the province to address the calls for "reconciliation"—a phrase non-Indigenous people seemed excited about, but that Indigenous people were disillusioned by. I covered racism in schools, cultural appropriation, MMIWG, the Sixties Scoop, deaths in foster care, racism in hospitals, and Indigenous babies apprehended by social workers—and showed how those topics were all intricately intertwined. I also talked about media's failures.

But not everyone loved it. In meetings, the executive had to defend the column and me—explaining that even though I was Indigenous and would be looking critically at systemic racism, I was not biased but rather a strong investigative journalist. Hearing her say that, I knew I had an ally and one that I would work with (and sometimes fight alongside) intensely for years to improve the way our colleagues viewed, interacted with, and reported on Indigenous people. When a white investigative journalist sat on my desk and screamed in my face that I was "just a token" because I was nominated for a prestigious award and to "fucking educate her," CBC leaders immediately moved to protect me and address the vile treatment in ways that I wish I could discuss more, but that are protected by privacy legislation. In a recent response to this event, the CBC told me it "has no tolerance for discrimination, harassment and disrespect in the workplace. This matter was immediately and thoroughly looked into; however for reasons of confidentiality, CBC cannot confirm nor comment on any specific details."

When another journalist suggested it would be a good idea for me to "cover the drunk Native people living on Commercial Drive," she told him that was racist and to self-reflect. When dozens of people (journalists and the public) formally complained about me, calling me an advocate or biased for being

Indigenous and covering Indigenous stories, she educated them, telling them how no white journalist would ever be held to the same ridiculous standards and how white fragility and white supremacy are at the root of the ways Indigenous journalists are viewed. If a white man who was a war correspondent was a veteran, surely he would be lauded for his expertise rather than being called biased.

And it was not just Indigenous journalists who were treated as subpar. I heard non-Indigenous reporters treat Indigenous survivors of residential school as if they were lying about their experiences and grill them as if they were shady politicians. I listened to a live CBC radio program in which the non-Indigenous host spoke to a residential school survivor with disdain, questioning her every experience in disbelief. I witnessed a white CBC reporter ask an Indigenous pregnant woman how often she drank wine or beer—over and over on camera, for eight minutes straight—even after she said she'd been sober for several years. I listened as a white CBC journalist asked a grieving mom, who'd lost her son only days before, to educate him on how the child-welfare system works. In its defence, in an email, the CBC told me it "is a microcosm of society, an evolving and imperfect institution made up of hundreds of employees in dozens of newsrooms across the country. Unconscious and conscious bias is a reality in all institutions like the CBC," and went on to list the number of programs it hosts that focus broadly on Indigenous people and communities.

I realized my industry was still not only retraumatizing Indigenous people but adding new traumas. And I spoke out about it, in emails to bosses, in tweets, and in meetings. I refused to see Indigenous people be dehumanized.

Still, the racism I was experiencing at work was starting to wear me down. In anticipation of making my way out of the journalism industry for my mental wellness, I started to audition as an audiobook narrator and decided to freelance for magazines to get by until I figured out a master plan. But my course was changed at the end of 2019, during a spiritual winter ceremony in the Lummi community, when a close friend, Vyna Brown, and her brother Saul told me an awful story they'd heard about two of their Haíɫzaqv (Heiltsuk) Bella Bella community members.

On a mild winter day in December, Maxwell Johnson and his 12-year-old granddaughter walked into a downtown Vancouver BMO branch, a bank Johnson had been with since 2014, to open an account for her. Since his granddaughter travelled at the time for basketball games and cultural events, he wanted to be able to transfer money from his to her own account. It would be her first account there. But immediately the teller became suspicious as she didn't recognize their government-issued Indian status cards. I would later discover through 9-1-1 transcripts I obtained that the manager of the bank called Indigenous Services Canada to ask about the cards. The records reveal that the federal ministry representative told the bank to call 9-1-1. In a surprising move, BMO told the 9-1-1 operator that two "South Asian people," one 50 and one a teen, were committing a fraud. Shortly after, two VPD officers arrived, handcuffed the pair behind their backs on a busy downtown street, and detained them there for an hour while the girl stood crying out of fear for herself and her grandfather. It was hard to believe, but when I got back to the city and made all the calls, I verified that it was all too real. I was the first reporter to interview Johnson and break the story. While he was emotionally drained from the incident, something that aggravated an already serious panic disorder, he was eager to share the story in hopes of shedding light on the racism and violence Indigenous people face when doing business that white people do without a second thought, every day.

People around the world were instantly captivated by the story. Most non-Indigenous people found it shocking. But Indigenous people in Canada found the story validating, because many of them had also been considered suspicious while trying to use a status card, while banking or doing business of any sort. Journalists in London from the BBC, in Washington from NPR, and in Toronto from CBC were keen to hear me tell the story and kept their eyes on it. It opened up an international conversation about how anti-Indigenous racism exists in many everyday and institutional settings, from banking to encounters with police and governments. Through my investigating, I learned that the bank manager suspected Johnson of fraud because she didn't trust that the money he had in his account was his, nor that his Indian status card was real.

I reported on several angles of the story and sought answers from the bank and the police, both institutions that at first would not speak to media, about why a 12-year-old girl and her grandfather were arrested while trying to open a bank account. While BMO apologized five days after I broke the story, the VPD refused to, saying the force acted in the right. BMO started an Indigenous advisory board, something it shared with the media, and while the VPD created new Indigenous-focused training hosted by Reconciliation Canada, it would not share it publicly (as I found out during an interview on another matter with Reconciliation Canada). In an interview with a CBC anchor, VPD chief Adam Palmer said the officers, Mitchel Tong and Canon Wong, "come from diverse communities… and are not racist and were not racially profiling."

In the middle of February 2020, I travelled with Haíɫzaqv camera operator Shawn Foss and my son to Johnson's Bella Bella community to witness and take part in their Washing Ceremony, held in their Haíɫzaqv Big House. Called Waglisla by the Haíɫzaqv, Bella Bella rests on the Pacific Ocean in the central coast region of B.C. The day we arrived, the water looked like shimmering silver in one section because the herring were running. Eagles and ravens flew overhead just feet away from us. At the time, I wrote, "Bella Bella is a 2,000-person-strong reserve that is culturally and resource rich, welcoming to visitors and politically powerful."

Like feasts in my territory, this ceremony took place in the Big House; some may see it akin to a longhouse, with a fire burning in the centre and rows of people sitting around it on wooden bleachers. I witnessed Johnson and his granddaughter be brushed off with cedar boughs by Elder Pauline Waterfall and others, working to take away and heal the pain that the BMO incident caused them. They were then "dressed" in regalia to symbolize a new day.

While the Haíłzaqv had invited a BMO representative to attend the ceremony, BMO chartered a plane and brought fifteen people (something some people found excessive and that others shrugged at). In the Big House, under giant totem poles and lit by the flickering of the fire, we all listened to Johnson speak directly to the BMO executives, describing how they had hurt him, his family, and his whole community. It was a powerful ceremony to witness. While I was witnessing (and at times directing Shawn about good places to shoot), to my surprise my son and I were called to the floor. As we made our way to the centre near Johnson and his granddaughter, the Elders and the drummers, I wondered what was going on. We stood, curiously looking around us, while Chief Councillor Marilyn Slett spoke, explaining that the Nation was gifting me with regalia—a royal-blue button blanket and fringed apron made by Elder Frances Brown and designed by Maxwell Johnson—in order to honour me for my work on stories of MMIWG. My son was also gifted a red blanket, which he was wrapped in. I felt stunned and held back tears. As I made my way back to our spot on the bleachers and sat beside Vyna's mom, I shared that I didn't feel I deserved it. She explained that this was a message from the ancestors to keep pursuing answers for the family members.

But CBC leaders in Toronto didn't see it that way. Instead of a spiritual gift, they viewed it more as a monetary transaction that could be seen by the public as a conflict of interest (for example, people might have seen it as a gift for me doing a positive rather than balanced story on Maxwell Johnson and his granddaughter's experience). I was not able to put my byline on the story about the ceremony, so a white male reporter who was not at the ceremony wrote the story, largely relying on me for the information and visuals I gathered, with his byline on it. Because I was used to journalists misunderstanding Indigenous people and cultures, I was not surprised.

In November 2020, Maxwell Johnson filed a human rights complaint against BMO and the Vancouver Police Board. In April 2022, Brian Neal, a retired provincial court judge appointed to the case by the Office of the Police Complaint Commissioner, found the VPD officers each committed two counts of abuse of authority by "recklessly arresting the complainants and by using unnecessary force by applying handcuffs." Neal ordered that Tong and Wong be suspended for several days. In September, Johnson settled his human rights case with the VPD. As part of the settlement, the Vancouver Police Board formally admitted officers discriminated against Johnson and his granddaughter based on their Indigenous identities and paid undisclosed damages to the Johnson family "for injury to dignity" and $100,000 to Haíłzaqv First Nation's restorative justice department, the latter to fund one year of community programming to support at-risk young women, including young women who suffer anxiety due to traumatic incidents.

In October 2022, Johnson and his Haíłzaqv community invited the two officers to take part in a cultural apology feast—one agreed to in the human rights settlement, and that the VPD were required to pay $25,000 for. It would be an opportunity for Johnson and his granddaughter to heal and have closure. But they never showed up. Instead, Chief Palmer, other high-ranking officers, and about ten other police board members came bearing gifts and attempted to stand in the officers' place at the event in the Haíłzaqv's Big House—their place of government and business. But the Haíłzaqv shared that in their culture, stand-ins are not permitted. I was at the Big House, along with my camera operator Shawn Foss and my son Namawan. It was tense. One of the hereditary Chiefs, Frank Brown, had words for Palmer. Across the Big House floor, he yelled out to the police chief, questioning his previous assessment that the officers in the handcuffing incident were not racist. He then walked across the floor and returned the gift Palmer gave to one of the hereditary Chiefs—a feast bowl. It was dramatic. And for me, as the Indigenous woman who broke the story, I felt anger from the police officials there. And it was not just a feeling. I saw at least two officers share on Twitter that they felt the media should not have been there covering this "private event." But for many Indigenous people, like the Gitxsan, the Sk̲wx̲wú7mesh, and the Haíłzaqv, having witnesses to share with those who couldn't be there is key.

The police not showing up, not respecting the Haíłzaqv culture, and even previously saying the officers were not racist in the handcuffing felt all the more exhausting, since all this happened after one of the more horrific examples of racism in policing in recent history unfolded.

IN MARCH 2020, shortly after I finished filming the Maxwell Johnson story, the world started to lock down as we sorted out the tragic nature of the global pandemic. Society's slowdown gave people time to think more deeply about the world around us and how we treated each other. While racism and racial violence against Black and Indigenous people is common, the killing of George Floyd by a Minneapolis police officer, Derek Chauvin, who knelt on Floyd's neck for nine minutes and twenty-nine seconds as he died on May 25, 2020, moved North America to reignite conversations about racism and the institutional violence that people of colour experience. Not long after his death, on June 4, 2020, Chantel Moore, a Tla-o-qui-aht mother living in New Brunswick, was shot and killed by Edmundston police after they were called to do a wellness check on her. Her death opened up more conversations about the police killings of Indigenous people in Canada. It took me back to my time in Prince George, when Judge Ramsay was committing his crimes and I was hearing allegations of police assaults against Indigenous women and girls. And it hurt to think of all the times when Indigenous people were killed or brutalized by police but no one has cared, not until the world watched the video of the Floyd murder, unedited, and could not look away or victim-blame.

According to a CTV analysis, "an Indigenous person in Canada is more than 10 times more likely to have been shot and killed by a police officer in Canada since 2017 than a white person in Canada." Public discussions about the harms institutions like the RCMP and VPD cause to Black and Indigenous people started to inspire another conversation about defunding the police. Public discussions also gave the Indigenous women I interviewed for a multiplatform CBC story a sense of safety to open up about their past experiences with racism and violence at the hands of police. And as the public discourse moved to the role the media plays in systemic racism, I could feel a release of all the pain, all the pressure, all the hatred that Indigenous women, especially family members of MMIWG, had experienced, and that I had directly experienced as a result of pushing to tell their stories. Maybe there was hope that we would not have to be constantly fighting for our place at the table as Indigenous women anymore. Maybe there was hope that I could still work in journalism and make a difference. And maybe this was an industry that I could stay in, succeed in, and even see changes in.

In the weeks that followed, a number of employees apologized to me for their racist behaviour toward me and my stories. And members of the public tweeted and emailed me, saying they wanted to learn and were willing to educate themselves. As 2020 came to an end, I was finally at a place where any Indigenous story I pitched, regardless of the complexity, was accepted and my producers trusted me to do the investigative journalism required for it to have impact. Today I rarely have to shield myself or other Indigenous women and girls from comments that may arise from hosts or other journalists, such as "Well, didn't Indigenous kids get taken away from their homes because they were bad homes?" or "Why are there so many drunk Natives in my neighbourhood?" because white people making those comments are slowly educating themselves, and being told by their superiors and peers that racism is no longer acceptable. It is hard now to imagine that racial violence and colonization were so normalized just a couple of years ago. Back then I was told not only that I was wrong, but that I was essentially breaking journalistic standards and practices by speaking out against racism—and even by telling stories about Indigenous people. Sometimes, breaking rules is necessary, especially when those rules have normalized and maintained colonial violence against Indigenous people, something the media has done for decades in Canada. And my refusal to accept the norm paid off.

In the spring of 2021, because no in-person awards galas were being held due to the pandemic, I found out on Twitter that I'd won an Academy of Canadian Cinema and Television award (Canadian Screen Award) for best local reporter of the year for my stories about Maxwell Johnson and his granddaughter being handcuffed in front of the bank. I did not expect it and immediately started to scream and cry for joy. Too emotional to talk on the phone, I left a series of blubbering voice memos for my colleagues and friends, thanking them for being beside me in this fight to tell stories about violence against Indigenous people with integrity. All in one instant, I felt that everything I had pushed through for all those years had actually been worth it. I had finally made it to the top of the mountain while carrying a virtual bag of potatoes and being shot at—or at least that was what it felt like—the whole way.

In the same year I won the best local reporter award, a program I hosted with CBC's Lien Yeung called *Unmasking Racism*, a town hall about racism in B.C., was also nominated for a Canadian Screen Award, for best news or information program. These honours signalled to me that people were listening, that our stories mattered, and that we are just as important as white people. It showed me that people were making room to talk about racism.

BY THE SPRING OF 2021, family members and advocates were still pressing governments to implement the action plan of the National Inquiry into Missing and Murdered Indigenous Women and Girls. Two years had passed since the commissioners released their final report. In June 2021, the federal government announced it would be releasing its plan. "Our goal here is to end the genocide," Denise Pictou Maloney, co-chair of the National Family and Survivors Circle—one of many groups, along with the federal and provincial governments, who developed the National Action Plan—told the CBC. Pictou Maloney's mother, Annie Mae Pictou Aquash of the Sipekne'katik First Nation, was murdered in 1975.

The Path Forward—Reclaiming Power and Place, the contribution of the National Family and Survivors Circle to the National Action Plan, identified thirty actions related to some of the inquiry's 231 calls for justice, including equitable funding, better data collection, and improved policing agencies. The Canadian government's 2020/21 budget earmarked $2.2 billion to implement the inquiry's calls. But family members I spoke to said its National Action Plan fell short. Melissa Moses, women's representative for the Union of British Columbia Indian Chiefs, said that the document Ottawa released was "an offensive performance by the government to skirt responsibility and glaze over the ongoing genocide of women and girls." Others called it vague and said there was no clear timeline, meaning it could take years before action is seen. The Native Women's Association of Canada was not a signatory on the National Action Plan, calling it a "toxic and dysfunctional process," and instead called on the United Nations to investigate how Canada is dealing with the genocide.

In May of 2021 I got another call that would change the way the world viewed Indigenous people in Canada. When Tk'emlúps te Secwépemc communications representative Racelle Kooy told me over the phone that a ground penetrating radar specialist found disturbances in the ground that could be 215 graves of Indigenous children who never made it home from residential school, I was floored. I was the first reporter from a mainstream outlet that the Tk'emlúps te Secwépemc's Kúkpi7 (Chief) Rosanne Casimir spoke to. I felt chills go up my spine as she explained to me her pain and shock at the findings. A later report from the ground penetrating radar specialist showed two hundred potential burial sites on the grounds of the Kamloops Indian Residential School, with 158 acres left to be surveyed.

In an instant, conversations about genocide were sparked again as Canadians and the world considered the violence Indigenous children experienced, some as young as 3, in these state- and church-run schools. On CBC's *The Current* and *Front Burner*, I spoke about the ways thousands of children had died, as documented already by the Truth and Reconciliation Commission in 2015. I shared the disturbing details of how a 9-year-old boy died of suicide, another child in the river, another from starvation, another from tuberculosis, another in a fire. Those who once treated so many Indigenous people with frank disregard in B.C. were now asking us for help to teach them about what happened. While it was exhausting to be educating a group who had seen Indigenous people as irrelevant until five minutes ago, it felt like this was the time to talk about everything from colonial violence to the Indian Act to genocide. That summer on Canada Day, instead of celebrating Canada by waving red-and-white flags, Canadians were wearing orange shirts to reflect upon those that never made it home or survived residential school. People were forced to unwind the tightly knit coil of lies that Canada was a country built on peace and diversity, and reckon with the truth. It was time to truly listen to Indigenous people.

And Indigenous people like me grieved as we recalled the traumas our families experienced. Even for those of us whose parents and grandparents didn't attend residential schools, we were forced to recount everything else they did live through, like segregation, racial violence, and the banning of our languages, feasts, and cultures. And we grieved the family members and friends who did attend or who were intergenerational survivors.

When I started my book in 2015, "racism" was a no-no to talk about in the journalism industry. In 2017, "colonization" was questioned in my stories. In 2019, journalists were not to give the reality of "genocide" in Canada any weight. In 2021, all these rules began to break.

THINKING OF THESE ENORMOUS CHANGES summons memories of long ago, of the time right after the rug was pulled out from under me, when I was thrust from relative safety into a

life of unpredictability and violence. I had to survive with little more than a sleeping bag and a pen. But like my ancestors, I
knew that somehow I could pull through this if I adapted, with
creativity, ingenuity, and support. I am still healing, but my experience of being abandoned and rejected placed me on a path to
guard others from the harms of mistreatment. As I climbed out
of the trenches of street life, I was drawn to expose the truth,
especially on topics that are explicitly shrouded in Canada, like
anti-Indigenous institutional racism. When society casts you as
the lowest sort, it is easier to see clearly through all the layers of
injustice. I knew that telling the truth was a revolutionary act in
a country that was built on removing, erasing, murdering, and
silencing those it worked so hard to displace.

But I also knew that on this path, I needed to come to terms
with my own truth. I needed to understand the patterns of violence I'd come to accept. I was longing to belong, but even more
I was searching to know who I was. Moving to Prince George
helped me to understand how even my own family, in many
ways filled with dysfunction, was keen to forget our past and
our history with colonization and displacement. Moving there
spurred an interest in deepening my grasp of my Gitxsan culture, through my uncle Neil and more recently another uncle,
Art Sterritt. Through my cousins and aunties, I also learned
more about how my grandpa and my dad grew up.

In 2022, while working on a CBC podcast called *Land Back*,
I travelled to my home territory, in Gitanmaax, one of our villages. I was terrified that my producers might see me not being
accepted by my own people (the trauma of the bullying, of my
family never wanting me, has really stuck). Speaking to one of
our Gitxsan legends, Dimdiigibuu (Ardythe Wilson), during a
long interview at the 'Ksan Historical Village, she told me how
respected some of my ancestors were—that they helped to protect our territory and our people from land theft. The day before
I left Gitxsan territory, I gave her and a Gitxsan Sim'oogit,

Hanamuxw (Don Ryan), a print of my artwork. In an email the day I left, Hanamuxw told me, "Your print is a legal, political and economic statement." As I drove down Highway 16 back to Vancouver, tears burned into my skin for hours as I thought about how much I needed to finally feel accepted and loved by my own people, and how much I'd missed out on that feeling for much of my life.

It reminded me, though, of all the work I had done to bring myself here, starting out as a youth moving off the street, trying to find the truth and my place in the world.

As I stepped into my power as a storyteller though radio in the Downtown Eastside of Vancouver and then campus radio in Prince George, I could feel my ancestors light my path and carry me into a role as a healer. The more stories I told of MMIWG, the more I realized that telling and hearing the truth is like salve to a wound that has long been neglected. And now, I was getting more comfortable with speaking my truth.

When I was younger, I was shy and insecure and hid the truth about myself; now I stand in front of television cameras telling the truth to the world.

At the start of this book, I spoke about Wiigyet, our Gitxsan transformational figure who teaches us of our humanity, who creates rivers while holding a mirror up to us to show that we make mistakes. But Wiigyet, being a trickster, also teaches us not to accept everything as it is or the way we know it. Wiigyet demonstrates that moral codes and rules we've taken it upon ourselves as humans to create will often shape and shift beyond our control. Through humour Wiigyet shows us that we often cannot control change—we have to keep an open mind and adapt to the transformation happening all around us. He teaches us that to grow, we need to break the rules we've set up for ourselves. My ancestors, who struggled through so many changes in their lives, fought against the rules and the norms in Canada. If we didn't break the codes of normalcy, we'd continue to believe that Indigenous women are less than any other group in Canada, that Indigenous people are inferior, and that European white supremacy is the gold standard. If we did not challenge those norms we'd be content with the idea that white people are the gatekeepers of knowledge, power, and policy. Fortunately, some Canadians have realized that without change, we'd continue to stay in a past that only served white men well.

Breaking those rules and living in the discomfort of it paid off, though. I feel that I am respected for standing up against racism, and for speaking truth to power. Since 2021, there are small shifts happening. In journalism, people are starting to realize how Indigenous reporters are over-scrutinized for having the same passion, compassion, contacts, and understanding about a story that a white reporter would be lauded for in doing a story about a white community. There are still many lessons journalists need to learn about not causing more harm to family members of MMIWG. Treating Indigenous survivors and those grieving tremendous losses with compassion and kindness is still very new. Being trauma informed is something we are just starting to talk about today.

There is still a great lack of sensitivity and understanding when it comes to our reporting on missing and murdered Indigenous women, girls, and two-spirit people. Their stories are still neglected in our coverage, and part of me feels responsible for that. Often, when I don't cover a story that is heavy and difficult, complex and thorny and full of complicated intergenerational trauma, like so many stories of MMIWG, I know that there is little chance anyone else will know how to properly cover it. It is why I feel that while we need more Indigenous journalists in our newsrooms, we shouldn't expect them to carry the weight that no one else can or wants to.

While I am critical and sometimes cynical, I am also hopeful and keen to look forward to a shift where Canadians can make the connections on their own, can call out and stand up against violence against Indigenous women, and create spaces that honour Indigenous women, our cultures, and our world views without feeling it is their place to save us.

There is hope in knowing change is possible.

Today, I see young Indigenous women, girls, and two-spirit people reclaiming their language, their culture, their lands, and their power. I am also witnessing us taking back joy, as the burden of addressing systemic racism and violence is shared more widely. In that vein I see young Indigenous women and two-spirit people lifting up and empowering each other to live our lives without the oppression of colonization. Loving ourselves and each other as Indigenous people is a radical act of decolonization in a world that teaches us to constantly self-hate.

I cannot wait to see us rise above with each other, not in a western sense of success but communally, with compassion, curiosity, and courage. Like the mighty rivers and streams that flow from the northwest to the west coast, we can never go backwards. It is my hope not just that all the family members I have written about here are afforded the justice they deserve, to have the closure they have been searching for all these years, but that as Indigenous women we can just live our lives without the burden of constantly fighting for our rights. That we can have the space and time to use our imagination, be curious, and wonder what it's like to live the way our ancestors did, with an abundance of love for each other, our children, and future generations.

Afterword

A Letter to My Son

BABY, WHEN I FIRST STARTED writing this book, you were just 5 little years old, with the light in your eyes, sprite in your smile, and giggle in your belly to prove it. When you looked into my eyes, yours shone like black pebbles in the sand, a part of the earth where the shore meets the land. You were proud to be Anishinaabe and Gitxsan, even though you didn't know what Indigenous, Native, or Aboriginal meant. With my coaxing and gentle pushes, you sang the Women's Warrior Song at a conference about "being a man" that confronted toxic masculinities. You listened attentively as we talked about ending violence against Indigenous women, and today in 2022, at 11 years old, after many weeks of us working from home, you've heard me speak about protecting Indigenous women, girls, and two-spirit people probably hundreds of times.

Like all moms I beam and glow when I think of you. From the time you were born, we had struggles mostly with poverty and solo mom life, but in my heart of hearts I knew if I just loved you more than anything I'd ever loved in my entire life, you would grow to realize that you can overcome any hurdle with just that. I'm a clichéd dreamer and believer. I've tried to explain what racism, human rights, and sexism are to you, but the words just don't come out right. Because just like with all my creations, I want to instill hope and beauty in you strong enough to overshadow the doom, pain, and unending cruelty on this planet. Right now, I don't want to burden you with the details of how many of your people—your family—have been abused and brutalized, or how Mommy was homeless when she was still a girl, how she was almost beaten to death. There are things I might never tell you, because I don't want to normalize these things for you, because they should never be normal in someone's life. They should always be jarring and signal the need to change.

How do I tell you that when you grow, you might not be liked as much because you are not white, and that your best friend is in the same boat because he is Black? How do I explain that our people are more likely to die young than anyone? How do I explain that we were violently removed from our traditional territories, penalized for being Gitxsan, and abused in schools that beat our mother tongue out of us? How do I explain that Mommy was almost killed? The words to describe these things escape me, even though my white friends seem to be able to explain residential school and all the injustices fine to their children. For me, for our people, it hurts because it happened to us. But I hang on to hope that history won't repeat itself, and that by teaching you, my son, to love, respect, and honour our women, change will come. To me, your generation, like mine was to my parents, is the hope. You are the future, the hope to hold and set free that truth you are learning and walking. Your name, to me, was not about being a warrior, but about justice and freedom. Namawan, after all, means "fair wind."

Yours is among the first generations to learn about residential schools, colonial violence, and the Indian Act in elementary school. At 11 years old, my son, you know more than many non-Indigenous people over 25. You are proud at age 11, unlike your mom, who hid her Indigenous roots for much of her childhood and teen years. While I didn't grow up with my culture and am estranged from many of my Gitxsan family, you, my baby, with me have learned our songs and dances together.

Loving yourself, my dear son, is an act of decolonization and resistance. While we have in our recent past been treated as subhuman, I am confident you will love and cherish who you grow up to be as an Indigenous man and treat Indigenous women and girls just the same because we are all rising together, holding our pens of healing, change, and light, together as one.

ACKNOWLEDGEMENTS

ABOVE ALL, I AM GRATEFUL to the ancestors that have guided the direction of this book with love and compassion. To the spirits whose lives were cut far too short, whom we will never forget, we honour you and will continue to help find justice for you.

I hold up my son Namawan, for all the dinners he made, all the dishes he washed, the loads and loads of laundry he folded, and all the love he gave me throughout this arduous seven-year journey to write this book. To my late mother Delphine for imparting wisdom to me, namely teaching me to never stay silent, and with my voice and my actions, to never let oppressive behaviours go unchecked. And to my aunt Mary, for helping me to see her. To my late uncle Neil Jr., whose deep research and writing about our Gitxsan people not only gave great insight into my understanding of my people, our land, lineage, and culture, but whose work continues to educate the public about all the great that Gitxsans are. To my cousin and our Gitxsan language teacher and Elder Dr. M. Jane Smith, who graciously provided language guidance for this book and who continues to support Gitxsans to help revitalize and maintain Gitxsanimx, our language.

I hold my hands up to all the family members who gave me hours and hours of their time over many years.

To Vanessa Hans, whose endless fight for justice for her mother, Levina Moody, inspired me to never give up and showed me what healing looks like. I am grateful for the years she gave to me to get her mother's story right, but more so to try to find answers about her mother's murder. To Gladys Radek and Tom Chipman, who continue to keep the spirit of Tamara Chipman alive and who continue to fight for justice for all missing and murdered Indigenous women and girls. To Brenda Wilson, whose strong and gentle Gitxsan spirit continues to generously give direction and love to so many family members, as she keeps the spirit of Ramona Wilson alive. To Bernadette Smith, who honours her sister Claudette Osborne-Tyo's memory while bringing to light the colonial violence Indigenous women and girls continue to experience in institutions in Canada. To Lorelei Williams, who continues to educate the public and journalists about how to better tell the stories of missing and murdered Indigenous women, while searching for justice for her aunty Belinda Williams and her cousin Tanya Holyk. And to all the countless Indigenous people who spent hours and days with me to ensure I told this story accurately, with cultural integrity, with respect, and with honour.

A big thanks also to family members and friends of missing and murdered Indigenous women and girls who provided important insights about their loved ones: David (Al) Moody, Sam Moody, Kyle Kematch, Wanda Good, Terri Brown, Ida Basil, and Wayne Leng.

A very special thanks to Dimdiigibuu (Ardythe Wilson) for her Gitxsan cultural and language help, to my dear friend Marissa Nahanee for her Skwxwú7mesh teachings, and to Jennifer Annaïs Pighin-Pete Joseph for her teachings on Lheidli T'enneh.

To Marci McDonald, whose early encouragement helped start the journey that led to this book. To my literary agent Samantha Haywood, who took a chance on me, believed in me and the story I wanted to tell, and who ultimately took a piece of writing that was a very rough work in progress and made it something that all Canadians could learn from and that Indigenous woman and girls will hopefully be inspired by. I'm grateful for how you honoured my story and my goal to seek justice for missing and murdered Indigenous women and girls, but yet gently encouraged me to be brave and share my own story. To my editor Jennifer Croll, who witnessed the struggles it took to get this work to publication, advocated for my success and wellness, and made my then okay writing into a powerful book that I hope will educate and empower. Without her, this book would never have reached the level it reached. To everyone at Greystone who supported me, championed my book, and made it beautiful: Jen Gauthier and Rob Sanders; Megan Jones and Makenzie Pratt; Jessica Sullivan and Paula Ayer—I couldn't have done this without you.

To my copyeditor Dawn Loewen, who showed me what being decolonized in heart and mind looks like and who of course made my writing so much stronger and more beautiful. She is a true gem to the literary world and someone who should model how to support Indigenizing literature. To my fact checker Sarah Berman, who spent months ensuring the accuracy of my truth and the truths of so many others. It was an exhaustive, mammoth project she undertook, and I am grateful.

A special thanks to Lindsay Kines for his help in guiding me through his reportage over the years. Thanks to Lorimer Shenher, who provided valuable insights about the Vancouver police and missing women's investigations. And a thank-you to the RCMP's Janelle Shoihet, who spent years answering my questions for this book, some of them long and complex and extremely detailed.

To the Canada Council for the Arts, that so generously funded the writing and fact checking of this book.

NOTES

In Memoriam

The names, ages, and other details for missing and murdered women came from a wide range of sources: newspaper articles, books, interviews, websites, *Forsaken: The Report of the Missing Women Commission of Inquiry*, Volume I (2012), and testimony from the National Inquiry into Missing and Murdered Indigenous Women and Girls.

Preface: Waiy woh, *it is time*

When 22-year-old Wet'suwet'en mother Tamara Chipman went missing: In-person interview with Tom Chipman in Terrace, B.C., August 3, 2016.

after more than a decade of loved ones demanding: Telephone interview with Ernie Crey, September 23, 2011; telephone interview with Terri Brown, October 7, 2015.

In 2014, Tina Fontaine, a diminutive 15-year-old Anishinaabe girl: "Tina Fontaine, 15, Found in Bag in Red River," CBC News, August 17, 2014.

The heartbreaking tragedy fell on the heels of a report: Royal Canadian Mounted Police, *Missing and Murdered Aboriginal Women: A National Operational Overview* (2014), rcmp-grc.gc.ca/wam/media/460/original/0cbd8968a049aa0b44d343 e76b4a9478.pdf

Indigenous women make up 4 percent of the female population in Canada: Paula Arriagada, *First Nations, Métis and Inuit Women* (Statistics Canada, 2016), www150.statcan. gc.ca/n1/pub/89-503-x/2015001/article/14313-eng.pdf.

Indigenous women and girls in Canada made up almost 25 percent of all female homicide victims: National Inquiry into Missing and Murdered Indigenous Women and Girls, *Reclaiming Power and Place: The Final Report of the National Inquiry into Missing and Murdered Indigenous Women and Girls* (Vancouver: Privy Council Office, 2019), 1a:55.

Reporters...were barred from using the word survivor: Experience of the author and of other journalists, including Waubgeshig Rice, who tweeted on June 2, 2021: "Before the apology in 2008, CBC sent a note to staff saying we couldn't use 'survivors' to describe people who went to residential schools, only 'former students'" (twitter.com/waub/status/1400121496987746306).

media were the first to rail against commissioners' use of the word genocide: Evan Dyer, "What Does It Mean to Call Canada's Treatment of Indigenous Women a 'Genocide'?," CBC News, June 5, 2019.

1 | Adaawk, *oral history*

the Xsan (Skeena River): The Xsan is also called Xsi-yeen.

Gitanmaax, Gitsegukla, Gitanyow, Kispiox, Gitwangak, and Sik-E-Dakh: Neil J. Sterritt, Susan Marsden, Robert Galois, Peter R. Grant, and Richard Overstall, *Tribal Boundaries in the Nass Watershed* (Vancouver: UBC Press, 1998), 5. Gitanyow has also been called Kitwancool; Kispiox is also called Anspayaxw, "people of the hiding place"; and Gitwangak is also known as Kitwanga or Gitwangax.

an area about five times the size of Prince Edward Island: Mike Priaro, "Bill C-48— Inland First Nation's Testimony to Commons Committee," Briefing Note for Hereditary Chiefs of Gitwangak and Gitsegukla, November 3, 2017, linkedin.com/pulse/bill-c-48-inland-first-nations-testimony-commons-committee-priaro/.

home to 400 to 700 people, or 800 to 2,500 if you include off-reserve members: "Census Profile, 2016 Census," Statistics Canada, www12.statcan.gc.ca/census-recensement/2016/dp-pd/prof/index.cfm?Lang=E.

Ansi'suuxs, or "place of the driftwood": Neil J. Sterritt, *Mapping My Way Home: A Gitxsan History* (Powell River, BC: Creekstone Press, 2016), 39.

my lineage stems from Kisgegas, a now abandoned village farther north: Sterritt, *Mapping My Way Home.*

for ten thousand years at least: Sterritt, *Mapping My Way Home,* 31.

Wiik'aax ("big wings"), the head of the House of Wiik'aax: Sterritt, *Mapping My Way Home,* 264.

The route started at Gitlax'aws: Known as Gitlaxksiip to the Gitxsan and as Grease Harbour to the Europeans. "Gitlaxksiip," BC Geographical Names, Government of British Columbia, apps.gov.bc.ca/pub/bcgnws/names/54542.html.

"they needed to disempower the women": Kim Anderson, *A Recognition of Being: Reconstructing Native Womanhood* (Toronto: Canadian Scholars, 2001), 58.

Scores of ships visited my Nation's territories and the northwest region from the 1700s to the 1800s: Hudson's Bay Company Archives, *Ships' Movements Books, 1719–1929,* Keystone Archives Descriptive Database, Archives of Manitoba, pam.minisisinc.com/scripts/mwimain.dll/144/LISTINGS_WEB2_INT/LISTINGS_DET_REP_FULL_GR/SISN%201689?sessionsearch.

a steamer ship known as the Brother Jonathan . . . was also transporting smallpox: Robert Boyd, *The Coming of the Spirit of Pestilence: Introduced Infectious Diseases and Population Decline Among Northwest Coast Indians, 1774–1874* (Vancouver: UBC Press, 1999); Joshua Ostroff, "How a Smallpox Epidemic Forged Modern British Columbia," *Maclean's,* August 1, 2017.

efforts colonists made to manage smallpox: William B. Spaulding and Maia Foster-Sanchez, "Smallpox in Canada," *The Canadian Encyclopedia,* last edited February 12, 2020, thecanadianencyclopedia.ca/en/article/smallpox.

little proof that the Hudson's Bay Company deliberately killed Indigenous people by gifting blankets infected with smallpox: Emailed statement from Michelle Rydz, Archivist, Hudson's Bay Company Archives, Archives of Manitoba, January 27, 2022.

the British had used blankets exposed to smallpox: Elizabeth A. Fenn, "Biological Warfare in Eighteenth-Century North America: Beyond Jeffery Amherst," *Journal of American History* 86, no. 4 (March 2000): 1552–1580.

a year before the smallpox epidemic, in 1861: Cole Harris, "The Native Land Policies of Governor James Douglas," *BC Studies* 174 (Summer 2012): 101–122.

miners passing through Hazelton en route to the Omineca goldfields: Sterritt, *Mapping My Way Home,* 162.

careless prospectors failed to extinguish a campfire: R. M. Galois, "The Burning of Kitsegukla, 1872," *BC Studies* 94 (Summer 1992): 59–81.

"Please do not come through our town": Sterritt, *Mapping My Way Home,* 176.

"the white men are always after the Indian": Sterritt, *Mapping My Way Home,* 178.

reality that dozens of women and girls have gone missing from or been murdered here since the 1970s: Telephone interview with former RCMP staff sergeant Wayne Cleary, April 11, 2016; news reports; and reports from family members.

"She was vulnerable": Facebook Messenger correspondence with Mary Audia, March and September 2020.

1997... case that would famously become known as the Delgamuukw case: Delgamuukw v. British Columbia, [1997] 3 S.C.R. 1010.

Neil J. Sterritt countered that argument with anthropological evidence: Part 14, 2b, "Aboriginal Jurisdiction and Ownership Before British Sovereignty," Delgamuukw v. British Columbia, 1991 CanLII 2372 (BCSC), CanLII, canlii.org/en/bc/bcsc/doc/1991/1991canlii2372/1991canlii2372.html.

Gradual Civilization Act of 1857: Bob Joseph, 21 Things You May Not Know About the Indian Act: Helping Canadians Make Reconciliation With Indigenous Peoples a Reality (Indigenous Relations Press, 2018), 116.

Amsiwaa (the word we use for white man): Dr. Jane Smith, provided via Facebook Messenger, October 28, 2022.

the experiences of some residential school survivors—at the St. Anne's residential school in Ontario: Jorge Barrera, "Ottawa Initially Fought St. Anne's Residential School Electric Chair Compensation Claims," CBC News, December 2, 2017.

2 | Nee dii sgithl ts'ixts'ik loo'y, I don't have a vehicle

behind the slopes of the Ts'edeek'aay mountains: Witsuwit'en name from "Place Names," Elder Doris Rosso (unpublished manuscript, June 4, 2014).

16-year-old Ramona was getting ready for a dance: Telephone interview with Brenda Wilson, December 2020.

Brenda was living on her own... made her way to a barbecue: Email correspondence from Brenda Wilson, January 24, 2022.

on June 13, 1990, Wet'suwet'en teen Delphine Nikal went missing: "Delphine Nikal," Missing and Murdered: The Unsolved Cases of Indigenous Women and Girls, CBC News, 2016.

Roxanne Thiara, 15, was last seen in Prince George in July 1994: "Roxanne Thiara," Missing and Murdered: The Unsolved Cases of Indigenous Women and Girls, CBC News, 2016.

Alishia Germaine, 15, was last seen at the Prince George Native Friendship Centre: "Alishia Germaine," Missing and Murdered: The Unsolved Cases of Indigenous Women and Girls, CBC News, 2016.

Lana Derrick, 19, was a college student: "Lana Derrick," Missing and Murdered: The Unsolved Cases of Indigenous Women and Girls, CBC News, 2016; in-person interview with Wanda Good in her Gitanyow band office, September 2016.

"We had to initiate all those searches": Interview with Brenda Wilson.

"Why did Matilda not benefit": Quoted by David Wilson, "An Indigenous Mother Searches for Answers on B.C.'s Highway of Tears," Broadview, November 1, 2004.

"It was another slap in the face" and "The way Indigenous women are seen": Interview with Brenda Wilson.

These pervasive stereotypes foster violence: Native Women's Association of Canada, "Fact Sheet: Root Causes of Violence Against Aboriginal Women and the Impact of Colonization" (2015), nwac.ca/wp-content/uploads/2015/05/Fact_Sheet_Root_Causes_of_Violence_Against_Aboriginal_Women.pdf.

Noreen Gosch's 12-year-old son Johnny: Daniel P. Finney, "Cleveland Case Lifts Hopes of Iowa Mother, Other Parents," USA Today, May 8, 2013.

Amber Alert system started in… 2002 *in Canada:* "Amber Alerts: When They're Used and How They Work," CBC News, August 19, 2009.

Indigenous, Hispanic, and Black children went missing at a higher rate: "2018 NCIC Missing Person and Unidentified Person Statistics," Federal Bureau of Investigation National Crime Information Center, fbi.gov/file-repository/2018-ncic-missing-person-and-unidentified-person-statistics.pdf/view; Federal Interagency Forum on Child and Family Statistics, *America's Children: Key National Indicators of Well-Being,* 2019 (Washington, D.C.: U.S. Government Printing Office, 2019), childstats.gov/pdf/ac2019/ac_19.pdf.

"missing white woman syndrome": Derecka Purnell, "The 'Missing White Woman Syndrome' Still Plagues America," *The Guardian,* September 29, 2021.

upwards of fifty-nine women… have gone missing or been murdered: Telephone interview with former RCMP staff sergeant Wayne Cleary, April 11, 2016.

RCMP officers acknowledged this disparity: RCMP documents on Nicole Hoar obtained via Access to Information and Privacy request, August 17, 2009 (obtained by author February 7, 2019).

Sisters in Spirit… compiled statistics on violence against Aboriginal women: Native Women's Association of Canada, *What Their Stories Tell Us: Research Findings From the Sisters In Spirit Initiative* (2010), nwac.ca/wp-content/uploads/2015/07/2010-What-Their-Stories-Tell-Us-Research-Findings-SIS-Initiative.pdf.

in March of 2010, the federal Conservative government under Stephen Harper cut funds: Robyn Sanderson Bourgeois, "Warrior Women: Indigenous Women's Anti-Violence Engagement With the Canadian State" (PhD diss., University of Toronto, 2014), 235.

It would take until 2014… for Ottawa to initiate the Missing Children/Persons and Unidentified Remains (MC/PUR) *database:* Emailed statement from national RCMP spokesperson Sgt. Tania Vaughan in Ottawa, July 17 and 18, 2019.

data was not restricted to Indigenous women (or even broken down by race): Legal Strategy Coalition on Violence Against Indigenous Women (LSC), *Analyzing the 2014 Royal Canadian Mounted Police* (RCMP) *Report, Missing and Murdered Aboriginal Women: A National Operational Review: A Guide for the Study of the RCMP Statistics in the 2015 Report* (2015), leaf.ca/wp-content/uploads/2015/06/2015-06-16-MMIW-LSC-2014-Fact-Sheet-final-version.pdf.

Out of the 32,759 missing persons: "Canada's Missing: 2019 Fast Fact Sheet," Government of Canada, February 27, 2020, canadasmissing.ca/pubs/2019/index-eng.htm.

"the information is gathered primarily through an electronic connection" and "Additional information may be entered directly by CMPUR members": "National Centre for Missing Persons and Unidentified Remains (NCMPUR)," Royal Canadian Mounted Police, last modified April 6, 2018, rcmp-grc.gc.ca/en/national-centre-missing-persons-and-unidentified-remains-ncmpur.

"there is some subjectivity in the original CPIC data": "Canada's Missing: 2019 Fast Fact Sheet."

"The most common probable cause of the missing person cases… was a kidnapping": Irwin M. Cohen, Darryl Plecas, and Amanda V. McCormick, "A Comparison of Aboriginal and Non-Aboriginal Missing Persons in British Columbia Where Foul Play Has Not Been Ruled Out" (research report, 2009),

ufv.ca/media/assets/ccjr/reports-and-publications/Missing_Aboriginal_
Persons.pdf.

Mary Teegee, executive director of Carrier Sekani Family Services, commented: Betsy
Trumpener, "RCMP Say Highway of Tears Killers May Never Be Caught," CBC
News, October 17, 2016.

Annette Poitras... lost her way while on a dog-walking hike: Lisa Johnson, "Missing Dog
Walker Annette Poitras Found 'Alive and Well' in Coquitlam, B.C., After Massive Search," CBC News, November 22, 2017.

53-year-old Frances Brown, a Wet'suwet'en woman... disappeared: Ka'nhehsí:io Deer,
"'She's With Me Every Step of the Way': B.C. Man Walks Across Canada for
Missing Aunt," CBC News, November 26, 2018.

the year before the dog walker went missing, Deanna Desjarlais... disappeared: Angela
Sterritt, "Body of Deanna Desjarlais, 27, Found in Surrey, B.C.," CBC News,
September 18, 2016.

One year later, an inquest found fault in the police investigation of Deanna's murder: British
Columbia Ministry of Public Safety and Solicitor General, *Verdict at Coroners
Inquest: Findings and Recommendations as a Result of the Coroner's Inquest Pursuant
to Section 38 of the Coroners Act, [SBC 2007] c 15, Into the Death of Desjarlais Deanna
Renee* (2018), gov.bc.ca/assets/gov/birth-adoption-death-marriage-and-
divorce/deaths/coroners-service/inquest/2018/desjarlais-deanna-renee-
2016-0225-0116-verdict-with_-coroner_-comments.pdf.

Seven months after Ramona went missing: Interview with Brenda Wilson.

"in an on-going criminal investigation, the cause of death may be important not to release":
Emailed statement from Staff Sergeant Janelle Shoihet, Senior Media Relations Officer, Communication Services, RCMP E Division HQ, December 22,
2020.

*Indigenous women are twelve times as likely to be murdered or missing as any other women
in Canada and sixteen times as likely to be murdered as white women:* National Inquiry
into Missing and Murdered Indigenous Women and Girls, *Reclaiming Power
and Place: The Final Report of the National Inquiry into Missing and Murdered Indigenous Women and Girls* (2019), 1a:55.

*When it comes to intimate partner violence, Indigenous women experience it more frequently
and more severely:* Jillian Boyce, *Victimization of Aboriginal People in Canada*, 2014
(Canadian Centre for Justice Statistics, Statistics Canada, 2016), www150.
statcan.gc.ca/n1/pub/85-002-x/2016001/article/14631-eng.htm.

*"Even when all other differentiating factors are accounted for, Indigenous women are still at
a significantly higher risk of violence":* National Inquiry, *Reclaiming Power and Place*
1a:56.

"If you are a mom and need formula": In-person interview with Wanda Good in her
Gitanyow band office, September 2016.

*First Nations people, under the Indian Act, also still do not have the legal authority to possess
land on their own reserves:* "Definition and Registration of Indians: Reserves,"
Indian Act, last amended August 15, 2019, Justice Laws Website, laws-lois.
justice.gc.ca/eng/acts/I-5/page-3.html - h-332074.

*The structure as it stands makes it difficult if not impossible to run or own businesses on
reserve land:* See, for example, Tina Faiz, "Clearing the Hurdles of On-Reserve
Start-Ups," CBC News, May 5, 2009.

3 | K'emk'emeláy, *the place of many maple trees*

Ch'ich'iyúy Elxwíkn: "About," Ch'ich'iyúy, accessed April 18, 2022, chichiyuy.ca/ about.

"*This was one of the names for Vancouver*": Facebook Messenger communication with Marissa Nahanee, January 23, 2021.

Lek'lek̓ 'i was one of the names to describe what is now called CRAB Park: Angela Sterritt, "Road Signs Along the Sea to Sky Highway Offer Insight Into the History of the Skwxwú7mesh People," CBC News, June 24, 2021.

səlilwətaɬ (Tsleil-Waututh): Spelling of name confirmed by Charlene Aleck, Councillor with Tsleil-Waututh Nation, August 25, 2022.

Deighton... had two Skwxwú7mesh wives during his life, one just a girl: Laura Sciarpelletti, "Indigenous Activists Say the Story of Gassy Jack Is Missing Sordid Details," CBC News, June 30, 2019.

the Downtown Eastside neighbourhood started to face a steep decline: Harold Kalman and Robin Ward, Exploring Vancouver: The Architectural Guide, 4th ed. (Vancouver: Douglas & McIntyre, 2012), 18.

the federal government's deficit-cutting agenda: Larry Campbell, Neil Boyd, and Lori Culbert, A Thousand Dreams: Vancouver's Downtown Eastside and the Fight for Its Future (Vancouver: Greystone Books, 2009), 6.

"that dumb little Indian": Telephone interview with Tom Littlewood, February 26, 2021.

Manitoba's Child and Family Services placed a 15-year-old Anishinaabe youth, Tina Fontaine: Caroline Barghout, "Tina Fontaine Met Social Workers, Police and Health-Care Workers—but No One Kept Her Safe," CBC News, February 23, 2018.

B.C.'s Ministry of Children and Family Development put a Métis 18-year-old, Alex Gervais, in a Super 8 hotel: "Teen in B.C. Provincial Care Dies in Fall From Hotel Window," CBC News, September 23, 2015.

report that found the Ministry of Children and Family Development had housed twenty-four children: Liam Britten, "Report Shows 'Disturbing' Number of Kids Still in Hotels, Child Watchdog Says," CBC News, June 1, 2016.

In 2016, the ministry banned the non-emergency use of hotels: Emailed statement from Shawn Larabee, Government Communications and Public Engagement, Ministry of Children and Family Development, January 26, 2022.

Lindsay Kines considered first to break MMIWG story in Downtown Eastside: Yasmin Jiwani and Mary Lynn Young, "Missing and Murdered Women: Reproducing Marginality in News Discourse," Canadian Journal of Communication 31 (2006): 895–917.

In 1997, Kines wrote a story about the disappearance of Janet Henry: Lindsay Kines, "Family Fears Worst as Woman Vanishes in East Vancouver," Vancouver Sun, July 24, 1997.

"At that time, I had no idea she was one of a larger number": Quotations and information from Lindsay Kines in this chapter are from Angela Sterritt, "A Movement Rises," Open Canada, November 20, 2015, and from email interviews with Kines in July 2016 and August 2019.

Wayne Leng... was searching for his friend Sarah de Vries: Sterritt, "A Movement Rises"; email interviews with Wayne Leng, February 2021.

police had a list of sixteen women: Lindsay Kines, "Police Target Big Increase in Missing Women Cases," *Vancouver Sun,* July 3, 1998.

Indigenous people make up less than 2.5 percent of the population in Vancouver: "Census Profile, 2016 Census: Vancouver [Census Metropolitan Area], British Columbia and British Columbia [Province]," Statistics Canada, www12.statcan.gc.ca/census-recensement/2016/dp-pd/prof/index.cfm?Lang=E.

"We set up talking circles": Telephone interviews with Terri Brown, October 2015 and January 2022; see also Sterritt, "A Movement Rises."

"after the charges were stayed": "Early Pickton Prosecution Fouled by Witness's Drug Habit," Canadian Press (on CBC News website), April 12, 2012.

Terri's youngest sister, Ada Elaine Brown, was found dead in a Prince George hotel room in 2001: Denise Ryan, "Terri Brown's Quiet Voice Raises Big Questions About Missing Women," *Vancouver Sun,* March 22, 2016.

"this death is classified as undetermined": Martha Troian, "Unresolved: Ada Elaine Brown," *Missing and Murdered: The Unsolved Cases of Indigenous Women and Girls,* CBC News, October 7, 2016.

"I was the interim president": Telephone interview with Michèle Audette, November 8, 2014.

"Family members had told us horror stories": Terri Brown, quoted in Sterritt, "A Movement Rises."

Not long after, on February 1, 2002, a Coquitlam RCMP officer: Wally T. Oppal, Commissioner, *Forsaken: The Report of the Missing Women Commission of Inquiry,* vol. IIA, *Nobodies: How and Why We Failed the Missing and Murdered Women Part 1 and 2* (Victoria: Government of British Columbia, 2012), 182.

Police found bodily remains and trace DNA evidence of thirty-three missing women: Mark Gollom, "How the Robert Pickton Case Sparked Changes to B.C. Missing Persons Investigations," CBC News, February 3, 2018.

From 2002 to 2005, Pickton was charged with twenty-six counts of first-degree murder: Robert Matas, "Pickton Trial Update," Globe and Mail, October 5, 2006.

"they'd been there all along": Lorimer Shenher, *That Lonely Section of Hell: The Botched Investigation of a Serial Killer Who Almost Got Away* (Vancouver: Greystone Books, 2015), 206.

changing of power from the Liberals to the Conservatives... felt like a door being slammed: Kenneth Jackson, "Stephen Harper's Longest War: Missing and Murdered Indigenous Women," APTN National News, September 9, 2015.

"Pickton should have been apprehended sooner": SisterWatch Project of the Vancouver Police Department and the Women's Memorial March Committee, *The Tragedy of Missing and Murdered Aboriginal Women in Canada: We Can Do Better* (Vancouver Police Department, June 2011), 5, vpd.ca/wp-content/uploads/2021/06/missing-murdered-aboriginal-women-canada-report.pdf.

murder risk for sex trade workers: SisterWatch, *Tragedy of Missing and Murdered Aboriginal Women,* 10.

"enough evidence for a search warrant": Catherine Galliford, quoted in Suzanne Fournier, "Corporal's Statement Blasts RCMP," National Post, November 24, 2011, pressreader.com/canada/national-post-national-edition/20111124/281569467537745.

From that year to 2002, fourteen women were brutally murdered: Fournier, "Corporal's Statement Blasts RCMP."

"It's an absurd system": Email interview with Lindsay Kines, July 2016.

"There's bad things going on on that highway": In-person interview with Gladys Radek in Vancouver, B.C., September 28, 2003.

She was granted the highest award ever given for injury to dignity: Jonathan Woodward, "Sweet Victory Worth the Four-Year Wait," Globe and Mail, July 15, 2005.

4 | Nilhchuk-un, *those who take us away*

"people of the confluence of the rivers": Facebook Messenger conversation with Jennifer Annaïs Pighin, January 25, 2022.

a judge had been violently sexually assaulting Indigenous girls: Jane Armstrong, "B.C. Judge Throws the Book at Sex-Criminal Colleague," Globe and Mail, June 2, 2004.

from 1992 to 2001 he paid Indigenous teenage girls—all living on the street—for sex: R. v. Ramsay, 2004 BCSC 756 (CanLII), canlii.org/en/bc/bcsc/doc/2004/2004bcsc756/2004bcsc756.pdf.

In 2004, Ramsay pleaded guilty to five charges: R. v. Ramsay.

Prince George Citizen news article from 2010: Frank Peebles, "Gang Summit Offers Hope," Prince George Citizen, November 1, 2010.

2013 Human Rights Watch report: Human Rights Watch, Those Who Take Us Away: Abusive Policing and Failures in Protection of Indigenous Women and Girls in Northern British Columbia, Canada (2013), hrw.org/report/2013/02/13/those-who-take-us-away/abusive-policing-and-failures-protection-indigenous-women.

"sex crime investigation involving underage prostitutes": "2nd Mountie Sues RCMP Over Sex Crime Probe," CBC News, September 17, 2008.

Ramsay finally met his fate during a May 2002 custody case: Ian Mulgrew, "Ex-Judge Pleads Guilty to Preying on Troubled Girls," National Post, May 4, 2004, accessed via ProQuest.

"The accused's conduct was utterly reprehensible": R. v. Ramsay, 9.

In 2003, a Métis man named Clayton Willey was arrested: Civilian Review and Complaints Commission for the RCMP, Report Following a Chair-Initiated Complaint and Public Interest Investigation Into the In-Custody Death of Clay Willey, January 31, 2012, crcc-ccetp.gc.ca/en/report-following-chair-initiated-complaint-and-public-interest-investigation-custody-death-clay.

"the RCMP must nonetheless take responsibility": Civilian Review and Complaints Commission, Report Following a Chair-Initiated Complaint, "Conclusion."

"I can tell you it was sickening": Grand Chief Stewart Phillip, quoted in Mark Hume, "Death in Custody: Release of Man's Arrest Tape Urged," Globe and Mail, November 17, 2009.

"Code of Conduct processes were initiated against two RCMP officers": Emailed statement from Staff Sergeant Janelle Shoihet, Senior Media Relations Officer, Communication Services, RCMP E Division HQ, February 7, 2022.

Nilhchuk-un, meaning "those who take us away": Carrier Sekani Tribal Council, "Nilhchuk-un: Those Who Take Us Away," news release, February 14, 2013, carriersekani.ca/nilhchuk-un-those-who-take-us-away/.

"the police were not perceived as a source for help": Marcel-Eugène LeBeuf, *The Role of the Royal Canadian Mounted Police During the Indian Residential School System* (Ottawa: Royal Canadian Mounted Police, 2011), 4, collections.irshdc.ubc.ca/index.php/Detail/objects/9436.

The social workers' logs I have seen: Documents obtained February 2019 via freedom of information requests to the B.C. Ministry of Children and Family Development from July 2009 until July 2018.

"high-risk youth/street youth intervention team": "Youth Community Response," Vancouver Police Department, accessed February 22, 2022, vpd.ca/community/youth-community-response/.

From June 2017 to March 2018, ninety-eight children and youth died... Thirty-five were Indigenous: Angela Sterritt, "Other Deaths Linked to B.C. Aboriginal Agency Running Group Home Where Indigenous Teen Died," CBC News, November 10, 2020.

In 2020, I wrote an awful and traumatic story about a 17-year-old Cree youth: Angela Sterritt, "'I Trusted Them With My Son': Mother of Indigenous Teen Who Died in B.C. Group Home Speaks Out for First Time," CBC News, October 22, 2020.

Recorded in 2012 in a police interrogation room in Kelowna: Angela Sterritt and Jason Proctor, "'Were You at All Turned On?': RCMP's Handling of Sexual Assault Interview Denounced," CBC News, May 15, 2019.

In a telephone interview that same year, Aden tells me: Telephone interview with Aden Withers, May 14, 2019.

The ministry admitted to fraud and negligence by Saunders: Chad Pawson, "More Civil Claims Filed Against Province, Former Social Worker in Negligence, Fraud Case," CBC News, March 15, 2019.

In a Kelowna Capital News story: Michael Rodriguez, "Rape Survivor, Aden Withers, Settles Civil Suit Against Kelowna RCMP," *Kelowna Capital News*, January 29, 2020.

"No survivor of sexual assault should ever fear that his or her case will not be taken seriously": Minister of Public Safety Ralph Goodale, quoted in Sterritt and Proctor, "'Were You at All Turned On?'"

In 2021... the force announced a mandatory cultural competency training course: "Royal Canadian Mounted Police 2020–2021 Departmental Results Report," Royal Canadian Mounted Police, rcmp-grc.gc.ca/en/2020-2021-departmental-results-report/full-report.

Top RCMP officials in B.C. at the time admitted... they didn't believe the girls then: Jane Armstrong, "RCMP Seek to Reinstate Case Against Constable," *Globe and Mail*, December 13, 2006.

the RCMP's adjudication board held a hearing to determine whether... Constable Justin Harris should be disciplined: "Hearing Dismissed for Mountie Accused of Having Sex With Teen Prostitutes," CBC News, October 4, 2006.

after Ramsay pleaded guilty in 2004, the allegations... were taken more seriously: Petti Fong, "Sex Allegations Heard for Years, Hearing Told," *Globe and Mail*, October 3, 2006.

Harris was suspended with pay in September 2004: Emailed statement from Justin

Harris, February 2, 2022; "B.C. Mountie Sues Over Suspension," Globe and Mail, February 14, 2008.

In 2007 Harris was reinstated on paper: "B.C. Mountie Sues."

"segued from a paid suspension to paid sick leave": Jane Gerster, "RCMP Officer Accused of Sexual Assault Has Been on Paid Leave for 16 Years," Vice World News, May 5, 2021.

"While it certainly is tragic": Emailed statement from Justin Harris, February 2, 2022.

"a tract of land, the legal title to which is vested in Her Majesty": "Definitions," section 2(1), p. 1, Indian Act, last amended August 15, 2019, laws-lois.justice.gc.ca/PDF/I-5.pdf.

the Department of Indian Affairs under Prime Minister John. A. Macdonald instituted a federal "pass system": "Highlights From the Report of the Royal Commission on Aboriginal Peoples: People to People, Nation to Nation," Government of Canada, September 15, 2010, rcaanc-cirnac.gc.ca/eng/1100100014597/1572547985018.

If caught without a pass, an Indigenous person could face a ten-dollar fine: Bev Sellars, Price Paid: The Fight for First Nations Survival (Vancouver: Talonbooks, 2016), 83.

federal government began a concerted effort to ban Northwest Coast Indigenous technologies like the fish weir: Mark Hume, "Turning to the Past Can Help Salmon Stocks of the Future," Globe and Mail, February 2, 2009.

Indigenous people were also fined for hunting for game in season: Tyler McCreary, Shared Histories: Witsuwit'en–Settler Relations in Smithers, British Columbia, 1913–1973 (Powell River, BC: Creekstone Press, 2018), 83.

a "local Indian" running a mill in the Skeena region was charged for having moose meat: McCreary, Shared Histories.

Indigenous people could not sell what was grown on their land: Truth and Reconciliation Commission of Canada, The Final Report of the Truth and Reconciliation Commission of Canada, vol. 1, Canada's Residential Schools: The History, Part 1, Origins to 1939 (Montreal and Kingston: McGill-Queen's University Press, 2015), 109, 110, 123, 128; James Daschuk, Clearing the Plains: Disease, Politics of Starvation, and the Loss of Aboriginal Life (Regina: University of Regina Press, 2013), 122.

"natives are to be given strict application of every by-law": McCreary, Shared Histories; "Squatter Indians May Be Forced From Townsite," Interior News, May 11, 1927, accessed via newspapers.com.

In 1869, through section 6 of the Gradual Enfranchisement Act: Bob Joseph, 21 Things You May Not Know About the Indian Act: Helping Canadians Make Reconciliation With Indigenous Peoples a Reality (Indigenous Relations Press, 2018), 28–29, 116; for the section of the act pertaining to loss of status, see paragraph 6 of the legislation on the National Centre for Truth and Reconciliation website, dev.nctr.ca/wp-content/uploads/2021/01/1869-Gradual-Enfranchisement-Act.pdf.

the 1951 Indian Act: Peter Kirby, "Marrying Out and Loss of Status: The Charter and New Indian Act Legislation," Journal of Law and Social Policy 1, article 6 (1985): 77–95.

In 1923, the B.C. government created the Women's and Girls' Protection Act: McCreary, Shared Histories.

Lovelace took her case to the United Nations Human Rights Committee: See Sandra Lovelace v. Canada, Communication No. R.6/24, U.N. Doc. Supp. No. 40 (A/36/40)
at 166 (1981), submitted by Sandra Lovelace, December 29, 1977, accessed via
University of Manitoba Human Rights Library, hrlibrary.umn.edu/undocs/
session36/6-24.htm.

Her efforts, along with those of Mary Two-Axe Earley, Yvonne Bedard, and Jeannette Corbiere Lavell: Janet Silman, Enough Is Enough: Aboriginal Women Speak Out (Toronto:
Women's Press, 1987).

a Wet'suwet'en woman named Florence Naziel: Gladys Radek, "Why I Volunteer," CBC
News, November 29, 2010.

Florence was the first person known to use "Highway of Tears": Morgan Hampton, "Red
Dress Day: A History of the Highway of Tears," Toronto Star, May 7, 2021.

"That walk was the one that set the template": Telephone interview with Gladys Radek,
December 16, 2021.

Thirty-three recommendations were listed: Lheidli T'enneh First Nation, Carrier Sekani
Family Services, Carrier Sekani Tribal Council, Prince George Native Friendship Centre, and Prince George Nechako Aboriginal Employment and Training
Association, Highway of Tears Symposium Recommendations Report (2006), 19, 21,
highwayoftears.org/resources/documents-and-reports.

B.C.'s information and privacy commissioner... launched an investigation: Mike Laanela,
"Triple Delete: Former Ministry Staffer George Gretes Charged in Scandal,"
CBC News, March 11, 2016.

"there's a cover-up going on": Mavis Erickson, quoted in "Highway of Tears: 'There's
a Cover-Up Going On,' Says First Nations Tribal Councillor," CBC News,
May 29, 2015.

Denham's investigation revealed: Mark Hume, "B.C. Government 'Triple Deleted'
E-mails Related to the Highway of Tears," Globe and Mail, October 25, 2015.

"get rid of" all emails related to the Highway of Tears: Elizabeth Denham, Access Denied:
Record Retention and Disposal Practices of the Government of British Columbia, Investigation Report F15-03 (Victoria: Office of the Information and Privacy Commissioner for British Columbia, 2015), 26, oipc.bc.ca/investigation-reports/1874.

"he sympathized with the families": Denham, Access Denied, 29.

"To watch as the government doesn't take it seriously": "Q&A: Tim Duncan Explains
Why Highway of Tears Emails Were Allegedly Deleted," CBC News,
May 28, 2015.

One month later the ministry announced a $3 million government action plan: British
Columbia Ministry of Transportation and Infrastructure, "B.C. Unveils Five
Point Action Plan for Safe Transportation Options Along Highway 16," news
release, December 14, 2015, news.gov.bc.ca/releases/2015TRANO179-002092.

"people in the communities along the Highway 16 corridor asked for safe, affordable travel
options": British Columbia Ministry of Transportation and Infrastructure,
"Increased Use Marks Highway 16 Plan's Second Anniversary," news release,
January 31, 2019, archive.news.gov.bc.ca/releases/news_releases_2017-2021/
2019TRANO006-000119.htm.

after more than sixty women and girls from the region had gone missing or been murdered:
Interview with Gladys Radek.

It took fifteen years, until 2021, for the B.C. government to announce it was bringing cell service: Lee Wilson, "It Took 15 Years of Advocacy to Get Cell Coverage on Highway of Tears, and Families Say There Is Still Much Work to Do," APTN National News, May 5, 2021.

"Took you long enough": Interview with Gladys Radek.

"This ongoing official RCMP investigation should determine the number of missing women": Lheidli T'enneh First Nation et al., Highway of Tears Symposium Recommendations Report, 31.

In 2007, the RCMP expanded its investigation from nine cases of missing or murdered women or girls to eighteen: Neal Hall, "Police Reveal Details of E-Pana Investigation Into 18 Female Unsolved Cases in Northern B.C.," Vancouver Sun, May 18, 2010.

5 | Nucwstimu, *quiet*

Yunesit'in, also known as Stone or Stoney: "Welcome to Yunesit'in," Yunesit'in Government, accessed February 23, 2022, yunesitin.ca/.

Levina, as she was called by her family: All information and quotations from Vanessa Hans in this chapter come from telephone interviews and correspondence with her from May 2016 to February 2021.

"Oh, and she was a great mom who loved children": Telephone interview with David (Al) Moody, January 18, 2022.

Her case, like Ramona Wilson's, is now among the investigations of the RCMP's Project E-PANA: "Project E-PANA," Royal Canadian Mounted Police, last modified December 13, 2016, bc-cb.rcmp-grc.gc.ca/ViewPage.action?siteNodeId=23&languageId=1&contentId=27048.

Few of the women's cases have been solved: Telephone interview with former RCMP staff sergeant Wayne Cleary, April 11, 2016.

"until such time that it has been settled"… "It is my understanding that there was at one time someone of interest": Emailed statement from Staff Sergeant Janelle Shoihet, Senior Media Relations Officer, Communication Services, RCMP E Division HQ, March 9, 2021.

two hundred pages of documents I obtained: Documents obtained from the RCMP via Access to Information and Privacy request, April 27, 2020.

A 1999 Coast Mountain News article: Angela Hall, "The Final Chapter in a Brutal Murder," Coast Mountain News, 1999, accessed via Vanessa Hans.

The RCMP tell me one of their members had a contact: Emailed statement from Staff Sergeant Shoihet.

A former Mountie, Mel McIntosh…says he was aware of Blohm: Telephone interviews with former RCMP officer Mel McIntosh, November 6, 2016, and December 6, 2019.

[John Brecknock] is originally from Alexis Creek: Telephone interview with former RCMP officer John Brecknock, July 22, 2019.

"one of the suspects killed himself in 1972": Hall, "The Final Chapter."

Brecknock's message…contained a link to a Williams Lake Tribune article: Angie Mindus, "Case Closed on a Brutal Murder," Williams Lake Tribune, December 12, 1998.

Statistics around lesser charges and sentencing of those who kill Indigenous women and girls: Lillian Dyck, Melanie Morrison, Kandice Parke, and Karissa Wall, "Indigenous Female Homicide Victims Study: Summary of Key Findings" (unpublished report, June 18, 2019), received as Microsoft Word file from Senator Dyck's office; Justin Brake, "People Who Kill Indigenous Women Punished Less Than Those Who Kill Non-Indigenous Women, Senator's Study Finds," APTN National News, November 28, 2018.

widespread notion that we do not matter as much as other Canadians: National Inquiry into Missing and Murdered Indigenous Women and Girls, *Reclaiming Power and Place: The Final Report of the National Inquiry into Missing and Murdered Indigenous Women and Girls* (2019), 1a:101.

"Indians" from or visiting Williams Lake were banned from businesses: Constance Backhouse, *Carnal Crimes: Sexual Assault Law in Canada, 1900–1975* (Toronto: Irwin Law, for the Osgoode Society for Canadian Legal History, 2008), 241.

In 1891, it became a residential school: Backhouse, *Carnal Crimes,* 234.

In 1955, at 6 years old, Rose Roper, a Secwepemc and Tŝilhqot'in child: These and other details about Rose Roper are from Backhouse, *Carnal Crimes.*

"Our objective is to continue until there is not a single Indian": Duncan Campbell Scott, quoted in "Until There Is Not a Single Indian in Canada," Facing History & Ourselves, accessed February 23, 2022, facinghistory.org/stolen-lives-indigenous-peoples-canada-and-indian-residential-schools/historical-background/until-there-not-single-indian-canada; National Archives of Canada, Record Group 10, volume 6810, file 470-2-3, volume 7, pp. 55 (L-3) and 63 (N-3).

In 1989, Roman Catholic priest Harold McIntee: Douglas Todd, "Priest's Sex Assaults Called Breach of Trust: Lengthy Jail Term Urged," *Vancouver Sun,* May 16, 1989, vancouversun.com/news/staff-blogs/one-of-canadas-first-big-convictions-for-residential-school-abuse.

In 1996, former St. Joseph's priest Hubert O'Connor was convicted: Tom Hawthorn, "Disgraced B.C. Bishop Dead of Heart Attack," *Globe and Mail,* July 27, 2007.

more than 4,100 children who attended residential school: "Student Memorial Register FAQ," National Centre for Truth and Reconciliation, accessed February 23, 2022, nctr.ca/memorial/national-student-memorial/student-memorial-register-faq/.

In 1902, an 8-year-old boy, Duncan Sticks: Truth and Reconciliation Commission of Canada, *The Final Report of the Truth and Reconciliation Commission of Canada,* vol. 1, *Canada's Residential Schools: The History, Part 1, Origins to 1939* (Montreal and Kingston: McGill-Queen's University Press, 2015), 533.

In 1920, another Indigenous boy who was around 9, Augustine Allen: Truth and Reconciliation Commission, *Final Report,* vol. 1, *The History, Part 1,* 540. Note that Augustine's surname is spelled "Allan" in the TRC report, but "Allen" in the National Centre for Truth and Reconciliation database, nctr.ca/residential-schools/british-columbia/cariboo-williams-lake/.

Gordon's Indian Residential School in Saskatchewan was closed in 1996: Winona Wheeler, "Not as Envisioned: Gordon's Indian Residential School," *Canadian Geographic,* January 14, 2021.

[Rose Roper's] father, as a result of his trauma, became a heavy drinker: Details in this paragraph from Backhouse, *Carnal Crimes*.

The press coverage from the time of Rose Roper's murder is telling: Details and quotations in this paragraph from Backhouse, *Carnal Crimes*, 247.

"a bit of Indian trash" and a "drunken native girl": Quoted in Backhouse, *Carnal Crimes*, 253.

Spiritual and community leaders have held two ceremonies for Levina: In-person interview with Sam Moody in Vancouver, B.C., August 6, 2017.

in 2018, a story out of Bella Coola: Bethany Lindsay, "B.C. First Nation Hopes Tiny Solar-Powered Homes Will Give Men in Need a Leg Up," CBC News, March 25, 2018.

6 | Gidi guutxwdiit seegidit, *caught a killer*

UBC's Alma Mater Society president Marium Hamid expressed a "profound regret": Kevin Ward, "AMS Apologizes to Indigenous Peoples," Indigenous Portal, University of British Columbia, November 7, 2018, indigenous.ubc.ca/2018/11/07/ams-apologizes-to-indigenous-peoples/.

the RCMP in B.C. started Project E-PANA, their task force dedicated to unsolved murders: "Project E-PANA," Royal Canadian Mounted Police, last modified December 13, 2016, bc-cb.rcmp-grc.gc.ca/ViewPage.action?siteNodeId=23&languageId=1&contentId=27048.

"spirit goddess that looks after the souls": "Project E-PANA," RCMP.

"When this project was put together it was an historical investigation": Telephone interview with former RCMP staff sergeant Wayne Cleary, April 11, 2016.

the criteria for a case to be selected for Project E-PANA: Emailed statement from Staff Sergeant Janelle Shoihet, Senior Media Relations Officer, Communication Services, RCMP E Division HQ, January 27, 2022.

Monica Jack was just a 12-year-old girl riding her bike: "Monica Jack," Missing and Murdered: The Unsolved Cases of Indigenous Women and Girls, CBC News, updated January 2019.

Bruce Hulan and other earlier E-PANA investigators: Neal Hall, "Police Reveal Details of E-Pana Investigation Into 18 Female Unsolved Cases in Northern B.C.," *Vancouver Sun*, May 18, 2010.

"it is wrong to attribute the women's vulnerability" ... "Often they were treated not as persons": Wally T. Oppal, Commissioner, *Forsaken: The Report of the Missing Women Commission of Inquiry*, Executive Summary (Victoria: Government of British Columbia, 2012), 16, 25.

a woman's Aboriginal identity should be taken into consideration: Government of British Columbia, *Provincial Policing Standards*, Section 5.0 – Specialized Investigations, Sub Section 5.1 – Missing Person Investigations, Subject 5.1.2 – Risk Assessment Process, revised September 15, 2018, www2.gov.bc.ca/assets/gov/law-crime-and-justice/criminal-justice/police/standards/5-1-2-risk-assessment.pdf.

"In the past people might hear that Jane Doe was missing": Bowen Osoko, quoted in Nicole Crescenzi, "What It Means to Be a 'High Risk' Missing Person on Vancouver Island," *Vancouver Island Free Daily*, February 8, 2020.

When I ask other RCMP officials if being Indigenous alone makes a person high risk, I am told no: Interview with Wayne Cleary.

The SisterWatch committee… has stated that Indigenous women face unique risks: Vancouver Police Department, The SisterWatch Program: An Evaluation and Best Practices Summary (n.d.), vpd.ca/wp-content/uploads/2021/06/sister watch-evaluation-1.pdf.

Indigenous women are about seven times as likely as non-Indigenous women to be killed by serial killers: Kathryn Blaze Baum and Matthew McClearn, "Prime Target: How Serial Killers Prey on Indigenous Women," Globe and Mail, November 22, 2015.

FBI's definition of serial murder as "the unlawful killing of two or more victims": Brian Fitzpatrick, "Serial Killers: How Is the Term Defined?," Regina Leader-Post, June 2, 2020.

A Globe and Mail analysis found that at least eighteen Indigenous women died: Blaze Baum and McClearn, "Prime Target."

"If there is such a thing as an ideal profession": Rene Chun, "Modern Life Has Made It Easier for Serial Killers to Thrive," The Atlantic, October 2019.

In 2014, Cody Legebokoff, a white 24-year-old: "Cody Legebokoff Sentenced to Life on 4 Counts of 1st-Degree Murder," CBC News, September 16, 2014.

all four women would be classified as "knowing their killer": Royal Canadian Mounted Police, Missing and Murdered Aboriginal Women: 2015 Update to the National Operational Overview (2015), rcmp-grc.gc.ca/wam/media/455/original/c3561a284 cfbb9c244bef57750941439.pdf.

in 2013 and 2014, thirty-two Indigenous women were homicide victims, and in 100 percent of the solved cases, they knew their killer: RCMP, Missing and Murdered Aboriginal Women: 2015 Update.

CBC journalist Andrew Kurjata wrote an analysis of the report: Andrew Kurjata, "Focus on 'Family Violence' in Cases of Missing, Murdered Aboriginal Women Misguided," CBC News, July 8, 2015.

as was pointed out during an RCMP news conference about their report: Connie Walker (@connie_walker), "Reporter: Is a john considered an acquaintance? RCMP: Yes. I'm paraphrasing here," Twitter, June 19, 2015, 12:45 p.m., twitter.com/ connie_walker/status/611967977202827264.

In a 2015 letter to Grand Chief Bernice Martial: Gloria Galloway, "70 Per Cent of Murdered Aboriginal Women Killed by Indigenous Men: RCMP," Globe and Mail, April 9, 2015.

Commissioners of the National Inquiry… debunked that finding: National Inquiry into Missing and Murdered Indigenous Women and Girls, Reclaiming Power and Place: The Final Report of the National Inquiry into Missing and Murdered Indigenous Women and Girls (Vancouver: Privy Council Office, 2019), 1a:648.

"It is a mistake, in my view, to limit the seriousness of this issue": Justice Glen Parrett, quoted in Mark Nielsen, "Judge Sentences Legebokoff to Life for Four Murders," Prince George Citizen, September 16, 2014.

E-PANA lost 99 percent of its annual budget between 2009/10 and 2017/18: RCMP document obtained via Access to Information and Privacy request, January 18, 2019.

E-PANA was "winding down": Interview with Wayne Cleary.

quantity of evidence E-PANA was dealing with was mammoth: Interview with Wayne Cleary.

"because all cases are technically always being investigated": Interview with Wayne Cleary.

Garry Handlen was arrested and charged: "Garry Handlen Found Guilty of Murdering Monica Jack 40 Years Ago," CBC News, January 17, 2019.

He is suspected of killing at least two other girls: CTV Vancouver, "New Details Emerge on Alleged Child Killer's History," CTV News, December 2, 2014.

RCMP investigators announced they believed that U.S. convict Bobby Fowler: CTVNews.ca Staff, "U.S. Convict Responsible for B.C. Teen's Murder, Suspect in 2 Others: Police," CTV News, September 25, 2012.

Brian Peter Arp was initially arrested in 1990: R. v. Arp, [1998] 3 S.C.R. 339, Case No. 26100, scc-csc.lexum.com/scc-csc/scc-csc/en/item/1664/index.do.

Edward Isaac, a Dakelh man, was charged with first-degree murder: Sheryl Thompson, "Man Charged in Girl's Murder," *Prince George Citizen*, August 12, 1986, Prince George Digitization, pgnewspapers.pgpl.ca/fedora/repository/pgc:1986-08-12/-/Prince%20George%20Citizen%20-%20August%2012,%201986; "City Girl's Killer Given Life Term," *Prince George Citizen*, May 12, 1987, Prince George Digitization, pgnewspapers.pgpl.ca/fedora/repository/pgc:1987-05-12/-/Prince%20George%20Citizen%20-%20May%2012,%201987.

he told me there are about six murders...that are now solved: Interview with Wayne Cleary.

B.C. Prosecution Service "was not at all interested": Emailed statement from Staff Sergeant Janelle Shoihet, March 9, 2021.

"The RCMP constructed a thorough timeline as to Bobby Jack Fowler's activities": Emailed statement from Staff Sergeant Janelle Shoihet, January 27, 2022.

"the investigation [E-PANA] is supported by the Special Projects Major Crime Unit": Emailed statement from Staff Sergeant Janelle Shoihet, August 21, 2019.

"Families that do their own searches are feeling a little bit let down": Grand Chief Sheila North, quoted in Kelly Geraldine Malone, "Manitoba Manhunt Shows Lack of Resources for Missing Indigenous Women: Advocates," *Vancouver Sun*, August 1, 2019.

"I've stopped counting": Telephone interview with Gladys Radek, December 16, 2021.

She says by 2013 she had counted more than four thousand MMIWG: National Inquiry into Missing and Murdered Indigenous Women and Girls, "Truth-Gathering Process – Part I, Public Hearings," Hearing 3 (September 26, 2017), 149, mmiwg-ffada.ca/wp-content/uploads/2018/10/20170926_MMIWG_Smithers_Public_Vol_4_combined_Pub_Ban.pdf.

"How many more serial killers will we learn about": Interview with Gladys Radek.

Patty Hajdu repeated the same number as Gladys: John Paul Tasker, "Confusion Reigns Over Number of Missing, Murdered Indigenous Women," CBC News, February 16, 2016.

7 | 'Et'doonekh, *it might happen*

"We didn't want [the women's march] just to be about Cheryl": Melodie Casella, quoted in Angela Sterritt, "Relatives of Woman Whose Death Sparked MMIW's Memorial March Want Changes in the Justice System," CBC News, February 13, 2017.

She connected with the women and the marches in this neighbourhood: Telephone interview with Gladys Radek, December 16, 2021.

she tells me she was "institutionalized since birth": Angela Sterritt, "A Movement Rises," Open Canada, November 20, 2015.

"It was a pretty emotional experience, my first child": In-person interview with Tom Chipman in Terrace, B.C., August 3, 2016.

"I remember her carrying me downstairs to a laundry room": In-person interview with Jaden, August 3, 2016.

Tamara had been living between his house in Terrace and her mom's in Rupert: Interview with Tom Chipman.

Eric Stubbs…tells me that finding Tamara would have been difficult: Telephone interview with Eric Stubbs, Director General of National Criminal Operations, RCMP, November 2, 2016.

Search parties of up to three hundred relatives and friends scoured: Interview with Tom Chipman.

During testimony at the national inquiry, a family friend: National Inquiry into Missing and Murdered Indigenous Women and Girls, "Truth-Gathering Process – Part 1, Public Hearings" (April 6, 2018), 30, mmiwg-ffada.ca/wp-content/uploads/2018/10/20180406_MMIWG_Vancouver_Public_Vol_101_Radek_et-al_Publication_Ban.pdf.

"It was very nerve-racking and scary": Telephone interview with Arnie Nagy, November 8, 2017.

Stubbs tells me police did conduct a ground search: Interview with Eric Stubbs.

In a local newspaper article, there's a photo of Stubbs: "City Bids Adieu to RCMP Supt. Eric Stubbs," *Prince George Free Press*, June 26, 2014.

"I tend to get in other people's problems": Email correspondence with Lloyd Thomas, November 1, 2016.

Ray Michalko…told me he helped Thomas set up an interview: Telephone interview with former RCMP officer Ray Michalko, October 7, 2016.

RCMP officers have said they believe everyone who was involved in Tamara's death is now dead: Interview with Eric Stubbs.

"She probably had PTSD from the cops coming down on her": Telephone interview with unnamed source (brother of possible witness to Tamara Chipman murder), March 18, 2021.

there is potentially a new piece of evidence: Telephone interview with Tom Chipman, January 23, 2022.

"Tamara Chipman's investigation has always been open": Emailed statement from Staff Sergeant Janelle Shoihet, Senior Media Relations Officer, Communication Services, RCMP E Division HQ, January 28, 2022.

In a second interview with him…at a Tim Hortons: In-person interview with Ray Michalko in Delta, B.C., January 12, 2017.

When I moved to Prince George in 2002, stabbings were not uncommon: "Crime Severity Index and Weighted Clearance Rates, Police Services in British Columbia," Geography: Prince George, British Columbia, Reference period: 2000–2006, Statistics Canada, doi.org/10.25318/3510006301-eng.

In 2011, Maclean's ranked Prince George as Canada's most dangerous city…a string of nine murders rocked the community: Ken MacQueen and Patricia Treble, "Canada's Most Dangerous City: Prince George," *Maclean's*, December 15, 2011.

Prince George and its sister city, Prince Rupert… were ranked among the worst places to live: Citizen Staff, "Prince George Among Worst Places to Live in Canada," *Prince George Citizen*, March 21, 2012.

"No one will ever know [what happened]": In-person discussion with Tom Chipman in Prince Rupert, B.C., September 23, 2018.

"Well, there's Nicole Hoar": Interview with Ray Michalko, January 12, 2017.

Of these, 64 percent were identified as missing due to "unknown" circumstances or suspected foul play: Royal Canadian Mounted Police, *Missing and Murdered Aboriginal Women: 2015 Update to the National Operational Overview* (2015), rcmp-grc.gc.ca/wam/media/455/original/c3561a284cfbb9c244hef57750941439.pdf.

In the early hours of 2011, Madison Scott, 20, went missing: Winston Szeto, "A Decade After Madison Scott's Disappearance, Parents Continue to Call for Witnesses," CBC News, May 28, 2021.

Immaculate (Mackie) Basil… disappeared in an eerily similar way: In-person interview with Ida Basil in Prince George, B.C., October 16, 2016.

"For this government to fund every organization": Telephone interview with Gladys Radek, November 1, 2015; Sterritt, "A Movement Rises."

8 | Ninchíms, *to question someone*

Wally Oppal was named the commissioner of the inquiry: Robert Matas, "Pickton Inquiry Details Kept From Aboriginal Groups, Grand Chief Says," *Globe and Mail*, September 27, 2010.

The aim of the Missing Women Commission hearings: Wally T. Oppal, Commissioner, *Forsaken: The Report of the Missing Women Commission of Inquiry*, Executive Summary (Victoria: Government of British Columbia, 2012).

the commission… no longer "represented a meaningful exercise"… "With its denial to fund legal counsel": Kasari Govender, quoted in Angela Sterritt, "Missing Women's Commission Flounders," *The Dominion*, September 26, 2011.

"To us it appears discriminatory": Jeannette Corbiere Lavell, quoted in Sterritt, "Missing Women's Commission Flounders."

"It would be the height of unfairness": Wally Oppal, quoted in Sterritt, "Missing Women's Commission Flounders."

"The government's decision means some of the best lawyers in Vancouver": David Eby, quoted in Sterritt, "Missing Women's Commission Flounders."

"These continue to be challenging economic times": Barry Penner, quoted in Sterritt, "Missing Women's Commission Flounders."

"In the big picture, setting aside the petty fault-finding": David Eby, quoted in Sterritt, "Missing Women's Commission Flounders."

if his jailhouse confession is true: "Pickton's Confession Elicited Through Police Lies, Court Told," CBC News, November 21, 2077.

the VPD "did not cause the failure of the investigation into Pickton": Doug LePard, *Missing Women Investigation Review* (Vancouver Police Department, 2010), 19, vpd.ca/wp-content/uploads/2021/06/missing-women-investigation-review.pdf.

the report says that more police attention is given to "women with more conventional lives"… sex trade workers have "little day to day accountability": LePard, *Missing Women Investigation Review*, 35.

"Some of the allegations of bias": LePard, Missing Women Investigation Review, 36.
"Folks were coming up and saying that women...were disappearing": Ernie Crey, quoted in Sterritt, "Missing Women's Commission Flounders."
In 1997, Karen Isaac of the Summit provided police with a list: LePard, Missing Women Investigation Review.
"the brutal murders of fifty-five Aboriginal women": Letter quoted in LePard, Missing Women Investigation Review, 59.
even lengthier than fifty-five names, at seventy-one: LePard, Missing Women Investigation Review.
nineteen of those were women he thought "appeared to have relocated": Constable Dave Dickson's report, quoted in LePard, Missing Women Investigation Review, 60.
According to Crey, a police liaison explained the mystery of the missing women: Sterritt, "Missing Women's Commission Flounders."
In the summer of 1998, Detective Constable Lorimer Shenher was assigned...In late August 1998, Shenher reported that nearly all of the cases: LePard, Missing Women Investigation Review.
in Shenher's own book: Lorimer Shenher, That Lonely Section of Hell: The Botched Investigation of a Serial Killer Who Almost Got Away (Vancouver: Greystone Books, 2015).
"Four of us decided that was crap"..."When the VPD brass first insisted": Email interview with Lorimer Shenher, January 28, 2022.
"They had enough evidence": Lilliane Beaudoin, quoted in CTV.ca News Staff, "Women's Relatives Demand Pickton Inquiry," CTV News, August 21, 2010.
"In cases that involve the ongoing genocide of our people": Jeannette Corbiere Lavell, quoted in Sterritt, "Missing Women's Commission Flounders."
"I also conclude that there is no evidence of widespread institutional bias": Oppal, Forsaken, Executive Summary, 95.
"As Aboriginal women, we have the role of leading": Jeannette Corbiere Lavell, quoted in Sterritt, "Missing Women's Commission Flounders."
"Um, it, it isn't really high on our radar, to be honest, Peter": Prime Minister Stephen Harper, quoted in "Full Text of Peter Mansbridge's Interview With Stephen Harper," CBC News, December 17, 2014.
Harper reiterated his line that, "first and foremost": Kathryn Blaze Carlson and Jill Mahoney, "Harper Rejects Calls for Aboriginal Women Inquiry," Globe and Mail, August 21, 2014.
"I think we should not view this as sociological phenomenon": Prime Minister Stephen Harper, quoted in Jennifer Ditchburn, "Reports Contradict Stephen Harper's View on Aboriginal Women Victims," CBC News, September 3, 2014.
"we also have no history of colonialism": Prime Minister Stephen Harper, quoted in David Ljunggren, "Every G20 Nation Wants to Be Canada, Insists PM," Reuters, September 25, 2009.
"I feel emotional, I can't believe this is actually happening": Lorelei Williams, quoted in Angela Sterritt with Andrew Friesen, "Lorelei Williams Carries Family Story of Missing and Murdered Indigenous Women," CBC News, February 3, 2016.
In August of 2016, Ottawa launched the $53.8 million independent inquiry: Kristy Kirkup, "Ottawa Launches Long-Awaited Inquiry Into Missing, Murdered Indigenous Women," Canadian Press (on Global News website), August 3, 2016.

This process would give family members the chance to heal: Jessica Murphy, "Canada
Launches Inquiry Into Murdered and Missing Indigenous Women," The
Guardian, December 8, 2015.

Carolyn Bennett criss-crossed the country: "Full Summary of What We Heard: Final
Report of the Pre-inquiry Engagement Process," Government of Canada, May
19, 2016, rcaanc-cirnac.gc.ca/eng/1463677554486/1534775555263.

"Is it ironic that I found my missing cousin one weekend": Facebook post by Michael
Hutchinson, quoted in Angela Sterritt and Martha Troian, "MMIW Commis-
sion Off to a Bumpy Start as Communications Director Let Go," CBC News,
February 4, 2017.

the inquiry lost at least twenty people: Marc Montgomery, "Another Resignation From
Troubled Inquiry Into Missing, Murdered Indigenous Women and Girls,"
Radio Canada International, July 3, 2018.

she pointed to what she called a "colonial" process: "Marilyn Poitras on Why She
Resigned as MMIWG Commissioner and Her Hopes for Change," CBC News,
July 16, 2017.

proceeding with the commission at "lightning speed": Marion Buller, quoted in Laura
Kane, "Indigenous Women's Inquiry Head Says Process Moving at 'Lightning
Speed,'" CBC News, July 6, 2017.

On May 30, 2017, I covered the first story heard at the first inquiry hearing: Angela Sterritt, "Family Still Seeks Answers 35 Years After Mary Johns Found Dead in
Serial Killer's Barber Shop," CBC News, May 31, 2017.

Bernée Bolton said these alterations were all choices made by the family members: Margo
McDiarmid, "MMIW Inquiry Won't Hear From Most Families Until the Fall,"
CBC News, May 10, 2017.

"My health started to fail": Telephone interview with Gladys Radek, January
28, 2022.

"You can't unravel genocide in two years": Gladys Radek, quoted in Andrew Kurjata,
"Skepticism and Hope as National MMIWG Hearings Come to B.C.'s Highway
of Tears," CBC News, September 26, 2017.

province with the highest number of missing people in the country: Jolene Rudisuela,
"More People Go Missing in BC Than Anywhere Else in Canada. No One
Knows Why," Capital Daily, May 5, 2021.

Most of the concerns were about aftercare: "An Open Letter Calling for the Refusal of
the MMIWG Inquiry Extension Request," Manitoulin Expositor, April 11, 2018,
manitoulin.com/an-open-letter-calling-for-the-refusal-of-the-mmiwg-inquiry-
extension-request/.

They said that the word genocide shouldn't be used: Rob Breakenridge, "Use of the
Word 'Genocide' Undermines the MMIWG Report," Global News, June 8, 2019.

United Nations definition of genocide: "Genocide: Background," United Nations Office
on Genocide Prevention and the Responsibility to Protect, accessed February
25, 2022, un.org/en/genocideprevention/genocide.shtml.

CBC journalist Evan Dyer's article: Evan Dyer, "What Does It Mean to Call Canada's
Treatment of Indigenous Women a 'Genocide'?," CBC News, June 5, 2019.

CBC has defended the article, saying that it "sought to explain…" and that "the piece included
multiple perspectives": Emailed statement from Chuck Thompson, Chief of Staff
to the EVP, Head of Public Affairs at CBC, July 20, 2022.

"the thousands of truths shared before the National Inquiry": National Inquiry into Missing and Murdered Indigenous Women and Girls, *A Legal Analysis of Genocide: Supplementary Report of the National Inquiry into Missing and Murdered Indigenous Women and Girls* (Vancouver: Privy Council Office, 2019), 1.

When I followed up with her in 2021: Telephone interview with Gladys Radek, December 20, 2021.

9 | 'Mnsaksit gilelix, *going on top*

"more of a perspective than a geographic place"... "endless stretch of land"... lii vyeu or "the old ones": Jean Teillet, *The North-West Is Our Mother: The Story of Louis Riel's People, the Métis Nation* (Toronto: HarperCollins, 2019), xiv, xv.

"homicide capital" and "most racist city in Canada": Laura Glowacki, "Winnipeg Struggles to Shake 'Murder Capital' Reputation," CBC News, August 17, 2016; Nancy Macdonald, "Welcome to Winnipeg: Where Canada's Racism Problem Is at Its Worst," *Maclean's*, January 22, 2015.

Smith's sister Claudette Osborne-Tyo was a 21-year-old mother: "'She Was Aboriginal. She Had an Addiction': Sister of MMIW Says Family Had to Push Police," *The Current*, CBC Radio, December 7, 2016; "Claudette Priscilla June Osborne," *Missing and Murdered: The Unsolved Cases of Indigenous Women and Girls*, CBC News, 2016.

"My sister had a criminal record": Unless otherwise noted, quotations and information from Bernadette Smith in this chapter are from Angela Sterritt, "A Movement Rises," *Open Canada*, November 20, 2015.

Project Devote launched in 2011... However, it didn't have much success: Darren Bernhardt, "Winnipeg Police Pull Out of Project Devote, Create New Model for Investigating MMIWG Cases," CBC News, March 6, 2020.

"ensure vulnerable Indigenous women and girls are not exploited": Bernadette Smith, quoted in Bernhardt, "Winnipeg Police Pull Out of Project Devote."

"In the nearly three years of involvement since the homicide death of Tina's father": Report by Manitoba's Advocate for Children and Youth, quoted in Cameron MacLean, "Systems Failed Tina Fontaine's Family Before She Was Born," CBC News, March 13, 2019.

Tina suggested to him that she wanted "to play": Raymond Cormier, in video clip in Katie Nicholson and Joanne Levasseur, "Raymond Cormier Denies Killing Tina Fontaine, Admits to Giving Her Drugs," CBC News, March 14, 2019.

Tina's was one of seven bodies: Chinta Puxley, "Manitobans to Drag Red River Again to Find Missing, Murdered Aboriginal Women," Canadian Press (on CTV News website), April 5, 2015.

In 2014, he [Ningewance] told the Winnipeg Free Press that he'd found the bodies: Kevin Rollason, "They Refuse to Give Up Hope: Volunteers Drag Red River to Aid Missing-Women Cases," *Winnipeg Free Press*, September 15, 2014.

"She [Tina] was very young"... "She [Amber] was small like Tina"... "But people have had enough": Interview with Kyle Kematch for Sterritt, "A Movement Rises."

"I didn't know Kyle, I didn't know Bernadette": Melvin Pangman, quoted in Kristy Hoffman, "Drag the Red Sets Out on New Boat to Search Fast-Moving Waters," CBC News, July 18, 2016.

"I went through the system myself": Bernadette Smith, quoted in Kelly Geraldine

Malone, "Change to Manitoba's Child Apprehension Laws Ensures Kids Can't Be Taken Solely Because of Poverty," Canadian Press (on CBC News website), November 6, 2018.

Poverty, referred to as "neglect" in reports written by social workers: Angela Sterritt, "Indigenous Kids Largely Apprehended Because of Poverty, Says Former Child Protection Worker," CBC News, November 21, 2017.

10 | Hilaḵanthl ayooḵhl lixs gyat, *breaker of laws of others*

on kʷikʷəƛəm (Kwikwetlem) territory—"red fish up the river": Kwikwetlem First Nation home page, kwikwetlem.com.

Walking around Buntzen Lake, a spiritually important place where səlilwətaɬ oral history: Chris Arnett and Jesse Morin, "The Rock Painting/Xela:ls of the Tsleil-Waututh: A Historicized Coast Salish Practice," *Ethnohistory* 65, no. 1 (January 2018): 101–127.

about 75–85 percent of the journalists were still white: Author recollection. Even in the recent Canadian Newsroom Diversity Survey in 2020–21, 75 percent of journalists in newsrooms are white (Canadian Association of Journalists, caj.ca/diversitysurveyresults).

In its defence, CBC told me, "Today at CBC there is widespread acknowledgement": Emailed statement from Chuck Thompson, Chief of Staff to the EVP, Head of Public Affairs at CBC, July 20, 2022.

"advocacy journalism"—a phrase that white journalists often applied: Pacinthe Mattar, "Objectivity Is a Privilege Afforded to White Journalists," *The Walrus*, updated February 10, 2022.

In a recent response to this event, the CBC told me it "has no tolerance for discrimination": Emailed statement from Chuck Thompson, Chief of Staff to the EVP, Head of Public Affairs at CBC, July 20, 2022.

In its defence, in an email, the CBC told me it "is a microcosm of society": Emailed statement from Chuck Thompson, Chief of Staff to the EVP, Head of Public Affairs at CBC, July 20, 2022.

I would later discover through 9-1-1 transcripts: Angela Sterritt and Bridgette Watson, "Indigenous Man and Granddaughter Handcuffed at Vancouver Bank File Human Rights Complaint Against BMO, Police," CBC News, November 23, 2020.

I learned that the bank manager suspected Johnson of fraud: Sterritt and Watson, "Indigenous Man and Granddaughter Handcuffed."

"come from diverse communities... and are not racist and were not racially profiling": Joel Ballard, "Vancouver Police Chief Defends Handcuffing of Indigenous Man and Granddaughter," CBC News, January 10, 2020; "VPD Chief Says Officers Weren't Profiling During Bank Incident," CBC, cbc.ca/player/play/1669536323953.

"Bella Bella is a 2,000-person-strong reserve": Angela Sterritt, "Indigenous Ceremony Tries to Right the Wrong Caused by Handcuffing of Grandfather and Granddaughter," Reporter's Notebook, CBC News, March 5, 2020.

a white male reporter who was not at the ceremony wrote the story: Rafferty Baker, "'You Hurt the Whole Community': Heiltsuk Nation Hosts BMO Managers at Washing Ceremony After Mistaken Arrests," CBC News, March 4, 2020.

found the VPD *officers each committed two counts of abuse of authority:* Decision of
  retired judge Brian Neal, quoted in "Police Officers Who Handcuffed
  Indigenous Man, Granddaughter Outside Bank Ordered Suspended for
  Misconduct," CBC News, April 6, 2022.
the killing of George Floyd by a Minneapolis police officer: Evan Hill, Ainara Tiefenthäler,
  Christiaan Triebert, Drew Jordan, Haley Willis, and Robin Stein, "How George
  Floyd Was Killed in Police Custody," New York Times, May 31, 2020.
Not long after his death, on June 4, 2020, Chantel Moore: Shane Magee, "New Bruns-
  wick Police Officer Who Fatally Shot Chantel Moore Won't Be Charged," CBC
  News, June 7, 2021.
"an Indigenous person in Canada is more than 10 *times more likely":* Ryan Flanagan,
  "Why Are Indigenous People in Canada So Much More Likely to Be Shot and
  Killed by Police?," CTV News, June 19, 2020.
"Our goal here is to end the genocide": Denise Pictou Maloney, quoted in Ka'nhehsí:io
  Deer, "Federal Government Releases Long-Awaited MMIWG National Action
  Plan," June 3, 2021.
Annie Mae Pictou Aquash … was murdered in 1975: Facebook Messenger correspon-
  dence with family member Robert Pictou, January 20, 2022.
The Canadian government's 2020/21 *budget earmarked* $2.2 *billion:* Deer, "Federal Gov-
  ernment Releases."
the document Ottawa released was "an offensive performance": Melissa Moses, quoted
  in Union of British Columbia Indian Chiefs, "Aspiration Not Enough to End
  Genocide: UBCIC Demands Government Action and Accountability for Crisis
  of MMIWG," news release, June 3, 2021, ubcic.bc.ca/_aspiration_not_enough_
  to_end_genocide_ubcic_demands_government_action_and_accountability_
  for_crisis_of_mmiwg.
calling it a "toxic and dysfunctional process," and instead called on the United Nations:
  Lorraine Whitman, quoted in Ka'nhehsí:io Deer, "Native Women's Associa-
  tion Leaves National MMIWG Action Plan Process, Calling it 'Toxic and
  Dysfunctional,'" CBC News, June 1, 2021; Native Women's Association of
  Canada, "NWAC to File Human Rights Complaint in Canada; Requests
  International Intervention and Investigation on the Genocide by OAS and
  UN on Federal Government's So-Called 'National Action Plan,'" news release,
  June 3, 2021, globenewswire.com/en/news-release/2021/06/03/2241626/
  0/en/NWAC-to-File-Human-Rights-Complaint-in-Canada-Requests-
  International-Intervention-Investigation-on-the-Genocide-by-OAS-and-
  UN-on-Federal-Government-s-So-Called-National-Action-Plan.html.
When Tk'emlúps te Secwépemc communications representative Racelle Kooy told me:
  Telephone interview with Racelle Kooy, May 29, 2021.
I was the first reporter from a mainstream outlet that the Tk'emlúps te Secwépemc's
  Kúkpi7 (Chief) Rosanne Casimir spoke to: Zoom interview with Rosanne Casimir,
  May 28, 2021.
two hundred potential burial sites on the grounds of the Kamloops Indian Residential School:
  "Tk'emlúps te Secwépemc Release Final Report on Unmarked Graves at For-
  mer Kamloops Residential School," Radio Canada International, July 15, 2021,
  ici.radio-canada.ca/rci/en/news/1809374/tkemlups-te-secwepemc-release-
  final-report-on-unmarked-graves-at-former-kamloops-residential-school.

INDEX

115–17, 131, 136, 143, 149; status of case, 115–16, 119; Sterritt's experiences as context for her writing about, 11; suspects, 116, 118, 119–21, 122–23. *See also* Hans, Vanessa
Moody, Jalissa, 132
Moody, Ron, 124
Moore, Chantel, 230
Morgan, Judith, 16
Moses, Melissa, 233

Nagy, Arnie, 161, 168
Nahanee, Marissa, 57
National Action Plan, 232–33
National Centre for Missing Persons and Unidentified Remains, 41
National Centre for Truth and Reconciliation, 127
National Family and Survivors Circle, 232–33
National Inquiry into Missing and Murdered Indigenous Women and Girls: announcement and launch, 106, 188–89; Audette, Michèle, 74; burden of creating put onto families, 191; closing ceremony, 202–3; colonialism within, 193, 195; criticisms from Indigenous women and families, 189–90, 197, 198; genocide, use of the word, 9–10, 201–2; hearings, 195–98, 200, 215; implementation of action plan, 232; media coverage, lack of, 7; MMIWG family responses, 124–25, 128, 161, 190–91, 197, 199; presentation of final report, 202–3; Radek, Gladys, 170–71, 196–97, 202–3; RCMP statistics debunked by commissioners, 142; reasons why Indigenous women are easier targets, 124; relationship of residential schools and MMIWG, 128; significance of hearings, 200; staffing issues, 192–94; Stephen Harper on, 187. *See also* calls for national inquiry into MMIWG; Sterritt, Angela

National Inquiry into Missing and Murdered Indigenous Women and Girls final report (*Reclaiming Power and Place*, 2019): genocide of Indigenous people, 9–10, 201, 202–3, 232–33; statistics on risk of murder or violence, 52
Native Women's Association of Canada, 41, 74, 76, 178, 233
Naziel, Florence, 103
Neal, Brian, 228
Nepinak, Shawn, 214
Neufeld, Murray, 119
Neumann, Frances, 195
New Democratic Party, 105
Nikal, Delphine, 36
Ningewance, Percy, 212
Nlaka'pamux, 144
North, Sheila, 151

Obstruction of Justice (Michalko), 166
O'Connor, Hubert, 127
Oppal, Wally, 138, 177–78, 184–85
Oppal Inquiry. *See* Missing Women Commission of Inquiry
Osborne-Tyo, Claudette, 207
Osoko, Bowen, 138–39
O'Sullivan, Gunargie, 67

Palmer, Adam, 226, 229
Parrett, Glen, 142
The Path Forward—Reclaiming Power and Place (National Family and Survivors Circle), 232–33
patriarchy, 100
Paulson, Bob, 142
Penner, Barry, 178–79
Phillip, Grand Chief Stewart, 89
Pickton, Robert (Willie): charges against, 73, 75, 177; Crime Stoppers tip, named in, 182; demographics of victims, 71–72; Gitxsan Elder at inquiry, 199–200; inclusion of cases in MMIWG count, 140; *Missing Women Investigation Review* on failure of investigation,